T0301687

# THE POSTWAR
# ECONOMIC ORDER

# THE POSTWAR ECONOMIC ORDER

## NATIONAL RECONSTRUCTION AND INTERNATIONAL COOPERATION

## ALBERT O. HIRSCHMAN

*Edited by*

MICHELE ALACEVICH AND
PIER FRANCESCO ASSO

Columbia University Press    *New York*

Columbia University Press
*Publishers Since 1893*
New York    Chichester, West Sussex
cup.columbia.edu

Copyright © 2023 Columbia University Press
All rights reserved

Library of Congress Cataloging-in-Publication Data
Names: Hirschman, Albert O., author. | Alacevich, Michele, editor. |
Asso, Pier Francesco, editor.
Title: The postwar economic order : national reconstruction and
international cooperation / Albert O. Hirschman ; edited by
Michele Alacevich and Pier Francesco Asso.
Description: New York : Columbia University Press, 2022. |
Includes index.
Identifiers: LCCN 2022010627 (print) | LCCN 2022010628 (ebook)
| ISBN 9780231200585 (hardback) | ISBN 9780231200592
(trade paperback) | ISBN 9780231553698 (ebook)
Subjects: LCSH: United States—Foreign economic relations—
Europe. | Europe—Foreign economic relations—United States. |
Marshall Plan. | Economic history.
Classification: LCC HF1456.5.E8 H57 2022 (print) |
LCC HF1456.5.E8 (ebook) | DDC 337.7304—dc23/eng/20220627
LC record available at https://lccn.loc.gov/2022010627
LC ebook record available at https://lccn.loc.gov/2022010628

Columbia University Press books are printed on permanent and
durable acid-free paper.
Printed and bound by CPI Group (UK) Ltd, Croydon, CR0 4YY

# CONTENTS

# EDITORS' ACKNOWLEDGMENTS AND A NOTE ON THE TEXTS

Albert O. Hirschman wrote the reports collected in this book while in the employ of the Board of Governors of the Federal Reserve System. Almost all of them appeared in the *Review of Foreign Developments*, which ran from 1945 to 1975. The reports, which were usually marked "Confidential" or "Restricted," are now in the public domain but remain the intellectual creations of Hirschman.* For this reason, we sought permission to publish the texts in this volume from Hirschman's daughter, Katia Salomon, whose enthusiasm for the project was invaluable to us. For comments on a previous version of our introductory chapter, we are extremely grateful to Ivo Maes, Elizabeth Leake, and three anonymous reviewers, who also commented on the structure of the book.

In editing the reports for publication, we have maintained Hirschman's admittedly idiosyncratic and very parsimonious punctuation, as well as his own spelling, hyphenations, format of

---

* The Federal Reserve confirms this point with the following statement: "The analyses and conclusions set forth in the RFD [*Review of Foreign Developments*] series are those of the authors and do not indicate concurrence by other members of the research staff or the Board of Governors." Board of Governors of the Federal Reserve System, "Other Research," FederalReserve.gov, https://www.federalreserve.gov/econres/otherresearch.htm.

bibliographic references, and occasional factual and grammatical errors. Only in these latter cases have we provided a correction or a "sic" in square brackets. Likewise, in the very few instances in which a proposition was clearly missing, we have added it in square brackets.

The first footnote to each chapter provides information that comes directly from the original source, such as the date and place of publication of the report, the level of access to the document ("Confidential," "Restricted," etc.), or whether the published article had been presented at a conference. Subsequent footnotes are by the editors of the volume.

Hirschman's own footnotes have been turned into the endnotes. Our additions to the endnotes are in square brackets in order to make the distinction between Hirschman's original material and our contributions clear. For example, as was common in those years, Hirschman was often very synthetic and cursory in providing references. Also, he did not use a consistent syntax for references throughout his reports, and at times he provided incorrect information, such as about the volume or year of publication of specific sources. We have left Hirschman's references as they are in the originals (errors included), but we have integrated and corrected them, adding additional information in square brackets. When possible, we kept Hirschman's and our interventions clearly separated, though we also had to be slightly inconsistent: there are instances in which brief square-bracketed interventions within Hirschman's references have been preferred for the sake of simplicity and readability.

# THE POSTWAR
# ECONOMIC ORDER

# ALBERT O. HIRSCHMAN AT THE FEDERAL RESERVE, 1946–1952

MICHELE ALACEVICH AND PIER FRANCESCO ASSO

Albert Hirschman is widely known as a founding father of development economics and one of the most important and influential social scientists of the twentieth century. His first proper job, however, was as an economist in charge of the Western European desk of the research branch of the Federal Reserve Board in Washington, DC. His major areas of expertise, developed throughout the 1930s, were international trade and industrial and monetary policies in Italy and France. In 1946, when Hirschman was hired at the Fed, development economics hardly existed, and he had no idea that he would later become a pioneer in the field. As the Fed years predate Hirschman's major works in development, political economy, and the social sciences, scholars have largely ignored them.[1] Yet this early phase of Hirschman's career is important for at least two reasons.

First, it contributes to our understanding of debates and policy decisions about European reconstruction and international

Portions of this chapter are from Michele Alacevich and Pier Francesco Asso,
"Albert Hirschman, Europe and the Post-war Economic Order,"
*History of Political Economy* (forthcoming).

monetary cooperation in the early postwar years. By examining Hirschman's work at the Fed, we are able to reconstruct those debates through the eyes of an expert and perceptive participant. Like Dean Acheson, Hirschman was "present at the creation" of the postwar international system, contributing novel and at times visionary analyses of European reconstruction, the Marshall Plan, exchange convertibility, and a proposal for a monetary authority that anticipated a number of important issues related to intra-European and transatlantic cooperation.

Second, those early analyses informed Hirschman's subsequent, more famous work on development. The essays collected in this book reveal a number of elements that illuminate his intellectual trajectory. During his years at the Fed, Hirschman sharpened his ability to examine processes of policy-making in difficult times, rejecting prefab recipes and developing a sensitivity for inverted sequential processes, inducement mechanisms, and apparently paradoxical solutions in uncertain environments. The roots of what would become the distinctive "Hirschmanesque" style of thought (to use an expression coined by Walter Salant) are clearly visible in this early period. So even though a discontinuity in his research subject is apparent (international trade and monetary policies in the 1930s and 1940s and development issues in the 1950s and 1960s), a continuity in terms of methodology and attitude was present.

We will discuss these two propositions in due course. Before we proceed, however, a few words are needed to summarize the trajectory of Hirschman's life until the end of World War II.

Born in 1915 in Berlin to an assimilated, high-bourgeois Jewish family, Otto Albert Hirschmann witnessed the collapse of the Weimar Republic. (Upon immigrating to the United States in 1940, he changed his name to Albert O. Hirschman, with one "n." To avoid complications, in this introduction we will use the American spelling throughout.) After the Nazis seized power in January 1933, Hirschman left Berlin for Paris, as he had been an activist in the youth movement of the Social Democratic Party of Germany and would have risked arrest had he stayed. For the remainder of the interwar years, he wandered across Europe studying economics (in Paris, London, and Trieste, where in 1938 he defended his BA), participating in underground antifascist activities (including smuggling documents between France and Italy), and taking part in combat, first as a volunteer in the International Brigades in Spain in 1936 and then as a volunteer in the French Army at the outbreak of World War II.

Throughout these years, Hirschman acquired a deep knowledge of the Italian and French economies, the monetary policies of these countries, and the system of bilateral trade agreements that spread throughout Europe in the interwar years. In the late 1930s, Hirschman developed a dense and articulate analysis of the monetary policies of France from 1928 through 1936 in his BA thesis, wrote several articles on the Italian economy for major French magazines, prepared a long memorandum on exchange controls in Italy for a conference of the League of Nations, and wrote a statistical note on equilibrium and bilateralism in international economic relations. Through these efforts, he was developing the professional profile of an economist well versed in statistical analysis, the political economy of some major European countries, and international trade relations.

The outbreak of World War II put this work on hold. Hirschman first volunteered in the French Army and then, to avoid being summarily executed as a traitor when Germany invaded France, entered clandestine life. In the second half of 1940, Hirschman was in Marseille, where he joined forces with the American journalist Varian Fry to help Jewish and leftist refugees flee Nazi-Fascist Europe. Under the cover of the Centre américain de secours, devoted to providing refugees with material necessities such as food and clothing, Hirschman (using the pseudonym of Albert Hermant) ran an underground scheme that organized the flight of several thousand refugees across the Pyrenees. When the police were about to seize him, Hirschman followed the same route, reached Lisbon, and (with a Lithuanian passport and a Rockefeller Foundation fellowship) arrived at the University of California at Berkeley.

Hirschman found his years in Berkeley exhilarating. Not only, as he later joked, was he glad to be "on the side of the victors for once" after many defeats, but he also wrote his first book, *National Power and the Structure of Foreign Trade* (completed in 1942 and published in 1945); participated in a vibrant intellectual community that included John B. Condliffe, Howard S. Ellis, William Fellner, and Alexander Gerschenkron; and met his future wife and life companion, Sarah Chapiro. Sarah, six years his junior, was the daughter of a bourgeois family of assimilated Lithuanian Jews and had spent several years in Paris before fleeing to the United States. The couple married in June 1941 and moved to a small bungalow that bordered the Berkeley campus. "With nature, Sarah, and the books," Hirschman wrote to his sister, "I feel very autarkic."[2]

When the United States entered World War II, Hirschman volunteered in the U.S. Army, serving two years in Europe. Upon his return, Albert, Sarah, and their two daughters, Katia and Lisa, moved to Washington, DC. After the war, the United States was preparing to manage the peace as the new global hegemon. New agencies were established, and governmental offices swelled to meet the new task. Not unreasonably, Hirschman thought that in the federal capital he would easily find a job as an expert on

European economies. Indeed, his credentials seemed impec-
cable. Not only was he a talented economist fluent in five lan-
guages (in addition to his native German, he spoke French like
a native and also spoke Italian, Spanish, and English), but he
had also been a committed antifascist and a volunteer in the
U.S. Army. Yet his applications were invariably rejected, and
for months Hirschman was unable to find a job. In the end, the
reason for the impasse—because there *was* a reason—was ser-
endipitously overcome thanks to the initiative of his Berkeley
colleague Alexander Gerschenkron.

Unbeknownst to Hirschman, his European past, specifically his antifascist allegiance, had become a liability in postwar
America. With the sudden onset of the Cold War, American
authorities suspected Hirschman of possible communist sympa-
thies, and, as an FBI file reported, U.S. government officers felt
"unable . . . to establish that his primary loyalty was to the Government of the United States."[3] Gerschenkron, however, had
become the head of the International Section of the Division
of Research and Statistics at the Fed and had the power to hire
his own staff. He knew Hirschman and had no qualms about
his trustworthiness. After all, Hirschman was not the first antifascist European intellectual to emigrate to the United States
and join one of its government's branches. Indeed, the Fed was
among the most active agencies in hiring émigré economists
who could provide essential expertise on their countries of origin, and many likened it to a university in exile.[4] Hirschman's
initial task was to study reconstruction and monetary issues in
France and Italy, though he soon became responsible for the
entire Western European region.

Not surprisingly, Hirschman's work at the Fed was influenced
and prompted by the unique problems of European reconstruction, which unfolded in phases around major issues such as the

dollar shortage and the urgency of jump-starting the European economies in 1947 and 1948; the working and the effects of the Marshall Plan; the attempts to overcome bilateralism and reactivate mechanisms of multilateral trade and intra-European cooperation in 1949 and 1950; and the relationship between the United States and the rest of the world. We have organized the book around these four phases.

The destructive consequences of World War II on Europe are well known. As remarked in the 1945 strategic bombing survey, between 1940 and 1945 the monthly bomb delivery capacity of Allied forces on Europe grew by a factor of 150, with a huge surge in 1944 and 1945.[5] In France, Germany, and Italy, between 70 and 90 percent of merchant marine vessels, locomotives, and railways were destroyed; all major canals, ports, and riverways became unnavigable; and 20 to 40 percent of buildings were damaged. Industrial production was 40 percent of prewar levels in France and Belgium and a mere 20 percent in Italy and Germany.[6]

As for the terrible accounting of human losses, fifteen to twenty million individuals lost their lives in Europe alone.[7] In the synthesis of one historian, "Europe in the aftermath of the Second World War offered a prospect of utter misery and desolation."[8]

Yet despite its immense destructive power, the war's impact on European productive capacities was limited, and initial reconstruction was quick. According to the United Nations, by 1947, a mere two years after the end of hostilities, industrial production in Europe had returned to its 1938 level and by 1948 surpassed the prewar level by about 13 percent (excluding Germany; including Germany, the figures are 83 and 96 percent, respectively).[9]

As far as France was concerned, the Monnet Plan, published in 1946, was at the forefront of economic debates, so it is not strange to find one of Hirschman's first reports devoted to it.

The first element that Hirschman underscored, however, was not so much the economic potential of the plan but its political dividend. As a student of interwar French history, Hirschman knew that France had historically been characterized by bitter political factionalism. Yet parties across the political spectrum rallied around the plan. Always alert to the political culture of the countries he visited, Hirschman noted, "It may be that the idea of a national economic goal appeals strongly to the French people because of the frustrating lack of direction from which they suffered during the interwar period."[10]

This political convergence would be impossible in Italy, burdened as it was by political deadlock, incomplete sovereignty, and the problems left by the legacy of the Fascist *ventennio*.[11] Yet despite a more favorable political landscape and the vision of the Monnet Plan, Hirschman saw several shortcomings in the French economic policies. Surely the simultaneous presence of price inflation, currency expansion, and credit shortage posed problems for policy-making. The government was forced to slow down the investment program envisioned by the Monnet Plan and, as Hirschman anticipated, adjust the exchange rate.[12] The problem was that the French government acted abruptly and unilaterally with a differential devaluation that privileged exports to the dollar area and made French multiple exchange rates more complicated than they already were. The move was poorly conceived, and no effort was made to explain it to foreign governments or the International Monetary Fund (IMF). Hirschman circulated an insightful analysis to explain the substantive reasons behind what he, too, considered a needlessly confrontational move.[13]

Italy's exchange rate policies, in contrast, seemed to Hirschman both well conceived and effective. He wrote, "The least that can be said about postwar Italian exchange rate and

exchange control policies is that they have displayed remarkable inventiveness."[14] The Italian government, Hirschman noted,
had hardly regained sovereignty over foreign trade and monetary policies when it introduced a bold scheme of incentives
to exporters that permitted them to retain or sell 50 percent of
their hard currency earnings, provided they would be used for
the purchase of licensed imports (this was called the "50 percent
system"). Despite a number of shortcomings, the system seemed
effective, both for the positive expectations that it helped create
about the country's future trade policy and for the flexibility it
afforded at a time when both world and domestic prices showed
wide fluctuations.[15]

Hirschman recognized the same flexibility and inventiveness
in the Italian policies to fight inflation, particularly in the credit
restrictions put in place between August and October 1947 by
Luigi Einaudi, the minister of the budget and the former governor of the Italian Central Bank (and, starting in May 1948, the
first president of the Italian Republic). Hirschman praised that
mix of orthodox and expansionary measures for its ability to foster economic growth while preserving monetary stability. Italy
simultaneously experienced monetary tightening and large-scale
governmental compensatory spending, and Hirschman did not
miss the irony of this: "It is certainly curious to notice how Einaudi's 'orthodox' policy actually led to more State intervention in,
and greater State control of, Italian economic life."[16]

But despite this apparent paradox, the combination of deflationary credit restrictions and expansionary subsidies in selected
fields (in particular in heavy industry) was indeed a rational
policy in the wake of the dramatic inflation that Italy had been
experiencing. Inflationary or deflationary policies, Hirschman
argued, were not right or wrong in absolute terms. Instead,
they should be regarded as different measures to be activated in

different phases of the process of reconstruction: "Initially, the 'open' postwar inflation . . . probably permitted reconstruction to proceed more rapidly than might have been possible under conditions of monetary stability. But as the pace of the inflation quickened, an increasing portion of the investment . . . was wasteful and often competed successfully with genuine reconstruction and modernization activities. It thus became actually easier *and possibly tempting* to carry on these activities in a deflationary environment."[17] The point of interest, in other words, was to devise a sequential process in which apparently incompatible policies responded to specific needs.[18]

Moreover, with an optimistic attitude that would become a signature of his work, Hirschman highlighted the possible beneficial and unintended consequences of a difficult situation. The temporary recession triggered by Einaudi's credit restriction had the effect of exposing the maladjustments of Italy's industrial sector, which had remained hidden during the expansionary phase, making it possible to correct them.

One final point must be highlighted with regard to Hirschman's analysis of Italy's path of postwar recovery. Though widespread agreement existed about the need for further investment, opinions differed on what the optimal level of investment should be. Some feared it was too little too late, whereas others were concerned that an excessive acceleration in the investment rate would lead to renewed inflationary pressure. Hirschman refused to embark on this line of research. "The answer to this question," he wrote, "can be found only by trial and error."[19] He continued, "Rather than to engage in a futile search for the 'correct' aggregate volume of investment, one should concentrate upon locating those investments which permit the breaking of important bottlenecks and will thereby lead to increases of output and improvements of performance out of proportion to the investment itself."[20]

Several important points stand out here. First, Hirschman understood clearly that the predicament of Italy's balance of payments was not necessarily a harbinger of chronic difficulties. As Harold James wrote (with reference to the balance-of-payments problem experienced by Western European countries), "It was not obvious to contemporaries that this was an indication of potential strength. Many treated it rather as the beginning of a permanent weakness."[21] Hirschman, however, saw it as a sign of economic dynamism and even an opportunity for structural adjustment. Second, Hirschman gave pride of place to processes of learning by doing and considered theoretical analyses to have only limited efficacy. A priori deductions, he claimed, could produce only extremely imprecise guesses.[22] Third, a static analysis was of no use, as it was impossible to ascertain the "correct" policy measure or the "correct" volume of investments. He feared that "much time may be lost in looking for a simple formula that will 'set things right.'"[23] The point, instead, was precisely to avoid this elusive quest for a univocal remedy and to recognize that "the necessity to walk on a very narrow path between deflation and inflation" required the development of new methods for using foreign aid and domestic policies. In other words, Hirschman argued, "the therapy to be prescribed is thus quite likely to be unorthodox."

Fourth, Hirschman's unorthodox and eclectic stance was predicated upon a deep understanding of widespread concerns about inflation rates and the rising public debt. Macroeconomic orthodoxy on these issues, he thought, was not so much wrong as incomplete, excessively rigid, and static. For fiscal and monetary policies to be successful, Hirschman argued, contextual and institutional variables, as well as the need to reestablish confidence in government policies and authorities, had to be factored in. Clearly, Hirschman profited from this experience, for when in the early 1950s he became an adviser to the Colombian government on monetary and budgetary policies, his approach to macroeconomic matters was very much the same.

Finally, this unorthodox therapy called not only for sequential solutions based on a method of trial and error but also for selective policies. In a situation in which available resources were severely limited, Hirschman recommended privileging those investments that, by breaking bottlenecks, would unleash idle resources and further investment opportunities. Ten years later, Hirschman coined a new label for this process—"backward and forward linkages"—that granted him a place among the pioneers of development studies.[24] But the concept was already crystal clear in his mind in 1948. The unexpected dynamism that the Italian economy showed in postwar reconstruction and the way the Italian people reacted to the right policy incentives in hard times would later serve as an inspiration to study how poverty and underdevelopment could be successfully tackled.

The lack of resources to support basic consumption and to reactivate production was a fundamental problem in early postwar Europe. Obviously, the problem had existed in the war years, but rationing, economic planning, and, for the sterling area, the Lend-Lease program (established in 1941) mitigated its effects.[25] These, however, emerged abruptly after the war. In its first annual report, drafted in a hurry after having opened for business in May 1946, even the IMF recognized that there was "a severe shortage of goods of all kinds that must be obtained from abroad" and that for several countries, "exchange restrictions are unavoidable . . . in order to assure that the most essential requirements for consumption and reconstruction will be met out of their limited foreign exchange resources."[26] But the problem was not so much limited foreign exchange as limited reserves of hard currency, that is, dollars. By the spring of 1947, the "dollar shortage" had become *the* problem for economists and government officers working on European reconstruction and recovery. (And the labels multiplied quickly; the problem was known variously as the dollar famine, the dollar grip, and the dollar crisis.)

Truth be told, not all agreed. Fritz Machlup, for instance, had maintained for years that the idea of a dollar shortage was "faulty."[27] In any event, even those who considered this a false problem felt compelled to write about it, and a veritable "flood of contributions" to the discussion of postwar international monetary problems quickly ensued.[28]

Alvin Hansen and Charles Kindleberger published a programmatic piece in April 1942 in which they argued that the primary economic goal of the postwar period should be the preparation of a daring plan of international cooperation based on expansionist policies to achieve full employment, a development program to raise productivity throughout the world, and a commitment to increase living standards worldwide.[29] According to Kindleberger, a "chronic world shortage of dollars" constituted a major obstacle to this plan, and in turn the dollar shortage was a clear symptom of the technical superiority of the United States as compared to the rest of the world.[30] In such a situation, Kindleberger maintained that orthodox solutions of international monetary stabilization would not work. The problems were structural, and only long-term capital lending and an in-depth reorganization of the productive system would create the bases for postwar prosperity.

This perspective was questioned by those who claimed that the removal of trade restrictions was actually the policy to be implemented. A prominent supporter of this perspective was Howard S. Ellis, who called for trade liberalization while maintaining international monetary controls on exchange rates and capital movements by a powerful international monetary authority.[31] At Berkeley, Ellis had read the manuscript for what would become Hirschman's *National Power* and referred explicitly to it to highlight that a monetary authority should be able to restrain the disruptive power politics of countries leveraging trade imbalances. In a 1948 article, Ellis remarked, "In plain English . . . a shortage of dollars exists if, at the going rate of exchange, demand exceeds supply."[32] Failure to proceed with exchange rate adjustments, Ellis concluded, distorted trade and sabotaged long-term stability. Likewise, in a 1947 pamphlet Roy Harrod described the idea of a dollar shortage as "one of the most absurd phrases ever coined," "nonsensical," and "one of the most brazen pieces of collective effrontery that has ever been uttered."[33] He went on, "The radical mistake . . . is to think of the remedies for our troubles primarily in terms of exports and imports. . . . The shortfall of exports . . . is merely a by-product of the excessive capital outlay. That outlay is absorbing labour and materials, which are required for, and could be used by, exporters."[34]

This interpretation gained some traction, for it resurfaced in the loan schemes that the World Bank, in particular the World Bank economist Paul Rosenstein-Rodan, devised for European countries between the late 1940s and the early 1950s. The rationale of the World Bank's "impact loans," aimed at supporting the balance of payments of borrowing countries against the "impact" of a domestic investment plan, seemed to follow Harrod's reasoning, as they contemplated a loan in dollars to support the balance of payments, which the central bank of the borrowing country was expected to match by opening a counterpart fund in domestic currency to finance domestic investments. As Harrod put it, "The proposition that is absolutely fundamental . . . and that must always be borne in mind is that *the adverse balance of current foreign payments must necessarily be identical in amount with, and is indeed the mirror image of, the excess of current domestic capital outlay over current domestic saving.*"[35] Impact loans were meant to address this problem.

In mid-1948, Hirschman offered a general assessment of the debate. Monetary explanations of the dollar shortage, he noticed, seemed to prevail over structural ones and offered a relatively easy solution (an adjustment of exchange rates) compared to that contemplated by scholars focusing on structural issues, such as changes in industrial configuration or trade patterns.

Yet Hirschman claimed that, precisely because the task of structural industrial reforms was difficult to confront, the difficulties encountered by European countries might offer an unexpected opportunity.[36] Present imbalances, he argued, could activate the political resources to restructure the national economy—a proposition that several governments would happily disregard in easier times.

Like Harrod, moreover, Hirschman posited that the causal relationship between inflation and balance-of-payments disequilibria worked both ways. Not only were balance-of-payments deficits caused by domestic inflation, but inflation was, in turn, a consequence of balance-of-payments deficits. Grants and loans aimed at jump-starting reconstruction and investment activities would eventually result in an increased flow of goods, but in the short run they might well have an inflationary effect. "Because of their 'bottleneck' nature," Hirschman explained, they created the conditions to employ idle domestic labor and raw materials while individual savings remained very low and speculation in inventories became common practice.[37]

Undoubtedly, this analysis made the effects of imports on domestic monetary dynamics less easy to forecast. But what was lost in immediate clarity was gained in realism, making it possible to classify imports according to their deflationary or inflationary impact. Replacement of damaged machinery would not have an inflationary effect, but new machinery would. Food-stuffs would have a deflationary effect unless they created the conditions to divert labor resources to new investment activities. Imported "essential luxuries" such as films and tobacco, characterized by rigid demand, high prices, and high consumption taxes, drained domestic purchasing power and thus had a strong deflationary effect. Hirschman's analysis was clearly relevant for a broader audience than just the Fed staff, and the report was soon republished by the *American Economic Review*.[38]

The focus on sequences, bottlenecks, and apparently contradictory measures that could nonetheless work in practice offered a useful compass for policy-making and complicated economic analysis. Working on dichotomous alternatives (e.g., monetary stability versus productive expansionism) was often misleading. It was more useful to develop a feeling for sequences or combinations of policies tailored to specific situations. All these elements, so visible in Hirschman's analyses of postwar European reconstruction, would become important features of Hirschman's trademark style of thought.

Important as they were, however, balance-of-payments problems were only one of a constellation of critical issues that hindered European recovery. Strictly related to them was the problem of currency inconvertibility.

The Marshall Plan, announced in mid-1947 and operative in 1948, "solved the Catch-22 of having to export in order to pay for imports but being unable to produce for export without first importing materials and machinery."[39] The Marshall Plan, in other words, helped jump-start domestic production and reactivate market mechanisms, since countries accessing American aid "had to commit to putting in place the prerequisites for a

functional market economy."[40] Moreover, by reducing the burden under which European countries operated, the resources
made available by the Marshall Plan helped defuse potential
social tensions and conflicting claims by laborers and enterprises, facilitating the domestic distributional compact of the
postwar period.

As we will see, another step to reinforcing this compact would
be the establishment of the European Payments Union (EPU)
in 1950.[41] But in 1948, while the domestic side of recovery was
in motion, international economic relations remained extremely
difficult. The problem of inconvertibility seemed intractable, and
the abrupt failure of the early British attempt to resume convertibility only worsened the prospects for a quick return to multilateralism and monetary stability. As Eichengreen wrote, "By the
late 1940s, Europe's trade resembled a spaghetti bowl of more
than two hundred bilateral arrangements."[42] These agreements
reproduced those used in the 1930s, with limited credit facilities to finance imbalances; once the credit limits were reached,
gold and dollar payments were required. As a consequence, in
the eventful year of 1947, the volume of intra-European trade
declined significantly. As one of the policy-makers involved in
international negotiations wrote, "The ghost of the 1930s was
still there, live and daunting."[43]

European governments made several attempts to build a
multilateral clearing arrangement, establishing a First Agreement for Multilateral Monetary Compensation in November
1947 (involving Belgium, Luxembourg, the Netherlands, France,
and Italy) and two Agreements for Intra-European Payments
and Compensation in October 1948 and June 1949 (for all countries in the Organisation for European Economic Co-operation
[OEEC]). The problem was so serious that U.S. authorities tried
to support the functioning of the 1948 and 1949 agreements by

allowing the use of Marshall Plan funds for intra-European trade settlements—a scheme known as the "Little Marshall Plan." The results, however, were modest, as these schemes were unable to overcome the structural imbalances between surplus and deficit countries and did not offer any compelling incentives to foster continental cooperation.

By the summer of 1948, Hirschman's duties encompassed more than the preparation of country reports on France and Italy (and occasionally other European countries such as Switzerland). Invitations to make critical assessments of broader systemic problems of intra-European cooperation multiplied. Tellingly, they arrived not only from the Fed but also from other agencies based in Washington, DC, most prominently the Economic Cooperation Administration (ECA), which was in charge of administering the Marshall Plan.

Hirschman offered original and stimulating contributions to the discussions that shaped the road to multilateralism and European integration under the stimulus of the Marshall Plan institutions. These were fields of research that had figured prominently in Hirschman's experience as a young economist in 1930s Europe. His early studies on trade policy and exchange controls provided strong evidence of the economic and political effects of international disintegration and of the discriminating use of the network of bilateral agreements that characterized European trade relations. In particular, Hirschman demonstrated that bilateralism was not merely a second-best solution in times of international liquidity shortages. Instead, the essence of bilateralism rested on a strategy designed to conquer and exert political supremacy and influence, and all the leading powers—not only Nazi Germany but also Great Britain—were more or less openly committed to this practice. What Hirschman's studies from the interwar period contributed most to that debate was a statistical tool for measuring the numerous varieties of bilateral agreements. The elaboration in 1939 of a "Hirschman index" of bilateralism soon became familiar in the scientific literature and reached a wider audience.[44] The quantitative evidence he carefully provided in *National Power* unveiled the subtle and widespread connections between international value chains and the escalation of nationalism. Since bilateral agreements had figured prominently in the disrupted postwar scenario, Hirschman's knowledge of their intricacies became particularly useful for understanding postwar trade relations.

Economists from the ECA and the State Department in Washington played a crucial part in steering Hirschman's research agenda toward these most challenging debates on the future of a new European order. At the beginning of 1949, as he later recalled, "my office was virtually transplanted from the Federal Reserve Board to the new ECA building. I much enjoyed taking part in this manner in the 'activism' of this group [Harold van Buren Cleveland, Theodore Geiger, and John Hulley], which constantly invented new functions for the Marshall Plan and its dollars."[45] In this stimulating environment, Hirschman found support for the view that the United States had a fundamental interest in European countries converging upon a unified economic and political platform, as this would allow the United States to deal with a politically consistent counterpart rather than multiple positions. A number of governmental offices in Washington, DC, embarked on the task of promoting ideas to realize this vision, and Hirschman became a regular attendee of ECA seminars and meetings.

On October 31, 1949, Paul Hoffman, the head of the ECA, gave a speech at the OEEC in Paris in which he emphatically insisted on the need for European "integration." The speech is remembered as the beginning of a new phase in the history of the Marshall Plan and of European integration. Among the ambitious goals that Hoffman listed were the reduction of intra-European trade barriers, the restoration of multilateral agreements, the coordination of monetary and fiscal policies, and, in due course, the formation of a single market. In the same weeks, the small group of ECA economists assisting Hoffman in Washington informally invited Hirschman to write a proposal for the establishment of a new European Monetary Authority.[46] Hirschman's proposal, submitted in November 1949, was an audacious though realistic attempt to devise a possible path toward European monetary cooperation in the postwar years.[47] To be sure, the idea was not original. In 1946, Theodore Geiger, then an officer at the U.S. embassy in London, emphasized the need for a European Clearing Union to overcome bilateralism, and one year later Robert Triffin and Raymond Bertrand coauthored a memorandum on the same subject. Similar questions were also discussed by the OEEC Payments Committee.[48] The Managing Board of the IMF and the Department of the Treasury, however, resisted proposals in this direction, and the ECA found itself fighting a somewhat solitary battle on this front.

It is possible that the lukewarm attitude of the IMF and Treasury toward schemes such as those proposed by Geiger and Triffin was at the root of a certain cautiousness on Hirschman's part. As he warned, times were not ripe for major institutional innovations or any substantial surrender of national sovereignty over monetary affairs. Moreover, on fiscal matters, distances between European countries appeared insurmountable, and the power of central banks over their national economies was unchallengeable. In 1947, Triffin and Bertrand proposed the introduction of an intra-European unit of account—the "European dollar" or "interfranc"—but Triffin was adamant, during the negotiations for the establishment of the EPU, that no existing currency should function as unit of account. He argued that this should be defined only by a gold content.[49] Hirschman concurred. The use of terms like "common currency," "common reserve bank," or "common monetary policy," he wrote, should be carefully avoided in official documents, let alone in the public debate, as they were simply futile.[50]

A move toward greater European integration was thus possible only if the United States could convince European governments to accept a functionalist approach. European integration could be realized in stages, with the first step being the creation of a European authority in charge of facilitating stronger policy coordination, if only as a reaction to "the failure of the partial attempts undertaken in the economic area."[51] By sowing the seeds of endogenous processes of integration and by building "new institutions in 'the interstices' of the national prerogatives," policy cooperation would foster economic convergence.[52] These processes, in turn, would become prerequisites for greater political unification.

Built upon this general background, the core of Hirschman's proposal discussed the internal and external functions with which to equip the new authority. Among the former, Hirschman emphasized the crucial importance of building an organization characterized by a high degree of transparency in its operations and statistical expertise. The authority should design and implement standard procedures and instruments for the production and elaboration of statistics across all member countries. Hirschman stated that it was of the utmost importance that "its decisions [were based] on comparable data."[53]

The coordination of national monetary policies implied that the new authority would hold advisory functions (and, in special circumstances, veto power) on the use of traditional instruments of monetary policies.[54] Fiscal policies were another sensitive matter, and it would be unrealistic to imagine that they could fall under the domain of the new European Monetary Authority. Yet Hirschman believed that the new institution could have important advisory functions in this area, discussing with national governments the general aims of fiscal policies and offering its help on matters of the sustainability of public debts. The authority could exert moral suasion to inhibit practices of excessive debt monetization through inflationary financing and develop forms of conditionality "to make it difficult for the national governments to pursue irresponsible fiscal policies."[55]

As for deficit financing, Hirschman recognized that it was quite unthinkable that the new authority could exert any fiscal moral suasion, not to mention any direct power, over national central banks. As a more realistic option, he suggested that the authority be allowed to lend funds for public projects functional to increasing European integration, particularly in the areas of infrastructures and public utilities.[56]

The second part of Hirschman's proposal discussed the authority's external functions or, in other words, its role in European intergovernmental governance. One basic function would be the partial pooling of Europe's foreign reserves for exchange intervention and the management of ECA dollars. The new authority would act as a European Exchange Equalization Account, not different from similar institutions already in existence at the national level. Moreover, the authority would be responsible for approving exchange rate variations and have the power to recommend parity changes if deemed necessary for greater stability and integration. Hirschman remarked that this would be a "bold step" that challenged IMF prerogatives, but he did not see—or decided to ignore—its disruptive potential. Indeed, he argued that "further steps in this direction" might be welcome.[57]

In general, Hirschman imagined the new authority more as a producer of public goods and services on behalf of the whole Continental area than as a policy-maker preoccupied with growth policies or with fostering international convergence. To this extent, he argued that the authority should incorporate the Bank for International Settlements, in particular its functions of managing intra-European monetary imbalances and exchange controls within and outside the area. Likewise, the authority should be responsible for managing European reserves to promote stability between European and extra-European areas. In the short run, this would help reduce pressures resulting from the dollar shortage, and in the long run (in particular after the end of the Marshall Plan) it would provide collateral for stabilization loans. Hirschman noted that the pooling of reserves would enhance confidence in European currencies and increase the leverage for obtaining stabilization loans from the international financial community.

Finally, the new authority should participate in negotiations on IMF loans to European countries (another sign of IMF weakness in Hirschman's eyes). This participation would be necessary to avoid reserves from one country being used to finance imports or investments in favor of another country, thus imposing an artificial process of convergence. This, he warned, would be the very end of the European project: "The best way to doom any move toward European Union is to conjure up the vision of equalization of the Swedish and Italian standards of living."[58]

Hirschman's proposal was a succinct document, providing no discussion of the intellectual lineage of its various components. However, it is clear that his analysis of the authority's external functions is indebted to Triffin's framework, though he also made some original contributions. Hirschman, for example, was the only one to propose the incorporation of the Bank for International Settlements by the new organization.

The governance of the authority was outside the scope of Hirschman's study, for he was aware of the novelty of "a central monetary authority without a central government."[59] Yet he was adamant on at least two defining points. First, only a majority-voting rule, as opposed to a unanimity rule, would guarantee effectiveness. Second, the governing body should be formed not only by national central bankers and government officials but also by "outstanding Europeans with knowledge of financial and economic affairs" who would represent "the interests of the European area as a whole."[60] This mix of civil servants and members of the professions and civil society would become, according to Hirschman, an important precedent for the architecture of other European institutions.

The proposal contained several novel elements, as well as a strong dose of political realism—in the words of Hirschman, it was a "half-way house."[61] The surrender of economic sovereignty would happen in phases, with the role of the authority being initially limited to the management of reserves and only later expanded to monetary, fiscal, and economic policies. At the same time, the real mission of the European Monetary Authority—or EMA's "goodwill," as Hirschman put it—would be the production of public services for the construction of a united Europe.[62]

At the end of 1949, the ECA economists endorsed Hirschman's proposal. They wrote that the proposal was "a first critical step toward the objective of a single market and a common market."[63] Moreover, as a historian wrote, even if the economic benefits were limited, "central bankers recognized that [Hirschman's] EMA proposal served a useful political purpose, demonstrating to a potentially skeptical Congress that Europeans were making real progress toward self-help."[64] The ECA, however, also needed to find a solution to the dollar shortage and needed to restore intra-European multilateral trade and payments. From this perspective, the new authority was too far ahead of its time, and the ECA thus focused on the smaller but more realistic goal of establishing a payments union.

By the time he completed his proposal, Hirschman felt more in agreement with the ECA than with his direct employer, the Fed, in particular as far as the ECA's attempt to restore a limited European area of multilateralism and convertibility was concerned. This was consistent with his history. Hirschman's European wanderings in the 1930s had put him in contact with Robert Marjolin, who after the war had become the OEEC general secretary and was a strong supporter of European multilateralism. Moreover, Hirschman was deeply influenced by the leaders of European federalist thought, beginning with his two brothers-in-law, Eugenio Colorni and Altiero Spinelli.[65] Finally, the message conveyed in *National Power* provided substance for second-best policies, regional integration, economies of scale, and the creation of a common market.

Historians have long acknowledged the role of the ECA and the OEEC in fostering not only European reconstruction but also cooperation. According to Eichengreen, the ability of European countries in the early postwar years to go through a rapid economic expansion based on "catch-up growth" and "convergence" was the result of a specific set of institutions particularly well suited to sustaining capital formation in an age of "coordinated capitalism."[66] The onset of the Cold War further emphasized the urgency of European cooperation. Indeed, many officers involved in the administration of the Marshall Plan agreed that perhaps the most important result of U.S. aid to Europe was not physical reconstruction but intergovernmental cooperation.[67]

With the establishment in 1950 of the EPU, the discriminatory policies that had suffocated trade relations in the early postwar years were, for the first time since the end of the war, superseded by a truly multilateral clearing system. If between 1945 and 1950 economic recovery was often endangered by a pervasive tendency to bilateralism, frozen balances, and new protectionist policies, the EPU paved the way to increasing trade and economic cooperation and became one of the pillars of the foundation of Europe's postwar "economic miracles."[68]

Already with his proposal for a European Monetary Authority, Hirschman had showed his unabashed support for European integration based on the reduction of trade restrictions and the restoration of multilateral payments. Though the project of the EPU was less ambitious, Hirschman nonetheless considered it crucial. "In the absence of positive steps," he wrote in a Fed report, "further disintegration is the likely course of affairs."[69] The EPU was thus a radical innovation in at least two respects. First, it created the conditions for higher flexibility in offsetting external imbalances, with a consequent reduction in the use of hard currencies. Second, it would guarantee a fair distribution of sacrifices among member countries and of mechanisms to redress imbalances between surplus and deficit countries. From this perspective, the EPU had a distinctly Keynesian flavor—greater than that of the wavering Bretton Woods institutions.

Yet Hirschman warned against the use of trade policy for the pursuit of full employment.[70] He wrote that the idea that "new restrictions may be imposed on trade to safeguard employment" was only a bad reformulation of the new economic theory, something that "Lord Keynes branded in his last article as 'modernist stuff gone wrong and turned sour and silly.'"[71] Multilateral trade relations, Hirschman argued, were the main path to increasing productivity, economies of scale, and investment opportunities, and it was this process that would ultimately lead to full employment. The return to multilateralism would augment the capacity of countries to exploit the dynamic forces inherent in international trade, as well as gains from specialization. Together with Folke Hilgerdt, Frank Graham, and other international economists, Hirschman emphasized the growing importance of the changing structure of foreign trade. In his view, intra-industry trade would soon become the main driver of growth in international exchanges, whereas traditional patterns based on a static division of labor between industrial and nonindustrial countries would not represent the future course of European trade and growth.

Hirschman knew that, in addition to this interpretative framework, the success of the EPU would rest on technical details. Several reports show his sophisticated analyses of Britain's participation and the problem of sterling balances accumulated by many European countries;[72] the old question of the relations between creditor and debtor countries and the difficulty of finding a compromise between those who believed that credit facilities were excessively generous toward deficit countries and those who believed that they were inadequate;[73] and the potential positive side effects of the EPU, such as the generation of productive externalities and the strengthening of the overall competitiveness of European firms in terms of economies of scale, enhanced innovation, and growth. The establishment of a European market, Hirschman argued, "would create greater adaptability and mobility; it would make possible the economies of large-scale productions; and, most important, it would increase competition and would be a spur to entrepreneurial efficiency and initiative. As a result, productivity would be substantially increased and Europe's competitive position in world markets would be immeasurably strengthened."[74]

Moreover, the EPU would also help strengthen the social compact between capital and labor, a fundamental ingredient for long-term growth. Under its umbrella, countries would be able to reduce the deflationary bias of conservative budgetary and fiscal policies, and they would be more effectively insulated from economic fluctuations originating abroad, particularly in the United States. Finally, if successful, the effects of the EPU would go well beyond the economic realm. Greater integration would be a solid basis for enduring peace, friendship, and cohesion. European multilateralism would lead "to the general strengthening of the competitive spirit and of entrepreneurial initiative and in the productivity effects of an improved morale that would come with a free and united Europe. . . . The success of European integration thus hinges on the continued vitality of the Western European society."[75]

The EPU was meant to promote European solidarity and the sharing of sacrifices among countries. In his last article before the launching of the EPU in August 1950, Hirschman anticipated that the new institution would provide a powerful contribution "to the creation of a single European market" and play a part "in the setting of a common defense effort."[76] As he hoped, the EPU promised to achieve the most difficult objective in the postwar scenario: to become "a genuinely alive international institution."

The establishment of the EPU stirred much controversy in the United States, in particular among different branches of government. The Department of the Treasury and the Department of Agriculture, as many commentators noted, opposed it fiercely, fearing anti-American trade discriminations. The establishment of the EPU strained the collaboration between the Fed and the ECA, and the group that had involved Hirschman at the ECA began to dissolve in 1950, when their boss, Paul Hoffman, left for the Ford Foundation. Though in 1950 and 1951 Hirschman continued to write on European matters, he also began to reflect on broader postwar economic issues that went beyond Europe. In two reports, he discussed how the industrialization of less developed regions would affect industrial countries—chief among them the United States—and, from the opposite perspective, how U.S. economic trends would affect the growth of less developed countries.

For their breadth of analysis and detachment from contingent policy issues, these reports stand out from Hirschman's production at that time. After three years in which he was deeply involved in policy analysis directly related to pressing current debates, here Hirschman made an attempt to examine some longer-term structural elements of global development. Also, these reports show clear linkages to Hirschman's studies before and during World War II on the relationship between the structure of international trade and national power politics and the field of studies that he would address in his next phase, the development of less economically advanced countries.

In 1982, Hirschman described "The Long-Run Effect of Development and Industrialization Abroad on the United States" as his first incursion into the new field of development economics, but this is somewhat misleading.[77] In fact, the article is more about reactions within the United States and other Western countries to the prospects of industrialization in less developed regions of the world. The historical record, Hirschman argued, offered several examples of the recurring fears that the catching up of less developed countries triggers in more advanced ones. Only the United States, Hirschman argued, continually supported the development of other regions. The rationale seemed clear, as the United States would benefit from the export of consumer durables, capital goods, and industrial raw materials to newly industrializing countries and at the same time was relatively insulated from a potential crisis in the markets of raw materials owing to the industrialization of less developed regions. Yet this explanation was not entirely convincing. After all, Hirschman reflected, the differences in the structure of foreign trade between the United States and, say, Germany, were not so great as to be able to explain different attitudes toward industrialization abroad.

As he had done in his studies of international trade in the 1930s and 1940s, and as he would do in his studies of development policies in Latin America in the 1950s and 1960s, Hirschman found a better explanation in the role of ideology and in cultural values: "The truth is that German writers took a certain delight in showing that the industrial countries were digging their own grave through the export of machinery and industrial techniques. This propensity for discovering apocalyptic historical vistas has been a general trait of German historical and sociological writing since the nineteenth century."[78] He noted, "These numerous prophecies of doom do not teach us so much about the real nature of industrialism, capitalism, and competition as about the state of mind of their intellectual authors, ill at ease in the industrial age, and therefore inordinately fertile in finding proofs for its inevitable dissolution." The United States, having a different relationship to capitalist development and lacking the many conflicts and strains that had characterized Europe, showed much less intellectual hostility toward the spread of industrial capitalism.

Tellingly, Hirschman, relatively new to the United States, was eager to write in the first-person plural when discussing the prospects of the country: "Instead of casting an uneasy eye toward the industrial advances of other countries, we have always believed in the possibilities of further economic and technological progress and in our ability to maintain industrial leadership."[79]

And not only were cultural traits "at least as important as the purely economic ones."[80] The rhetoric of economic discourse was also important, and Hirschman devoted several pages to dissecting rhetorical figures such as "the market-destroying effects," according to which the newly industrialized country starts to compete in third markets and perhaps even in the market of the very country that originally supplied it with the capital necessary for industrialization. "Is it not natural enough then to cast the industrializing country in the role of the snake reared and nursed at the bosom of the older industrial countries?" Hirschman asked.[81] But, he noted, the substance of the issue was more rhetorical than real.

Hirschman claimed that data showed a different picture and that the alleged conflict between countries of old and new industrialization was a flawed proposition. International statistics unequivocally showed that imports of manufactured goods increased with the process of industrialization and that two-thirds of international trade consisted of the exchange of foodstuffs and raw materials against other foodstuffs and raw materials and of manufactures against other manufactures. Hirschman had already demonstrated this pattern in his 1945 book with reference to the interwar period; now it helped describe the implications of the postwar industrialization of less developed regions.[82] In conclusion, he argued, "*on balance* industrial countries have nothing to fear, and much to gain, from the industrialization of other countries."[83]

Hirschman also highlighted the geostrategic dimension of this process. In a bipolar world, he argued, the Western world, in particular the United States, should not miss the opportunity to use technical and financial aid as a means to keep less developed regions away from the allure of Soviet-style economic growth. He wrote, "Undeveloped countries . . . do not need to buy economic progress at the exorbitant political and human cost which has been paid by the Russian people."[84] Further, Hirschman did not abandon his hope for federative processes in Europe and elsewhere. In his view, what was then *international* trade might become the *interregional* trade of later times.

In another essay, Hirschman and his colleague Robert Solomon again addressed the question of the relationship between the United States and the rest of the world—this time, however, focusing not on the effects on the U.S. economy of industrialization abroad but on how the U.S. economy would affect foreign countries.[85] Not unlike Hirschman's 1945 book, this report discussed the unbalanced relationship between one large and powerful economy and a number of much smaller and weaker countries. Not only was the United States the country that produced and consumed the most in the world, but the rest of the world was also highly dependent on the U.S. economy, as both a final market and a source of supplies. This unbalanced relationship was not merely quantitative; for less developed countries, access to U.S. technology and financial markets would often mean the difference between development and backwardness. The strength of democratic capitalism in its " 'competition of performance' with Totalitarian Planning" rested on the ability to export modernization.[86] What, then, would be the consequences of a possible slowing down of growth in the United States?

Once again, Hirschman aimed at separating fact from rhetoric. As he put it, "A certain amount of fiction has grown up around the general theme of the devastating foreign effects of a U.S. depression."[87] Based on his studies of the balance of trade of European countries and of transatlantic economic and monetary relations, Hirschman showed how a U.S. depression would not only provoke problems in other countries but also open up unexpected possibilities. These might include an improvement of the terms of trade in favor of countries importing from the United States or the implementation of stabilizing policies and other countermeasures that would make them more independent from fluctuations in the United States.

These two reports mark the virtual end of Hirschman's work at the Fed. Throughout 1951, he continued to analyze the working of the EPU, for example publishing a report on the surplus condition of Belgium, amid increasing conflicts on the appropriate policies to support European recovery.[88] But he was beginning to feel that his work was becoming increasingly repetitive. He later recollected, "A considerable polemic occurred within the government. . . . This type of conflict did not seem to go away, and at a certain point I got tired of circling around the same problems."[89] Also, in conjunction with rising McCarthyism, his social-democratic and antifascist activism in Europe in the 1930s made him suspect to the FBI. Though unaware that the FBI had opened a file in his name, Hirschman must have felt that the atmosphere was changing, and he started to look for a new job. In 1952, the opportunity to go to Colombia as an economic adviser arose, and he seized it.

Hirschman's Colombian experience was initially frustrating. He clashed repeatedly with the head of the 1949 World Bank mission to the country, the Canadian economist and prominent New Dealer Lauchlin Currie, and felt somewhat underused. As Hirschman wrote to a World Bank high officer, "I did not give up my Federal Reserve position to advise on the raising or lowering of reserve requirements in Colombia."[90] From that experience, however, he would distill the theory at the basis of his 1958 book, *The Strategy of Economic Development*. The successful reception of the book catapulted Hirschman from being just one economic expert in a so-called underdeveloped country to being recognized as one of the most original contributors to the thriving field of development economics.

If in 1948 landing a job was for Hirschman a daunting task, *Strategy* gave him tenure and recognition. First at Columbia (1958–1964), then at Harvard (1964–1974), and finally at the Institute for Advanced Study in Princeton (after 1974), Hirschman became one of the most stimulating and admired social scientists of the twentieth century and the author of classics such as *Exit, Voice, and Loyalty* (1970), *The Passions and the Interests* (1977), and *The Rhetoric of Reaction* (1991).

In general, the reports that Hirschman wrote during his years at the Federal Reserve offer valuable insights into several issues. First, they provide an insider's perspective of the way the debate on postwar European reconstruction and monetary problems took shape. Economists had the difficult task of interpreting an economic landscape that was very uncertain and quickly evolving, and, even more than Hirschman's theoretical proficiency, it was his ability to develop a feeling for specific measures and ad hoc policies that made the reports capable of elaborating thought-provoking analyses and effective, though often only temporary, solutions.

Together with Robert Triffin, Guido Carli, Per Jacobsson, Alec Cairncross, and a few others, Hirschman can be credited as one of the architects of the new system of European trade relations and multilateralism. As the reports collected in this book show, he contributed to the theoretical foundations of the EPU, which soon became the most successful symbol of European integration and, as Richard Bissell claimed, "the supreme organization achievement of the Marshall Plan."[91] By February 1951, less than six months after the foundation of the EPU, member countries reduced trade barriers considerably, and by 1955 the share of quota-free European trade was at 90 percent. Between 1952 and 1958, three-quarters of the member countries' balances were successfully offset with a limited use of dollar payments.[92] Throughout the 1950s, intra-European trade increased from $10 billion to $23 billion—much faster than production—fueling the recovery of Western Europe.[93]

The EPU became much more than the first international monetary institution to function effectively after the war. As Hirschman wrote in his recollections, the EPU was "a different and higher form of altruism than the simple commodity aid that had been the essence of the Marshall Plan. It permitted and encouraged temporary discrimination against imports from the US, providing a significant exception to the rule of no discrimination."[94] Though less ambitious, the EPU was an effective embodiment of the spirit that characterized Hirschman's project of a European Monetary Authority in the fall of 1949.

His reports also document an important phase in the formation of Hirschman as a monetary and economic analyst. By the mid-1930s, Hirschman had become a "freelance economic researcher with a specialty on the Italian economy, living in Paris."[95] In 1938 and 1939, he worked on exchange controls in Italy and trade bilateralism in Europe under the supervision of John B. Condliffe, whom he would join at UCLA in 1940. Thanks to these formative experiences, Hirschman was able to develop an accurate interpretation of the postwar predicament of monetary and trade authorities and a feeling for the rationale behind policy choices that at first sight might look contradictory, inconsistent, unwise, or simply unorthodox. Clearly, it helped that he was European himself, as he immediately understood the skepticism of European policy-makers toward the quick elimination of trade barriers and discriminatory policies that had been proposed by several U.S. quarters. The special assistant to the U.S. secretary of state, for instance, had argued that "responsible statesmen *do* advocate . . . the elimination after the war of those unconscionable trade barriers which inescapably choke the flow of international trade."[96] But European authorities tended to see the origins of the current malaise in the disruptions that originated from the 1929 crash of the New York Stock Exchange. As a Chatham House report summarized, Americans "mistake the symptoms for the disease."[97] Hirschman's ability to "read" the European mindset also well equipped him to interpret policy choices in postwar Europe, such as the often apparently disorderly processes of monetary stabilization.

These considerations help explain one further reason for the importance of the Fed years in his professional formation. The analytical framework and the attitude for which Hirschman would become famous as a development economist in the late 1950s, based as they were on unbalanced processes of development and other similar metaphors (e.g., putting the cart before the horse and inverted sequences), took shape one decade earlier in his work as an analyst for the Federal Reserve. In other words, those early writings formed a crucial stage in the development of Hirschman's analytical tools, from his interwar studies on exchange controls, through his early postwar analyses of European monetary and trade policies, to his late-1950s exploits in the relatively new field of development. In a sense, this book shows how Hirschman became Hirschman.

## NOTES

1. Partial exceptions are Albert O. Hirschman, *Potenza nazionale e commercio estero: Gli anni trenta, l'Italia e la ricostruzione*, ed. Pier Francesco Asso and Marcello De Cecco (Bologna: Il Mulino, 1987), published in Italian, which offers a selection of Hirschman's writings on Italy and

chapters from *National Power*, and Jeremy Adelman, *Worldly Philosopher: The Odyssey of Albert O. Hirschman* (Princeton, NJ: Princeton University Press, 2013), which carefully describes the vicissitudes of Hirschman's life at the end of the war but offers only a cursory discussion of his work at the Fed. For a discussion of the Fed years, see Michele Alacevich, *Albert O. Hirschman: An Intellectual Biography* (New York: Columbia University Press, 2021). *National Power* was long overlooked, too, except by international political economists who rediscovered it in the 1970s; see Benjamin J. Cohen, *International Political Economy: An Intellectual History* (Princeton, NJ: Princeton University Press, 2008).

2. Hirschman to his sister Ursula, July 21, 1941, as quoted in Adelman, *Worldly Philosopher*, 195.

3. As quoted in Adelman, *Worldly Philosopher*, 289.

4. Nicholas Dawidoff, *The Fly Swatter: How My Grandfather Made His Way in the World* (New York: Pantheon, 2002).

5. United States Strategic Bombing Survey, *The Effects of Strategic Bombing on the German War Economy* (Overall Economic Effects Division, October 31, 1945), 1.

6. Barry Eichengreen, *The European Economy Since 1945: Coordinated Capitalism and Beyond* (Princeton, NJ: Princeton University Press, 2007), 54–55; Herman van der Wee, *Prosperity and Upheaval: The World Economy, 1945–1980* (Berkeley: University of California Press, 1986), 26.

7. Paul Bairoch, *Storia economica e sociale del mondo: Vittorie e insuccessi dal XVI secolo a oggi*, vol. 2 (Turin: Einaudi, 1999), 985; see also Angus Maddison, "Economic Policy and Performance in Europe, 1913–1970," in *The Fontana Economic History of Europe: The Twentieth Century*, part 2, ed. Carlo M. Cipolla (London: Collins, 1976).

8. Tony Judt, *Postwar: A History of Europe Since 1945* (New York: Penguin, 2005), 13.

9. Based on this kind of evidence, Milward concluded that "the great boom started in 1945"; see Alan S. Milward, *The Reconstruction of Western Europe, 1945–51* (Berkeley: University of California Press, 1984), xv. See also United Nations, *World Economic Report 1948* (Lake Success, NY: United Nations, 1949), 137.

10. Hirschman's dissertation has been published as Otto Albert Hirschmann, *Il franco Poincaré e la sua svalutazione* (Rome: Edizioni di Storia e Letteratura, 2004). See also Albert O. Hirschman, "France

and Italy: Patterns of Reconstruction," *Federal Reserve Bulletin* 33, no. 4 (April 1947): 366 (republished in this volume as chapter 4; the quote is at p. 98).

11. Hirschman, "France and Italy."

12. Albert O. Hirschman, "Public Finance, Money Markets, and Inflation in France," *Review of Foreign Developments* (July 29, 1947): 8–15 (republished in this volume as chapter 5).

13. Albert O. Hirschman, "The French Monetary Move," *Review of Foreign Developments* (February 10, 1948): 1–7.

14. Albert O. Hirschman, "Italian Exchange Rate Policy," *Review of Foreign Developments* (December 16, 1947): 6.

15. Hirschman's report earned him a note from the then director of the Economic Research Department of the Bank of Italy (and future governor of the Bank of Italy) Paolo Baffi: "I read your article on the new system of Italian exchange rates with the greatest pleasure. In my opinion, no one, whether in or outside of Italy, knows how to be as sober, balanced, and acute as you on this subject" (authors' translation). Paolo Baffi to Albert O. Hirschman, January 16, 1948, Archivio Storico Banca d'Italia, Carte Baffi, governatore onorario, cart. 24, fasc. 11, as reproduced in Paolo Baffi, *Via Nazionale e gli economisti stranieri: 1944–1953,* ed. Beniamino Andrea Piccone (Turin: Nino Aragno Editore, 2017), 81. See also Hirschman, "Italian Exchange Rate Policy," 6–11; on the 50 percent system, see Albert O. Hirschman, "Exchange Control in Italy— I," *Review of Foreign Developments* (March 11, 1947): 11–17 (republished in this volume as chapter 2).

16. In *Worldly Philosopher,* Adelman mistakenly interprets this consideration as a demonstration that Hirschman disagreed with Einaudi's policy. See also Albert O. Hirschman, "Credit Restrictions and Deflation in Italy," *Review of Foreign Developments* (April 20, 1948): 8 (republished in this volume as chapter 6; the quote is at p. 116).

17. Hirschman, "Credit Restrictions and Deflation in Italy," 8 (in this volume, p. 116; emphasis in the original).

18. Robert Triffin, who would visit Italy in early 1949 as an envoy of the IMF, also viewed Italy's recovery positively. He wrote, "It is impossible not to be deeply impressed by the most remarkable progress realized in the last year and a half. In many ways, Italy is clearly and rapidly approaching a 'pre-stabilization' stage in monetary and economic

recovery" (Robert Triffin, "Italy's Progress in 1948," RD-804, March 4, 1949, Baffi Papers, Pratiche, no. 30, f.1, Archivio Storico Banca d'Italia, as quoted in Ivo Maes, *Robert Triffin: A Life* [Oxford: Oxford University Press, 2021], 78). Like Hirschman, Triffin noticed the apparent paradox of mutually opposed policies of credit restrictions for private businesses and easy credit for (mainly state-owned) selected industrial sectors, highlighting the need to move to a new phase characterized by budgetary discipline (see Maes, *Robert Triffin*, 78–79).

19. Albert O. Hirschman, "Economic and Financial Conditions in Italy," *Review of Foreign Developments* (December 14, 1948): 13.

20. Hirschman, "Economic and Financial Conditions in Italy," 13.

21. Harold James, *International Monetary Cooperation Since Bretton Woods* (New York: Oxford University Press, 1996), 74.

22. Hirschman, "Economic and Financial Conditions in Italy," 1–17.

23. Hirschman, "Economic and Financial Conditions in Italy," 3.

24. Albert O. Hirschman, *The Strategy of Economic Development* (New Haven, CT: Yale University Press, 1958).

25. For contemporary discussions of the dollar problem and the postwar international monetary system, see for instance Robert B. Bryce, "Basic Issues in Postwar International Economic Relations," *American Economic Review* 32, no. 1, part 2 (1942): 165–81; and Geoffrey Crowther, "Anglo-American Pitfalls," *Foreign Affairs* 20, no. 1 (1941): 1–17.

26. International Monetary Fund (IMF), *Annual Report of the Executive Directors* (Washington, DC: U.S. Government Printing Office, 1946), 11.

27. This criticism, however, would not be particularly effective with commodities whose price elasticity of demand was very low, such as tin and rubber, or with general inputs to industrial production (Crowther, "Anglo-American Pitfalls"). See also Machlup in Gottfried Haberler, Karl L. Anderson, Antonin Basch, Imre de Vegh, Heinrich Heuser, Folke Hilgerdt, Michael L. Hoffman, et al., "Problems of International Economic Policy," *American Economic Review* 32, no. 1, part 2 (1942): 209.

28. H. W. A. "The United States in the World Economy," *Bulletin of International News* 21, no. 6 (March 18, 1944): 217.

29. Alvin H. Hansen and Charles P. Kindleberger, "The Economic Tasks of the Postwar World," *Foreign Affairs* 20, no. 3 (1942): 466–76.

30. Charles P. Kindleberger, "International Monetary Stabilization," in *Postwar Economic Problems*, ed. Seymour E. Harris (New York: McGraw-Hill, 1943), 375–95.

31. Howard S. Ellis, "Removal of Restrictions on Trade and Capital," in *Postwar Economic Problems*, ed. Seymour E. Harris (New York: McGraw-Hill, 1943), 345–59.

32. Howard S. Ellis, "The Dollar Shortage in Theory and Fact," *Canadian Journal of Economics and Political Science* 14, no. 3 (1948): 359. For other criticisms, see Arthur I. Bloomfield, "The Mechanism of Adjustment of the American Balance of Payments: 1919–1929," *Quarterly Journal of Economics* 57, no. 3 (1943): 333–77; and Arthur I. Bloomfield, "Induced Investment, Overcomplete International Adjustment, and Chronic Dollar Shortage," *American Economic Review* 39, no. 5 (1949): 970–74.

33. Roy Harrod, *Are These Hardships Necessary?*, 2nd ed. (London: Rupert Hart-Davis, 1947), 42–43.

34. Harrod, *Are These Hardships Necessary?*, 33.

35. Harrod, *Are These Hardships Necessary?*, 35 (emphasis in the original).

36. Albert O. Hirschman, "Inflation and Balance of Payments Deficit," *Review of Foreign Developments* (August 24, 1948): 6–8 (republished in this volume as chapter 8).

37. Hirschman, "Inflation and Balance of Payments Deficit," 7 (in this volume, p. 132).

38. Albert O. Hirschman, "Disinflation, Discrimination, and the Dollar Shortage," *American Economic Review* 38, no. 5 (December 1948): 886–92.

39. Eichengreen, *The European Economy Since 1945*, 65.

40. Eichengreen, *The European Economy Since 1945*, 66.

41. Standard references on the EPU are Robert Triffin, *Europe and the Money Muddle: From Bilateralism to Near-Convertibility, 1947–1956* (New Haven, CT: Yale University Press, 1957); and Jacob J. Kaplan and Günther Schleiminger, *The European Payments Union: Financial Diplomacy in the 1950s* (Oxford: Clarendon, 1989). A new wave of literature on the EPU was occasioned by the collapse of the Soviet Union and the related question of whether the EPU might work as a template for monetary arrangements among former socialist countries. A fine, short introduction to that debate is Barry Eichengreen, *Reconstructing*

*Europe's Trade and Payments: The European Payments Union* (Manchester: Manchester University Press, 1993).

42. Eichengreen, *The European Economy Since 1945*, 73; see also William Diebold Jr., *Trade and Payments in Western Europe: A Study in Economic Cooperation, 1947–51* (New York: Harper, 1952).

43. Guido Carli, "The Return to Convertibility of European Currencies," *Giornale degli Economisti e Annali di Statistica* 47, nos. 11–12 (1988): 525–36; see also Thomas H. Oatley, "Multilateralizing Trade and Payments in Postwar Europe," *International Organization* 55, no. 4 (2001): 949–69.

44. Otto Albert Hirschmann, "Étude statistique sur la tendance du Commerce extérieur vers l'équilibre et le bilateralism" (paper presented at the twelfth session of the International Studies Conference, "General Study Conference on Economic Policies in Relation to World Peace," Paris, 1939 (available at https://colornihirschman.org/dossier/article/75/etude-statistique-sur-la-tendence-du-commerce-exterieur-vers-lequilibre-et-le-bilateralisme). An English translation from the original French by Pier Francesco Asso is available as Albert O. Hirschman, "Statistical Study of the Trend of Foreign Trade Toward Equilibrium and Bilateralism," *Political Economy: Studies in the Surplus Approach* 4, no. 1 (1988): 111–24, http://www.centrosraffa.org/pe/4,1/4,1.5.%20Hirschman.pdf. See also Pier Francesco Asso, "Bilateralism, Trade Agreements, and Political Economists in the 1930s: Facts and Theories Underlying Hirschman's Index," *Political Economy: Studies in the Surplus Approach* 4, no. 1 (1988): 83–110.

45. Albert O. Hirschman, "Fifty Years After the Marshall Plan: Two Posthumous Memoirs and Some Personal Recollections," in *Crossing Boundaries: Selected Writings* (New York: Zone, 1998), 39; see also Albert O. Hirschman, "Trespassing: Places and Ideas in the Course of a Life. An Interview by Carmine Donzelli, Marta Petrusewicz, and Claudia Rusconi," in *Crossing Boundaries: Selected Writings* (New York: Zone, 1998), 78–79.

46. Hirschman's paper was also written as a follow-up to the proposal for a "reserve bank for Europe," prepared by the Financial Subcommittee of the European Assembly that met in Strasbourg in August 1949. See Albert O. Hirschman, "Proposal for a European Monetary Authority" (henceforth, "Proposal"), Albert O. Hirschman Papers, box 65, folder 7, "Federal Reserve Correspondence and Papers," Mudd Library,

Princeton University, henceforth, AOHP (republished in this volume as chapter 14).

47. On November 2, 1949, Harold van Buren Cleveland transmitted Hirschman's memorandum to the program secretary "for study and comment."

48. Ivo Maes and Ilaria Pasotti, "The European Payments Union and the Origins of Triffin's Regional Approach Towards International Monetary Integration," *History of Political Economy* 50, no. 1 (2018): 155–90; see also Kaplan and Schleiminger, *The European Payments Union.*

49. Robert Triffin and Raymond Bertrand, *The Unresolved Problem of Financing European Trade*, IMF Staff Memorandum no. 160 (Washington, DC: International Monetary Fund, December 29, 1947), 4; see also Maes, *Robert Triffin.*

50. Hirschman, "Proposal."

51. Hirschman, "Proposal," 1 (in this volume, p. 198).

52. Hirschman, "Proposal," 1 (in this volume, p. 197).

53. Hirschman, "Proposal," 3 (in this volume, p. 200).

54. Hirschman, "Proposal."

55. Hirschman, "Proposal," 4 (in this volume, pp. 201–202).

56. Hirschman, "Proposal."

57. Hirschman, "Proposal," 5 and 1 (in this volume, pp. 203 and 197).

58. Hirschman, "Proposal," 5 (in this volume, p. 204).

59. Hirschman, "Proposal," 8 (in this volume, p. 209).

60. Hirschman, "Proposal," 8 (in this volume, p. 208).

61. Hirschman, "Proposal," 2 (in this volume, p. 198).

62. Hirschman, "Proposal," 8 (in this volume, p. 208).

63. Harold van Buren Cleveland, Theodore Geiger, and John Hulley, "Proposal for the Establishment of a European Monetary Authority (EMA)," April 17, 1950, AOHP.

64. Timothy W. Wintour, *The Buck Starts Here: The Federal Reserve and Monetary Politics from World War to Cold War, 1941–1951* (PhD Dissertation, Kent State University, December, 2013), 341.

65. Eugenio Colorni (1909–1944), killed by the Fascists in 1944, was a philosopher and antifascist activist. Altiero Spinelli (1907–1986) was one of the authors of the Ventotene Manifesto and in the postwar years a member of the European Commission and of the European Parliament.

66. Eichengreen, *The European Economy Since 1945.*

67. See, for example, Richard M. Bissell Jr., with Jonathan E. Lewis, and Frances T. Pudlo, *Reflections of a Cold Warrior: From Yalta to the Bay of Pigs* (New Haven, CT: Yale University Press, 1996); on the European side, see Guido Carli, *Cinquant'anni di vita italiana* (Rome: Laterza, 1996). Further useful analyses can also be found in Gianni Toniolo, *Central Bank Cooperation at the Bank for International Settlements, 1930–1973* (Cambridge: Cambridge University Press, 2005); and Leland Yeager, *International Monetary Relations. Theory, History and Policy* (New York: Harper & Row, 1976).

68. Jossleyn Hennessey, Vera Lutz, and Giuseppe Scimone, *Economic "Miracles". Studies in the Resurgence of the French, German and Italian Economies since the Second World War* (London: Institute of Economic Affairs, 1964).

69. Albert O. Hirschman, "Multilateralism and European Integration," *Review of Foreign Developments* (April 25, 1950): 18 (republished in this volume as chapter 17; the quote is at p. 245).

70. As shown in John Ikenberry, "Rethinking the Origins of American Hegemony," *Political Science Quarterly* 104, no. 3 (1989): 375–400, this proposition gained wide currency during the negotiations over the International Trade Organization and then in the approval of the General Agreement on Tariffs and Trade.

71. Hirschman, "Multilateralism and European Integration," 18 (in this volume, p. 233).

72. See also Barry Eichengreen, Stanley Fischer, and Vittorio Grilli, "A Payments Mechanism for the Former Soviet Union: Is the EPU a Relevant Precedent?," *Economic Policy* 8, no. 17 (1993): 318.

73. See also Martin Daunton, "Britain and Globalization Since 1850: III. Creating the World of Bretton Woods, 1939–1958," *Transactions of the Royal Historical Society* 18 (2008): 1–42; Oatley, "Multilateralizing Trade and Payments."

74. Hirschman, "Multilateralism and European Integration," 13 (in this volume, p. 240).

75. Hirschman, "Multilateralism and European Integration," 19 (in this volume, p. 245).

76. Albert O. Hirschman, "The European Payments Union," *Review of Foreign Developments* (August 15, 1950): 8 (republished in this volume as chapter 18; the quote is at p. 262).

77. Albert O. Hirschman to H. W. Singer, March 29, 1982, AOHP; Albert O. Hirschman, "The Long-Run Effect of Development and Industrialization Abroad on the United States," *Review of Foreign Developments* (July 25, 1950): 1–17 (republished in this volume as chapter 20).

78. Hirschman, "The Long-Run Effect," 7 (in this volume, p. 281).

79. Hirschman, "The Long-Run Effect," 8 (in this volume, p. 282).

80. Hirschman, "The Long-Run Effect," 8 (in this volume, p. 282).

81. Hirschman, "The Long-Run Effect," 9 (in this volume, p. 283).

82. Albert O. Hirschman, *National Power and the Structure of Foreign Trade* (Berkeley: University of California Press, 1945).

83. Hirschman, "The Long-Run Effect," 12 (in this volume, p. 285; emphasis in the original).

84. Hirschman, "The Long-Run Effect," 14 (in this volume, p. 287).

85. Albert O. Hirschman and Robert Solomon, "The Influence of U.S. Economic Conditions on Foreign Countries," *Review of Foreign Developments* (September 12, 1950): 1–20 (republished in this volume as chapter 21).

86. Hirschman and Solomon, "The Influence of U.S. Economic Conditions," 10 (in this volume, p. 303).

87. Hirschman and Solomon, "The Influence of U.S. Economic Conditions," 9 (in this volume, p. 302).

88. Albert O. Hirschman, "The Problem of the Belgian Surplus in EPU," *Review of Foreign Developments* (September 25, 1951): 1–4.

89. Hirschman, "Trespassing," 80.

90. Albert O. Hirschman to J. Burke Knapp, September 20, 1952, as quoted in Michele Alacevich, *The Political Economy of the World Bank: The Early Years* (Stanford, CA: Stanford University Press, 2009), 57.

91. Bissell Jr., with Lewis, and Pudlo, *Reflections of a Cold Warrior*, 64.

92. Pierre-Hernan Rojas, "At the Origin of European Monetary Cooperation: Triffin, Bretton Woods, and the European Payments Union," in *Political Economy and International Order in Interwar Europe*, ed. Alexandre M. Cunha and Carlos Eduardo Suprinyak (London: Palgrave-Macmillan, 2021), 139–78.

93. Barry Eichengreen and Jorge Braga de Macedo, *The European Payments Union: History and Implications for the Evolution of the International Financial Architecture* (Paris: OECD Development Center, 2001).

94. Hirschman, "Fifty Years After the Marshall Plan," 42–43.

95. Albert O. Hirschman, conversation with the author (Asso), 1988; see also Asso, "Bilateralism, Trade Agreements, and Political Economists in the 1930s," 83–110.

96. Francis B. Sayre, "Keen Comments on World Economy Today: Necessity for Large Foreign Trade 'Indisputably Clear,'" *Foreign Commerce Weekly* 10, no. 5 (1943): 13 (emphasis in the original).

97. H. W. A. "The United States in the World Economy," 218.

# I

# PATTERNS OF EUROPEAN RECONSTRUCTION

## MACROECONOMIC CHALLENGES

# 1

## HIGHER INTEREST RATES
## AND THE CREDIT SHORTAGE
## IN FRANCE

On January 9, the Bank of France split the discount rate which, since January 1945, had stood at 1–5/8 per cent. While raising it only slightly to 1–3/4 per cent for Treasury bonds and short-term commercial bills financing genuine sales, the rate was increased to 2–1/4 per cent for all other commercial bills, such as, e.g., bills mobilizing banking overdrafts. The rates for advances were raised concurrently. Furthermore, the National Credit Council, an organ given large powers of supervision and direction of banking and investment by the Banking Nationalization and Reorganization Law of December 2, 1945, has reinforced its qualitative credit control. The main innovation consists in requiring conclusive proof for credit need from the applicant when the amount of credit requested exceeds a given limit (reported to be 30 million francs). Besides submitting complete information as to his past and present financial position, the applicant must also furnish a prospective budget and explain in particular why the amount sought could not be procured by a reduction of inventories.

---

These measures, which were foreshadowed by the recommen-
dations of the *Financial Inventory* issued in December by the
Ministry of Finance under the direction of Robert Schuman, are
the logical monetary complement to the attempt to provoke, by
the recent officially decreed 5 per cent price cutback, a liquidation of inventories and thereby a cumulative downward movement of prices. Officials were, however, at pains to point out that
no massive credit deflation is intended; the intention is rather to
provide for discrimination between credit requests for "productive" and "speculative" purposes. Apparently the Bank has profited from its experience during July 1946 when a selective credit
policy was first recommended and was coupled with an almost
total cessation of open market purchases by the Bank of France.
This sudden reversal greatly disturbed the bill market by raising
doubts as to the liquidity of Treasury bond investments and contributed to an excess of redemptions over subscriptions in the
following months. That the Bank of France is not acting with
similar rashness this time is indicated by the increase of its open
market portfolio from 37.7 to 39.2 billion francs during the first
week in January.

The new measures have served to dramatize a development
with which observers of the Paris money market have been
familiar for some time. The high state of liquidity which was
characteristic of the market throughout the German occupation was, it is true, further strengthened during the first year of
liberation, mainly as a result of the currency exchange which
brought about considerable preventive conversions of currency
holdings into bank and savings deposits. On January 20, 1945,
the discount rate was lowered from 1–3/4 per cent to 1–5/8 per
cent, the lowest rate in the history of the Bank of France. However, the first signs of change were seen as early as a few weeks
after the exchange of currency. The exceptional factors which

had led to a rapid increase of bank deposits at the expense of the note circulation ceased to operate. At the same time, expanding economic activity and wage increases reduced the liquid resources of industrial and commercial enterprises which were often forced to redeem their Treasury bond holdings and to have more frequent recourse to banking credits in the forms of discounts and overdrafts. An important factor in this situation is the slowness with which the French Treasury settles its obligations. Not only are cash payments often considerably delayed, but in many cases the State pays its contractors in bills with a maturity of one year which the contractors must discount with the banks in order to obtain cash. Credit requests for the purpose of holding stocks in anticipation of price increases placed further burdens on the banking system.

Under these conditions the Bank of France saw its rediscount portfolio rise rapidly and, in addition, was compelled to intervene on the open market by consistent purchases in order to make the market at all receptive to short-term Treasury issues. The following table [table 1.1] shows these two items and the note circulation as they appear at different dates in the Bank's balance sheet.

TABLE 1.1 BANK OF FRANCE, MAIN MONETARY POLICY OPERATIONS, 1945 TO 1946 (IN MILLIONS OF FRANCS)

| Date | Open-market portfolio | Rediscount portfolio | Note circulation |
|---|---|---|---|
| August 2, 1945 | 11,059 | 11,897 | 444,476 |
| December 27, 1945 | 17,979 | 25,852 | 570,006 |
| June 27, 1946 | 24,982 | 46,204 | 629,181 |
| December 26, 1946 | 37,618 | 79,389 | 721,865 |

*Source*: Bank of France, balance sheets, various dates.

Further evidence of tightening credit supply conditions was offered by the poor reception of a reconstruction loan issue by the Credit National in July 1946 and by the slow but steady rise of long-term interest rates. As is seen from the table, recourse to the credit facilities of the Bank of France expanded considerably in the second half of 1946. This period was highlighted by the excess of redemptions of Treasury bonds over subscriptions, by consequent direct advances of the Bank to the State, and by a particularly rapid rise of prices.

The simultaneity of price inflation, currency expansion, and credit shortage has given rise to rather confused comments, the most characteristic one being a release of the Ministry of Finance in August 1946 which stated that "in contrast to an opinion widely spread, France is not at present in a period of monetary inflation. . . . in relation to the pre-war period the rate of increase of the note circulation is indeed clearly below that of the cost of living. . . . it does not seem that there is a plethora, but rather a contraction of the means of payment. . . . the volume of means of payment is inadequate in relation to the requirements of the country" (*Monde*, August 29, 1946).

One cannot help remembering, in this connection, the thesis of many German economists (Helfferich in particular*) that there really was no inflation in Germany in 1920–23 since all experience testified to the scarcity of the circulating medium and since, relative to the rise in price of gold or of domestic goods, the volume of the German currency in circulation had actually

---

* Karl Theodor Helfferich (1872–1924) was a German politician, economist, and financier. During World War I, he held a series of important Reich offices and, after 1918, became a leading right-wing politician in the Weimar Republic. As creator of the plan to stabilize the mark in 1923, he played a major role in ending the catastrophic postwar inflation. See John G. Williamson, *Karl Helfferich, 1872–1924: Economist, Financier, Politician* (Princeton, NJ: Princeton University Press, 1971).

contracted. There is no need to re-expose this sophism after the masterful job done by Bresciani-Turroni in his well-known work on the German inflation.[1†] It is interesting to note here, however, that according to Bresciani-Turroni a shortage of working capital was first felt in Germany in the late stages of 1922, that the rise in prices started to outdistance the rise in currency circulation (in relation to 1913) in December 1920 while in countries with moderate post-World War I inflations such as France and Italy prices never caught up with the increase in money supply.[2]

The similarity between the present French situation and the later stages of the German inflation should not lead to too dark a view of French prospects. It must be recalled that French production had to recover from an extremely low level after liberation and that shortages of working capital and scarcity prices were therefore bound to occur. Secondly, there exist even today large-scale hoardings of cash on the part of French farmers waiting for the opportunity to buy machinery and cattle and of consumers hoping for prices to come down again, and the shortage of business cash is therefore due more to imperfection in the monetary flow than to anticipatory price markups caused by a universal scramble for real assets.

Finally, the measures used are evidence that the French Government has revised its former complacent position (particularly characteristic of M. Pleven's term as minister of finance) that monetary and banking policy can hardly make any contribution to the solution of the inflationary problem and that all that can

---

† Costantino Bresciani-Turroni (1882–1963) was an economist and banker. He contributed to the Dawes Plan of 1924 and was a financial adviser to the Agent General for Reparation Payments, who was responsible for establishing the plan for Germany's payment of reparations following World War I. In the postwar years, he was the chair of the Banco di Roma and the Italian executive director of the International Bank for Reconstruction and Development.

be done is to wait for increased production to bring prices down. It has recently been pointed out that private borrowing exerted a by no means negligible influence on the various inflationary processes after the first World War.[3] The new French policy of interest rate discrimination and of qualitative credit control presents an interesting attempt to reconcile the aims of expanding production, of preventing the use of bank credit for commodity hoarding and speculation, and of actually speeding up the turnover of inventories.

## NOTES

1. C. Bresciani-Turroni, *The Economics of Inflation*, London, 1937, pp. 155–182 [Costantino Bresciani-Turroni, *The Economics of Inflation: A Study of Currency Depreciation in Postwar Germany* (London: George Allen & Unwin, 1937)].

2. *Op. cit.* [Bresciani-Turroni, *The Economics of Inflation*], pp. 162, 165, and 366.

3. League of Nations, *The Course and Control of Inflation*, 1946, pp. 28–32 [League of Nations Economic, Financial, and Transit Department, *The Course and Control of Inflation: A Review of Monetary Experience in Europe After World War I* (Geneva: League of Nations, 1946)].

# 2

# EXCHANGE CONTROL IN ITALY—I

On January 27, an agreement between the American and Italian governments established a new rate of exchange for United States Government expenditures in Italy. This rate is intended to provide American military and civilian personnel with approximately the same amount of lire per dollar as is obtained by Italian exporters earning dollar exchange. Since March 1946, Italian exporters have had to surrender only 50 per cent of their hard foreign exchange proceeds to the Italian exchange control agency at the official rate (225 lire to the dollar);[1] they obtained the right to dispose freely, at whatever price the market might set, of the other half provided that it was used within a specified time-limit for the import of certain commodities. Supposing a "free export rate" of 425 to the dollar, the exporter would therefore obtain $0.5 \times 225 + 0.5 \times 425 = 375$ lire for each dollar earned through exports. In order to give similar advantages to United States Government personnel in Italy, the rate of 225 will be averaged on the 25th of each month with the average free export rate for the preceding 30 days. The resulting rate will be applicable during the following month to

---

United States Government expenditures. It amounted to 378 lire per dollar for February.

Simultaneously with the announcement of this monetary agreement, an Italian decree extended the benefit of the so-called "50 per cent system" to all non-commercial transactions (including tourists' expenditures, remittances, and investments) with all hard-currency countries. This will generalize the awkward cross-rates which have been prevailing on the free export exchange market where the Swiss franc has normally been quoted higher, and the pound sterling lower, than their official rates to the dollar.

The complicated, if ingenious, system which has been devised, while actually extending the "50 per cent system" from commercial to all foreign receipts, has been interpreted as the beginning of the end of the Italian experiment in multiple rates and limited freedom of foreign exchange. Ever since the fall of 1946, government officials and the financial press have forecast, discussed, advocated, or bemoaned its impending abolition to be carried out through the establishment of just such an average rate as has now been set for United States Government expenditures. This seems a proper moment, therefore, to review and appraise the "50 per cent system."

Freedom for exporters to retain part of their foreign exchange proceeds as a means of stimulating exports was urged by the First National Meeting of Foreign Traders at Milan in March 1946. The demand was quickly met by two decrees, dated March 15 and April 13, 1946, which authorized exporters to utilize or sell 50 per cent of their "free" currency proceeds (i.e., excluding currencies of countries with which payments agreements were in force) within 90 days. For this purpose foreign exchange accounts were to be opened at authorized banks; to the second decree was appended a list A of commodities which could be imported simply upon proof of the availability of free foreign exchange and list B of commodities the importation of which required in addition a regular license. The system got rapidly underway, possibly as a result of the experience which Italian industrialists, particularly in the textile field, had gained with a very similar system during the immediate pre-war years.[2] Since May 1946 "free export rates" for the United States dollar, the British pound, and the Swiss franc have been regularly quoted by the financial press.

The system, as established in March/April 1946, went through two distinct phases. The first was one of extension and liberalization, the second one of gradual restriction. The first phase, which lasted through August 1946, was marked by an extension of the time limit to a maximum of four months (Decree of May 31, 1946); and by admission to the benefits of the system of proceeds from repairs of foreign ships and of freight receipts (August 1946).

Soon thereafter, on September 3, 1946, the first restrictive measures were taken. These were intended mainly to prevent unduly slow turnover of the foreign exchange controlled privately under the system. The time limit within which utilization is mandatory was cut down to 60 days and a general limit of 120 days starting from the moment of acquisition of foreign exchange was set for the actual physical importation of the goods purchased. The most important further restriction was the shift, ordered on September 26, 1946, of cotton and wool from list A of freely importable commodities to the regime of ministerial license applicable to commodities on list B. The reason for this step was probably that the Italian textile industry was then already at or near capacity and that the authorities intended to check an excessive building-up of raw material inventories.

Finally, in October 1946, the 50 per cent system was largely abolished insofar as manufacturing for foreign account was concerned. This practice, particularly important in the textile industry, consists in importing raw materials from a foreign firm which keeps title to the material as it is being transformed into finished goods specified by and deliverable to that firm. In this way the Italian manufacturer has no initial outlay for raw materials and is paid only for "value added." The restrictive legislation adopted in October allowed the exporter the benefits of the 50 per cent system when value added exceeded the value of the foreign raw material used.

The following table [table 2.1] shows the development of the exchange rate for "free export" dollars and pounds sterling

TABLE 2.1 LIRA'S EXCHANGE RATES AND THE RATE OF INFLATION

| | Dollar | | Pound Sterling | | Wholesale Price[a] | | |
|---|---|---|---|---|---|---|---|
| | Export rate | Bank note | Export rate | Bank note | Official | Black market | Cost of Living (1938 = 100)[b] |
| Jan. 1946 | — | 382 | — | 1,119 | 2,305[c] | 4,633[c] | 3,096 |
| May 1946 | 364 | 333 | 1,446 | 920 | 2,289 | 4,588 | 2,899 |
| June 1946 | 377 | 366 | 1,593 | 1,057 | 2,314 | 4,429 | 2,823 |
| July 1946 | 478 | 401 | 1,864 | 1,222 | 2,351 | 4,430 | 2,811 |
| Aug. 1946 | 505 | 483 | 1,847 | 1,369 | 2,573 | 4,683 | 2,898 |
| Sept. 1946 | 596 | 530 | 1,965 | 1,464 | 2,665 | 4,838 | 2,677 |
| Oct. 1946 | 601 | 520 | 1,957 | 1,448 | 2,805 | 5,108 | 2,935 |
| Nov. 1946 | 569 | 600 | 1,651 | 1,690 | 2,953 | 5,502 | 3,037 |
| Dec. 1946 | 565 | 679 | 1,516 | 1,869 | 3,179 | 6,599 | 3,295 |
| Jan. 23, 1947 | 533 | 605 | 1,587 | 1,700 | | | |

[a] Indexes calculated by the Società Edison; both indexes include prevailing free market prices of unregulated commodities.
[b] Index of "cost of subsistence for middle classes" calculated by the Centro per la Statistica Aziendale.
[c] Index for February 1946; January index not available.

compared with black market rates for bank notes and with wholesale prices and the cost of living. While at first the bank note rate was inferior to the export rate, the opposite relationship has prevailed since the middle of November 1946. The export rate has not experienced the violent fluctuations of the black market quotations which brought the value of the dollar note to a maximum quotation of 755 on December 3. These latter fluctuations were caused by sudden and variously motivated flights from the lira in a thinning market while no such elements acted on the export rate. The sharp rise of the export rate until September seems to have been in anticipation of the rise of the price level during the later months of the year. Soon after a temporary leveling-off of prices during the early part of 1946 it was indeed generally felt that the de facto devaluation of 125 per cent which had taken place in January had not been sufficient, that demands for wage increases could not be held back and that Treasury Minister Corbino's "orthodox" financial policy was doomed to failure.* Furthermore, the peace treaty negotiations on which Italian public attention was then focused led to a general pessimistic feeling about Italy's economic future. Since September the export rate for dollars has displayed remarkable stability which may be explained partly by the impact of rising prices in the United States, and partly by the restrictive legislation mentioned above. The measures adopted eliminated or reduced certain classes of demand for the export currencies while leaving the supply relatively unaffected.

---

* Epicarmo Corbino (1890–1984) was an economist and politician (Italian Liberal Party), a member of the Italian Constituency Assembly, and an opponent of the drastic monetary reforms proposed by the Left parties. He was minister of industry, labor and trade (1944) and then treasury minister (1945–1946) in the first and second De Gasperi cabinets.

In attempting to appraise the Italian experiment in limited freedom of foreign exchanges, it should first be pointed out that the emergence of the experiment was greatly favored by the almost total absence of efficient State controls at the moment Italy recovered her sovereignty in matters of foreign trade from the Allied Commission on January 31, 1946. Furthermore, the UNRRA [United Nations Relief and Rehabilitation Administration] program guaranteed the most essential imports for the whole of 1946 and thereby reduced the risks inherent in the decision to leave allocation of half of the foreign exchange earned by exporters to competitive forces. These two conditions have now come, or are about to come, to an end and this alone makes the survival of the 50 per cent system precarious. But both friends and foes of the system agree that it has given Italian exports a powerful fillip during 1946. Its immediate effect was to transfer excess profits from importers (where they generally accrue in exchange control systems) to exporters, a shift which is certainly welcome when a country is struggling with foreign exchange difficulties. As a result of competitive bidding on the part of importers, exporters disposed of their foreign exchange at very advantageous prices. This actually stimulated exports to the extent of diverting many essential goods, particularly textiles, from home consumption and thereby increasing prices in certain sectors of the economy. An increase in the general price level, however, should result from this process only to the extent that the system permitted the creation of a foreign exchange reserve in the hands of exporters (which could easily be taken over by the State should it decide to abolish the "50 percent system") or the necessary rebuilding of raw material inventories.

According to data supplied by the Association of Italian Joint-Stock Companies (*Italian Economic Survey*, December

1946, p. 14<sup>†</sup>), foreign exchange proceeds from exports not yet utilized amounted at the end of November 1946 to 14.9 million dollars, 7.5 million pounds sterling, 1.9 million Swiss francs, and smaller amounts of other free currencies. It is understood that in December there was a further substantial increase in these figures. The relatively large amount of sterling holdings results from the difficulties of acquiring freely importable (List A) commodities in the sterling area and this fact may also account for the gradual but steady deterioration of the sterling cross rate relative to the dollar evident from the table on page 56 [table 2.1]. While on the black market for bank notes the pound has consistently been valued somewhat below three dollars, the export currency market reflected during the first two months approximately the official cross rate; only in November did the value of the pound fall below three dollars.

On the whole, the "50 per cent system" seems to have contributed greatly to Italian economic recovery in the past year; it has made Italian producers definitely export-conscious and has resulted in the allocation of certain imports according to efficiency of the producers rather than by reference to some fictitious base period or simply by favoritism. It has made underbilling of exports with the intent of accumulating foreign exchange abroad much less attractive than under conditions of strict exchange control. Finally, it has oriented Italian export

---

† The Association of Italian Joint-Stock Companies ("Associazione fra le Società Italiane per Azioni") was founded in 1910 and regularly published reports and studies on the Italian economy. See Gianni Toniolo, Fernando Salsano, Giangiacomo Nardozzi, Giandomenico Piluso, Antonio Pedone, Franco Gallo, Antonio Padoa-Schioppa, Piergaetano Marchetti, Fulvio Coltorti, Gustavo Visentini, and Carlo Carboni, eds., *Tra imprese e istituzioni: 100 anni di Assonime* (Rome: Laterza, 2010); and Pier Francesco Asso, Fabio Lavista, and Sebastiano Nerozzi, "Banks, Firms and Economic Culture: Economists and Research Centres in Interwar Italy," in *An Institutional History of Italian Economics in the Interwar Period*, vol. 2, ed. Massimo M. Augello, Marco E. L. Guidi, and Fabrizio Bientinesi (Cham, Switzerland: Palgrave Macmillan, 2020), pp. 179–209.

trade toward the hard currency countries, a welcome development since the deficit of Italy's balance of payments is primarily
a hard currency and even a dollar deficit. Bresciani-Turroni, in
an article published by the *Corriere della Sera* in Milan (January
16, 1947) has advocated the continuance of the system because of
its proven elasticity and adaptability to cost and price changes,
which in the present unsettled state of the Italian economy are
inevitable and even desirable.

According to unofficial preliminary estimates for 1946 now
coming from Rome, Italy's exports have made an excellent showing by reaching the level of 350–400 million dollars of which 230
million went to free-currency countries. Thus Italy bids fair to
be the country for which the universal underestimate of exports
during 1946 in balance-of-payments forecasts is highest, on a
percentage basis. Indeed various forecasts had put the exports
for 1946 at 125 to 175 million dollars, that is, at 25 per cent to 50
per cent of the actual result.[3]

In spite of its indubitable contributions to Italy's economic
recovery, the "50 per cent system" seems definitely in jeopardy.
Among its enemies are the Italian bureaucrats and "total planners" to whom any kind of economic freedom is anathema. They
have valuable allies in the countries with which Italy has clearing
agreements. These countries have to pay the official exchange rate
(225 lire to a dollar) for their imports from Italy while importers
in free-currency countries take advantage of the export rate. This
has led to the temptation for clearing-agreement countries to use
some of their free-exchange resources in their trade with Italy, as
Sweden has recently done in order to acquire some Italian manufactures of special value for the Swedish economy. Italian pro-
ponents of the "50 per cent system" have thus been able to claim
that the 50 per cent system has not only freed Italian trade from
the shackles of exchange control, but has also contributed to the

expansion of the free zone of multilaterally conducted international trade generally (*Il Sole*, January 24, 1947).

The incentive for Italian exporters to direct their sales to free-currency countries and the reluctance of importers in exchange-agreement countries to buy Italian goods at the official rate of exchange has [sic] led to a reversal of the Italian position on clearing accounts from a creditor to a debtor status.[4] Poland, in particular, has recently complained about Italian prices being far too high if converted at the official rate rather than the free export rate.

Further pressure for abolition of the "50 per cent system" is exerted by the British, mainly because of the unfavorable dollar-pound cross rate which has prevailed in the Italian exchange markets. Furthermore, some Italian newspapers have intimated that the ranks of the enemies of the 50 per cent system are due to be swollen by the International Monetary Fund, of which Italy is soon to become a member. The I.M.F. is, of course, opposed in principle to multiple exchange rates, but it seems unlikely that in this particular instance the Fund would press for immediate abolition. In view of high priority import requirements, there can be no question of leaving to the exporters 100 per cent of the foreign exchange earned. Reestablishment of a unique rate at the present time, therefore, could only mean reversion to the obligation for exporters to surrender all foreign exchange to the authorities. Such a development would clearly run counter to one of the main purposes of the Fund, which is to assist member countries in the relaxation and eventual removal of exchange controls. While it is true that even a nation's currency system cannot indefinitely remain "half slave and half free," it would appear better to leave it provisionally in this condition pending the creation of the bases for a system of total freedom—when the only practical alternative is a return to total regulation.

If it is desired to keep the essential features of the present system while removing from it the stigma of multiplicity of exchange rates, this can easily be done by adopting the device—familiar in South America—of letting the exporter sell to the importer not the foreign exchange itself, but the *right to buy* foreign exchange which is then acquired at the official exchange rate from the monetary authorities.

Opponents of the system have pointed out that Italian exports would not suffer if, as they propose, the new single rate is set half-way between the official and the export rate, so that the lira proceeds of the Italian exporter would remain unchanged. To this it is easy to reply (1) that this might be true for the moment the rate is set, but that subsequent cost, price, and demand changes could soon make exports very unattractive—or excessively profitable; (2) that exporters value not only the high lira proceeds they obtain for 50 per cent of their foreign exchange, but also, and quite importantly, the very right of relatively free disposition over this amount, i.e., the freedom from administrative control, the freedom to utilize the exchange themselves if they should so desire, the goodwill derived from ceding it to some supplier, etc.

Finally, the question might be asked: supposing that a single rate has to be set, does the free export rate provide an indication as to the probable level of the equilibrium rate? Official utterances and articles in the press have frequently given the impression that the equilibrium rate necessarily lies half-way between the official rate and the export rate. This, of course, would hold true only under very special conditions of demand which are highly unlikely to obtain. Nevertheless, it is certain that the level and movements of the free export rate provide incomparably more valuable indications as to the probable equilibrium level of the lira, than do black market quotations for bank notes, fluctuations of which have been largely determined by psychological factors and resulting capital movements.[5] The present system permits the monetary authorities to gauge the intensity of specific demands for foreign exchange at prevailing international prices through the device of adding to or subtracting from the list A of commodities which can be freely acquired abroad with the exporters' free exchange, thereby increasing or decreasing the number of bidders in the free export exchange market. Gradual addition of even more commodities to the free list, coupled with a concomitant increase in the supply of free exchange through successive raising of the percentage of foreign exchange earnings retained by exporters, might actually be one answer to the baffling problem of how to achieve conditions of relative monetary freedom in an orderly fashion and without undue exchange rate fluctuations.

It is the conclusion of this article, therefore, that the abolition of the "50 per cent system" at the present time is undesirable since it would:

(1)   increase the area of restriction in Italian and international trade and finance;

(2)   have unfavorable effects upon Italy's exports and balance of payments; and

(3)   deprive the Italian authorities of a valuable signpost and of a possible method for attaining a new equilibrium of exchange rates in a system of freer international payments.

## NOTES

1.  Cf. this *Review*, June 3, 1946 [J.H.F., "Relaxation of Foreign Exchange Control in Italy," *Review of Foreign Developments*, June 3, 1946]. Nominally, the official rate still stands at 100 lire to the dollar and is raised to 225 by a so-called "equalization quota" of 125 per cent which is uniformly applicable to all official foreign exchange transactions.

2. Between 1937 and 1939 from 50 to 75 per cent of foreign exchange earnings were left to various classes of exporters of manufactured products. The economic implications of this policy were excellently analyzed by G. Demaria, "I rapporti di cambio manovrato in regime di autarchia corporativa," *Giornale degli Economisti* LIII (1938), pp. 1–16 [Hirschman cited the wrong volume; the correct one is Giovanni Demaria, "I rapporti di cambio manovrato in regime di autarchia corporativa," *Giornale degli Economisti* 78, no. 1 (1938): 1–16]; and by G. [Giorgio] Boggio, "Contingentamenti e cambi specifici," *Rivista Italiana di Scienze Economiche* XI (1939), pp. 970–996.

3. Other European controlled economies are discovering the advantages of giving exporters the incentive of relatively free disposition of some portion of their foreign exchange earnings. Thus, France has recently made a timid step in the direction of Italy's system by allowing exporters of textiles and automotive products to retain 10 per cent of their exchange earnings for the purchase of industrial equipment. In Spain, exporters have been permitted since August 30, 1946, to retain one-third of their export proceeds for imports of raw materials, provided that one-fourth of the exchange delivered to the Exchange Control authorities (i.e., one-sixth of the total) is in free foreign exchange. In neither France nor Spain do exporters have the possibility of selling the retained exchange to importers.

4. This reversal is partly due to prepayments by Italian importers who, acting on the basis of rumors of impending devaluation, hastened to settle all their commitments at the present rate. As a result, payments by importers were limited in January 1947 to 200,000 lire; payments in excess of this amount had to be authorized by the Italian Exchange Control Agency.

5. It so happens that purchasing power parity calculations based on cost-of-living indexes for November/December 1946 and taking 1938 as the base year yield a parity quite close to the average between the official and free export rates.

# 3

# EXCHANGE CONTROL IN ITALY—II

A previous article in this *Review*[1] has dealt with the system which permits Italian exporters to utilize or sell in the free market 50 per cent of their free exchange proceeds. The present note will analyze another feature—or regulated loophole—of the Italian exchange control: the system of the so-called "franco valuta imports." To purchase franco valuta means to import without asking the Exchange Control authorities for foreign exchange (and to enter a firm commitment not to do so once the commodities have been imported). This is, of course, possible only if the imports are matched against a transfer of capital (or a gift) from abroad. Except insofar as they are financed directly through credits granted by foreign exporters, franco valuta imports are therefore merely a variety, or an extension, of the concept of trade carried on through private barter or compensation. Although recent legislation has drastically curtailed the system, it remains an interesting episode in the history of exchange control.

Franco valuta imports were authorized early in 1946, largely, as in the case of the 50 per cent system, upon the urgings of the

Convention of Foreign Trade held in Milan in March 1946. Detailed regulation started in April. A list, identical with list A of the 50 per cent system,[2] detailed the commodities importable upon the sole commitment not to ask for foreign exchange, while the importation of other commodities required an import license in addition. Franco valuta imports were authorized only from free currency countries; this restriction excluded Continental European countries with which payments agreements had been concluded. The "free" list was amended subsequently, one of the most important changes being the permission, granted as of July 1, 1946, to import coffee and cocoa franco valuta *without* ministerial license.

Subsequent legislation has gradually and severely restricted the system. On September 6, 1946, it was decreed that, in addition to the commitment not to ask for foreign exchange, proof was required that the imports were financed in one of three specified ways:

(a)   Through transfer of capital from foreigners or Italians residing abroad. In this case, the importer paid the amount in lire due into an untransferable account in the name of the foreign resident, this account being subject to restrictive rules with respect to types and amount of expenditures authorized.

(b)   Through repatriation of Italian holdings abroad which were not subject to surrender to the Government or which were subject to such surrender but were accumulated before March 26, 1946 (the date of the inauguration of the 50 per cent system). The latter undeclared holdings were to be repatriated through franco valuta imports within six months and for this purpose were granted immunity from penalties for failure to declare and surrender them. The time-limit for this immunity has since been extended another six months, i.e., to September 6, 1947.

(c)   Through gifts from abroad.

Finally, on February 21, 1947, all franco valuta imports against transfers of foreign capital ([a] above) were prohibited since it was held that the extension of the 50 per cent system to foreign investments, which had taken place in January, provided foreign capitalists with a sufficiently attractive rate.

As is generally true with respect to private compensations, the rates of exchange at which the franco valuta imports are financed are different for each transaction. All that can be said in this respect is that prices quoted in Italy for many commodities such as coffee and cocoa permitted an importer to pay a rate of exchange of 800 lire to the dollar and still make a handsome profit. In general, the rates at which the franco valuta transactions have taken place are believed to have exceeded the black market rates for dollar bank notes by a margin of about 150 lire. As to the importance of the transactions, various estimates have put them at as much as 15 per cent of commercial imports in terms of lire and at between $10 and $20 million during 1946.[3]

Interaction between the 50 per cent and the franco valuta systems has been evident in several respects. A commodity which could be imported by means of the free foreign exchange earned by exporters naturally would not be imported at the higher franco valuta rates. For this reason, the list of commodities freely importable through the franco valuta system and list A of commodities freely importable by means of free export currencies, which were identical at first, gradually had to be separated; while certain commodities were added to the former, the scope of the latter list became more restricted. Little is known as to the practices followed in issuing import licenses to the two categories of importers, but it appears likely that importers who could avail themselves of the franco valuta mechanism have been given preferential treatment. Every restriction of franco valuta imports has caused a tension in the free export rates since demand that was previously satisfied through the franco valuta system was forced to enter the bidding for the available free export currencies.

There has been much discussion of the merits and demerits of the system of franco valuta imports. Its partisans have pointed out:

(1)    that it provided the many Italians who had violated the exchange control regulations in the 'thirties with a convenient method of repatriating their foreign resources which generally were held under the names of foreigners residing abroad;

(2)    that it made possible some influx of foreign capital without the actual establishment of a preferential rate of exchange for capital imports; and

(3)    that the repatriation of Italian foreign holdings and the influx of foreign capital would never have taken place at all at the low official rate of 225 to the dollar. Therefore, the imports made possible by these transfers represented a net addition to the amount of goods available in Italy even though they might not have corresponded to the Government's idea of what was most needed by the Italian economy.

The opponents of the system pointed out that the system worked not only as an amnesty for past violations of exchange control, but even more as an encouragement to new violations.

(1)    Exporters have been reported to have undervalued their products and to have repatriated foreign holdings thus acquired through franco valuta imports.

(2)    Purchasers of bank notes in the foreign exchange black market apparently have found it profitable to ship the notes acquired to their countries of origin and to reconvert them into lire or into imported merchandise through the system. In general,

capital flight may have been encouraged by the certainty given to would-be exporters of capital that they could repatriate, through franco valuta imports, their foreign holdings at a profitable rate of exchange and whenever convenient.[4]

(3)   The most important source of the franco valuta transactions is said to have been purchases by Americans of real estate or business interests in Italy against dollar credits in the United States (*Il Sole*, March 8, 1947) which are then transferred through the franco valuta system. This practice deprived the State of valuable foreign resources.

(4)   Furthermore, the system discriminated against the Italian emigrant and his family in Italy since, because of the small amounts sent and because of lack of business connections, he could not but transmit funds at the unfavorable official rate. One of the main purposes of the recent extension of the 50 per cent system and the concomitant restriction of franco valuta imports was to do away with this iniquity.

In general, it was pointed out, the imports which have taken place through the system were chiefly certain eagerly sought consumption goods of a semi-luxury character; the system therefore has catered to the few rich and possibly increased the internal stresses afflicting Italian society.

All in all, it seems that the system may have served a useful purpose in the beginning as a temporary amnesty for exchange control violators during Fascism and as a means of reestablishing Italian foreign trade connections. But its usefulness would appear to have come largely to an end, and its harmful aspects have gradually outweighed its possible benefits. Recent restrictive legislation will practically terminate the system by September of this year. It remains to be seen, however, whether the plea of the latest Convention of Foreign Trade, just concluded at Milan, to abolish that legislation and to reauthorize franco valuta imports on a more liberal basis will be heeded by the Italian Government.

## NOTES

1. [*Review of Foreign Developments*], March 11, 1947 [republished in this volume as chapter 2].
2. See *loc. cit.*, page 11 [*Review of Foreign Developments*, March 11, 1947, p. 11, chapter 2 of this volume, p. 54].
3. Because of the high rates of exchange applied, franco valuta imports occupy a larger share in total lire imports than in total dollar imports.
4. The counter-argument is, of course, that as long as general political and economic instability makes some measure of capital flight almost unavoidable, it is essential to provide some built-in mechanism through which the capital can be repatriated—whenever one particular cause for alarm to capitalists has ceased to operate.

# 4

# FRANCE AND ITALY

## Patterns of Reconstruction

During the winter of 1946–47 economic recovery from the destruction wrought by the war suffered a temporary relapse all over Europe. The dramatic coal crisis in Great Britain has called renewed attention to the acute power shortage that prevails throughout Europe. Largely for lack of adequate fuel and power, European countries have been unable in recent months to maintain even the inadequate rate of industrial production achieved last fall, while at the same time they have faced impending food shortages, and remained in the grip of chronic monetary and financial instability. Neither France nor Italy was able to escape from this general predicament. At the same time, however, adoption of the Constitution in France and the signature of the peace treaty for Italy strengthened the feeling in these two major Continental nations that the insecurity of the immediate postwar period might finally be coming to an end.

When Germany collapsed, both France, victim of German spoliation for over four years, and Italy, battleground of the opposing armies for almost two years, were economically

Confidential. *Federal Reserve Bulletin* 33, no. 4 (April 1947), pp. 353–66.

prostrate. In 1945, national output in both countries was estimated at 40 to 50 per cent below the 1938 level. At the end of
the war both countries were suffering from disruption of transportation and drastically lowered productivity in agriculture
and industry owing to physical exhaustion of labor, destruction and undermaintenance of capital equipment, and drastic
reduction of supplies of raw materials and fertilizers. In addition, the swollen money supply, which was a heritage of war
and occupation, was generating acute inflationary pressures.
This, together with the general administrative disruption, led
to a near-breakdown of the official allocating and rationing
machinery.

Old economic ills peculiar to each country were aggravated
by the war: France's manpower problem became more acute
through the loss by agriculture and industry of one million
workers between 1938 and 1946. In Italy, the dangerous economic
and social cleavage between the relatively wealthy North and the
rest of the country was accentuated by the concentration of war
destruction in Central and Southern Italy.

## REVIVAL OF OUTPUT

Recovery in the immediate post-liberation period in European
countries has been aptly compared to the process that takes place
in an anthill that has been disrupted. Such activities as removing mines and debris, rebuilding bridges, and repairing damaged
railroad tracks, industrial plants, and dwellings have tended to
be carried out through numberless individual, local, and regional
initiatives, although even this "spontaneous" process could not
have occurred or would have been considerably delayed without
outside aid.

*Industrial production.* These early rehabilitation activities laid the groundwork for the more complex tasks of industrial recovery, in which the availability of fuel and raw materials acquired dominant importance. Industrial production began to assume significant proportions in France in the second half of 1945, and in Italy toward the spring of 1946. September and October 1946 were the best postwar months for Italy and France, respectively, with production indexes (based on 1938) reaching 68 for Italy and 93 for France. Output declined in the following months owing mainly to the effect of weather conditions on the production of hydroelectric power. There are indications that production began to rise again in several branches of French industry as early as January, whereas the relapse in Italian industrial activity, which relies more heavily on water power, was both more severe and more persistent. [Table 4.1 provides the production indexes for France and Italy for January and October 1946.]

In both countries the industries that have reached the highest levels of activity as compared with prewar are those directly concerned with electric power generation, transportation (trucks and rolling stock), and, to a lesser degree, with exports (textiles). A lag is evident in Italian iron and steel output, which had been overexpanded during the thirties, while Italian cement production is held back by coal shortages. The earlier start of industrial recovery in France is reflected both in the generally higher levels of output attained and in the slower rate of growth during 1946.

*Coal shortage.* French coal output has attained high levels, surpassing even the prewar production of one million tons a week. At the time of liberation, French domestic production was reduced to a rate of only 30 million tons a year. A major effort on the part of the miners, spurred by various incentives, and the use of over 50,000 German prisoners, led to a more rapid recovery of coal production in France than in any other European country.

### TABLE 4.1 INDUSTRIAL PRODUCTION

| Industry | France | | Italy | |
|---|---|---|---|---|
| | Jan. 1946 | Oct. 1946 | Jan. 1946 | Oct. 1946 |
| General index[a] | 65 | 93 | 28 | 66 |
| Selected industries: | | | | |
| Coal | 100 | 118 | 61 | 84[b] |
| Electricity | 134 | 132 | 109 | 131 |
| Pig iron | 38 | 74 | 4 | 20[b] |
| Steel | 45 | 87 | 25 | 55 |
| Passenger automobiles | 4 | 30 | 5 | 32 |
| Trucks | 111 | 206 | 115 | 202 |
| Railroad cars | 300 | 527 | 118 | 339 |
| Cement | 56 | 130 | 13 | 44 |
| Glass | 87 | 119 | 114 | 175 |
| Cotton spinning | 51 | 91 | 30 | 67[b] |
| Artificial fibers | 98 | 175 | 4 | 63 |
| Paper | 40 | 78 | 24 | 46 |
| Sulphuric acid | 55 | 76 | 39 | 60 |
| Sodium carbonate | 52 | 131 | 20 | 72 |

*Note*: Index numbers, 1938 = 100.
[a] For France, index calculated by the Institut National de la Statistique et des Etudes Economiques; for Italy, estimate based on two indexes, one given by the Italian Confederation of Industry, the other by the Institute of Economic Studies of Milan.
[b] September figures.

In the month of October 1946, output reached 118 per cent of the 1938 level in spite of a 25 per cent drop in average output per worker. Total coal supplies for the year 1946 remained, however, about one-sixth below prewar, since only half the normal imports were obtainable; France relied upon imports for about one-third of her total coal consumption before the war. Italy, with her weak position further impaired through the loss of the

Arsa mines in Istria, is producing only about one-tenth of her prewar consumption of 14 million tons, and has therefore been particularly vulnerable to the general European shortage of coal.

British coal, the chief outside source of supply for both France and Italy before the war, has not been available on any substantial scale. Deliveries from the Ruhr have remained disappointingly small; Ruhr coal production has not yet reached more than 50 per cent of the prewar level, and there has been a continuing problem of allocation as between German requirements and foreign needs. Silesian coal, for which Italy, unlike France, had been an increasingly important market before the war, failed to reach either country in significant quantities. Despite the high shipping costs involved, the United States has therefore been the principal source of European imports in recent months; shipments of American coal, however, have been erratic and have remained below schedules because of the coal and maritime strikes.

Thus coal has been and still is the major bottleneck of production in both France and Italy. Moreover, high priorities have been established for the requirements of mines, railroads, power plants, and food processing industries, and, as a result, general manufacturing has been forced to bear the brunt of shortages and irregularities of supply.

*Manpower problems.* In France shortage of manpower ranks with the scarcity of coal as a major economic problem, whereas Italy has approximately two million unemployed. An agreement has been reached, after considerable delay, for the immigration into France of 200,000 Italian workers during 1947. Italian labor is also in great demand in other European countries, and large numbers might be absorbed by South America. An agreement was signed in February with Argentina that may result, during the next five years, in the emigration of 250,000 Italian workers.

Unemployment in the North should be largely eliminated by expanding industrial activity, but the chronic overpopulation of the agricultural South can probably be absorbed only by a combination of further industrialization, agricultural reform, and emigration.

The manpower shortage in France is due partly to a long-term decline in the employable population, but mainly to an internal shift away from industry and toward government employment and the distributive trades. Output in various industries (such as mining, iron and steel, and machinery) is already limited by the lack of available manpower, and this condition will be accentuated by the scheduled departure of a large proportion of the 440,000 German prisoners of war lent to France by the United States, and of 17,000 Polish workers, half of whom are miners. The seriousness of the situation has led the trade unions to accept a return to the 48-hour week (with pay for 50 hours) from the 40-hour week which they had secured in the thirties after prolonged struggles.

*Agriculture and food consumption.* Varying weather conditions in the past two seasons make appraisal of agricultural recovery difficult. After the disastrous droughts of 1945, favorable weather prevailed in 1946, resulting in wheat crops of 6.1 million tons for Italy and of 6.7 million for France. These figures are 46 and 70 per cent, respectively, above those for 1945, but still 20 and 15 per cent below average prewar levels. In France, this year's harvest is likely to be severely affected by the extensive winter killing of wheat during the recent cold waves. Prewar production levels can be restored only gradually in both countries through increased availability of fertilizers, draft animals, and agricultural machinery. Relatively large food imports will therefore be required during the next few years.

In both countries serious problems were created by the diversion of grains from human to animal consumption, either through increased sowings of fodder grains at the expense of wheat or through direct animal feeding of wheat. This development was caused both by the relatively low official price of wheat and by the comparative ease with which animal products could be marketed through illicit channels.

The following table [table 4.2] shows approximate levels of food consumption for urban consumers in both countries. The French calory totals conceal the seriousness of specific shortages, particularly of dairy products and eggs. In Italy, the insufficiency of caloric consumption is aggravated by the even more inadequate supply of protective foodstuffs.

On the whole, despite the physical and human obstacles to recovery, economic activity has made substantial progress since the end of the war. The most important repairs of industrial plant have been carried out, inventories have been gradually rebuilt, and consumption levels raised. However, much remains to be done and even these limited accomplishments have been placed in periodic jeopardy by grave disturbances arising from unsolved monetary and financial problems.

### TABLE 4.2 ESTIMATED AVERAGE DAILY CONSUMPTION BY URBAN CONSUMERS (IN CALORIES)[a]

|  | France | Italy |
| --- | --- | --- |
| 1938 | 2,600 | 2,400 |
| 1946 | 2,200 | 1,750 |
| Official 1946 rations | 1,250 | 900 |

[a] Exclusive of wine.

## THE COURSE OF INFLATION

In both France and Italy rationing systems, as well as price and other economic controls, were instituted at the outbreak of the war. Despite the magnitude of the wartime inflationary forces and the difficulties of obtaining public compliance with government regulations, these controls functioned with a fair degree of success as long as the essentials of life were available through the rationing systems. In the course of liberation, however, the general disorganization of distribution transformed the black market, formerly a source of luxuries for the well-to-do, into an essential part of the distribution system. The more complete breakdown of controls in Italy led to abandonment of rationing for all commodities except bread, pasta, fats, and sugar. In France, shifts in basic policies led to several cycles of relaxation and tightening of controls, as in the case of bread, meat, and wine. Gradually, a tendency emerged for the official prices of rationed goods to rise toward the black market prices, but the continued existence of dual price levels and shifts in the comparative importance of the two markets in consumers' budgets serve to complicate analysis of the inflationary process.

The character of monetary developments was quite similar in the two countries although the expansion of money supply since 1938 was about nine-fold in France and more than forty-fold in Italy at the end of 1946. In relation to wholesale price movements two periods can be distinguished for France: a period of rapid increase in the money supply which left the rise in prices far behind, followed by a period during which the prices rose faster than the money supply. By the end of 1944, prices had increased by 175 per cent as against an increase in the money supply by more than 400 per cent. During the two subsequent years, the opposite relationship prevailed, as is shown in the accompanying chart [chart 4.1]. Between

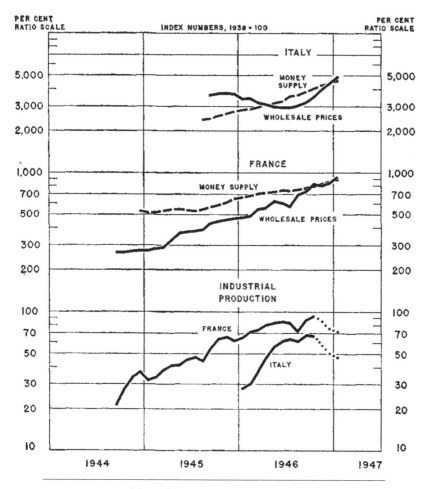

PER CENT
RATIO SCALE

INDEX NUMBERS, 1938 = 100

PER CENT
RATIO SCALE

ITALY

MONEY SUPPLY

WHOLESALE PRICES

FRANCE

MONEY SUPPLY

WHOLESALE PRICES

INDUSTRIAL PRODUCTION

FRANCE

ITALY

1944    1945    1946    1947

CHART 4.1 Money Supply, Prices, and Industrial Production
in France and Italy Since Liberation

Money supply—France: Includes currency circulation and bank and postal
checking deposits; total bank deposits estimated by doubling deposits of big
four banks; Italy: Includes currency circulation and bank and postal checking
deposits; adjusted for circulation of bankers' checks and similar instruments.
Wholesale prices—France: Provisional index of official wholesale prices
of the Statistique Générale de la France with 1938 weights; Italy: Wholesale price index calculated by the Center for Business Statistics, Florence.
Industrial production—See footnote a to table on page 74 [table 4.1]; figures
beginning November 1946 are estimated on basis of fragmentary data.

For each country, the various series are shown for the months for which
data are available since liberation (France, September 1944; Italy,
April 1945). Latest figures shown are for January 1947.

December 1944 and December 1946, prices increased by over 200 per cent and the money supply by only 70 per cent, closing the gap between the two.

In Italy, the rise in wholesale prices had already surpassed the expansion of the money supply by the time of liberation. Subsequently, the cycle repeated itself once more. During the first half of 1946 the money supply increased substantially, whereas prices actually declined slightly; from July until the end of the year a new series of price rises was accompanied by a relatively slower increase in the money supply.

Neither country has followed the example of several smaller European nations in forcing the transfer to blocked accounts of excess currency holdings and bank deposits owned by the public.[1] Measures of this type were widely debated in France and finally rejected in favor of a simple exchange of old against new currency issues designed (1) to ascertain for the purposes of a capital levy (the so-called national solidarity tax) the amount of liquid funds held by individuals, and (2) to cancel the notes that were not presented for exchange (including those looted by the Germans). Within this limited scope the operation was quite successful. In Italy an exchange of currency was in turn proposed, shelved, announced as impending, and finally renounced in March 1947.

The main obstacle in both countries to a more far-reaching currency reform appears to have been the political power held by the peasants, who are known to have hoarded huge quantities of bank notes. In France and Italy it would probably be necessary at least to offer government bonds in substitution for the blocked portion of currency holdings and bank deposits, and to the extent that the bank notes or deposits are already firmly held, this would mean incurring to no purpose a substantial added interest burden. But the main argument on the part of Ministers Pleven and

Corbino,\* the most active opponents of blocking measures in France and Italy, was that increased output of goods and services would take the pressure off prices and that, in the meantime, no action should be taken that might hamper business in financing increased production. Adherents of this view apparently believed that the idle currency and deposits were being hoarded because of a genuine preference for liquid assets, and not because there was nothing to buy. If, however, these idle means of payment were only being held in anticipation of the return of consumers' goods to the market, the first stages of industrial recovery might have been expected to usher in a period of great upward pressure on prices rather than to relieve the price tension. Price developments, particularly during the second half of 1946, suggest that blocking measures in anticipation of this critical period might have served a useful purpose, even if price controls and rationing had been a great deal more effective than they actually were.

Business enterprises have lately shown a marked need for bank credit in both countries. It is extremely difficult to distinguish in this process between credits called for by rising prices and higher levels of economic activity and those designed to finance, directly or indirectly, speculative activities such as the accumulation of excessive inventories. But there is little doubt that the expansion of bank credit to private borrowers has created a new source of inflationary pressure. In France, the monetary authorities have recently attempted to discriminate against speculative transactions by instituting differential discount rates on advances by the Bank of France and by requiring business

---

\* René Pleven (1901–1993), a politician and among the closest collaborators of General Charles de Gaulle, was the minister of colonies (1944), finance (1945–1946), and defense (1949–1950) and then prime minister (1950–1951); in this capacity, he proposed the so-called Pleven Plan for a European Army. On Corbino, see chapter 2, footnote 1.

enterprises seeking bank credit to prove that they cannot raise the necessary funds by accelerating their sales.

However, the excess of public expenditures over revenue, rather than expansion of bank credit for business purposes, has remained the principal and continuing source of inflationary pressure.

## THE INTRACTABLE DEFICIT

As might be expected at a time of low national income and large reconstruction expenditures, budgetary deficits have proved to be the most recalcitrant of all postwar problems. In both France and Italy, each new Minister of Finance has sought to introduce drastic corrective measures, but each time within a few months a new crisis has arisen. Long-term and short-term borrowing, fiscal reform, increases in tax rates, and capital levies—all these have been attempted with considerable ingenuity but with varying success.

The following table [table 4.3] shows estimates of public expenditures and receipts in France and Italy for recent years. The receipts figures exclude, however, substantial amounts of special revenues realized by the Governments concerned through the sale to the public of imported goods (or foreign exchange) financed from foreign sources. Such foreign financing includes grants, credits, and, in the case of France, liquidation of official gold and exchange reserves. Only the remaining deficits have had to be financed by internal borrowing.

In spite of strenuous efforts, the French and Italian Governments have had to resort to direct advances from their central banks in order to finance their needs. This traditional method of inflationary finance, however, has been kept within relatively modest limits and has amounted to only about 10 and 15 per cent, respectively, of the total increase in the public debt since liberation in Italy and France. In both countries early post-liberation bond

## TABLE 4.3 FRENCH AND ITALIAN PUBLIC EXPENDITURES AND RECEIPTS (IN BILLIONS OF FRANCS AND LIRE)

|  | 1938 | 1945 | 1946 | 1947 |
|---|---|---|---|---|
| France[a] |  |  |  |  |
| Expenditures[b] | 107.5 | 535 | 877 | 1.150[c] |
| Receipts | 54.6 | 221 | 485 | 550 |
| Deficit | 52.9 | 314 | 392 | 600 |
|  | **1938–39** | **1944–45[d]** | **1945–46** | **1946–47[e]** |
| Italy[f] |  |  |  |  |
| Expenditures | 39.9 | 332 | 509 | 900 |
| Receipts | 27.6 | 48 | 128 | 290 |
| Deficit | 12.3 | 284 | 381 | 610 |

[a] French fiscal year begins January 1.
[b] Including deficits of local bodies and subsidies to nationalized enterprises, as well as certain reconstruction expenditures not provided for in the budget.
[c] Official estimate composed of 660 billion francs ordinary, 360 billion extraordinary, and 130 billion special account expenditures; 40 per cent of non-ordinary expenditures have been made contingent upon the balancing of the ordinary budget.
[d] Liberated territory only.
[e] Latest estimates, inclusive of reconstruction expenditures of 300 billion lire, given by the Italian Minister of Finance.
[f] Italian fiscal year begins July 1.

issues were successful, and financing thereafter has proceeded mainly through short-term issues, supported when necessary by central bank purchases in the open market. In view of the extended powers of the French and Italian Governments over the banking systems, non-renewal of short-term Treasury paper is no longer, as was true during the inflation of the twenties, the constant dread of finance ministers. Nonetheless, an excess of redemptions over subscriptions occurred in France in the second half of 1946 partly as a result of increased demands for bank credit on the part of business.

While no such difficulties were apparent in Italy, the rapid rise in the volume of floating debt during 1946 was causing concern to the Government. A somewhat unusual issue of perpetual bonds was launched in Italy toward the end of 1946 with the double purpose of consolidating a portion of the short-term debt and of raising new money. Holdings of these securities were declared exempt from the capital levy which was then impending and has since been enacted. This provision permitted the Finance Ministry to set the interest yield on the loan as low as 3.6 per cent, or about one and one-half per cent below the long-term market rate. The loan attracted 231 billion lire, of which 119 billion was short-term paper tendered for exchange, leaving 112 billion of cash subscriptions. The simultaneous decrease in banks' reserves with the Bank of Italy indicates that the banks may have provided around one-fourth of the cash subscriptions in addition to their participation in the consolidation.

In addition to the task of reconstructing war-ravaged economies, the fundamental cause of the budgetary predicament, there has been a number of specific obstacles to fiscal recovery in both countries:

(1)  The war left in its wake an overexpanded government apparatus. In France, in particular, this situation has caused official concern in view of the lack of manpower in industry. The gradual dismissal of 50,000 wartime civil servants ordered by the Blum Government in December 1946 marked the first real attempt to remedy the situation.

(2)  In order to keep consumers' prices down, substantial subsidies have been paid to producers in France on a large number of food and industrial products and transportation services; in Italy, direct subsidies are granted mainly on wheat. In 1946, these payments absorbed from 20 to 25 per cent of total French and Italian budgetary receipts. Expenditures for subsidies have recently been reduced since it is held in both countries that their contribution to the general inflationary process through the budget deficit has been outweighing their retarding effect on the rise in prices of specific commodities.

(3)  In both countries widespread tax evasion has been a corollary of
     "under-the-counter" sales and other black market transactions.

(4)  The Treasuries of both countries have been burdened by heavy
     obligations arising from the deficits of local and regional bod-
     ies, numerous semi-autonomous agencies, and the railroads.
     In France the first year of operation of a number of national-
     ized enterprises ended with sizable deficits which had to be
     financed by the Treasury.

(5)  Revenues have not kept pace with the constant advance of
     prices because of difficulties in adapting the tax system. In
     both countries reassessment of real property lagged behind the
     rise in values, while the pay-as-you-go principle was only par-
     tially applied in income taxation.

(6)  In France, the budget continues to be burdened by heavy mili-
     tary expenditures (26 per cent of all expenditures in 1946), the
     scheduled reduction of which in 1947 is rendered problematical
     by events in Indo-China. A special factor in Italy, on the other
     hand, is the large outlays for the unemployed.

The discussion of both the inflationary and the budgetary
problems would be incomplete without reference to a number
of hopeful symptoms. In both countries, tax receipts more than
doubled between January and November 1946, while the rate
of increase of ordinary expenditures has been materially slower.
An important factor in dealing with the general inflationary
situation is the growing conviction shown by the workers and
their representatives that increases in nominal wages are futile
under present circumstances. In Italy a six-month labor "truce,"
stabilizing wages and outlawing strikes, was signed between the
trade unions and the employers in October 1946. In France, the
unions have abandoned their plea for a general wage increase
after having obtained an adjustment of sub-standard wages. No
final judgment can yet be rendered on the attempt, initiated by

the Blum Government in January 1947 and recently followed by the Italian Government, to lower prices through direct administrative decree, but it is already clear that the accelerated rise in French prices, which in the latter part of 1946 threatened to turn into a runaway inflation, has been arrested.

## INTERNATIONAL FINANCIAL POSITION

The harassing difficulties of the domestic monetary and financial situation are matched by another no less fundamental problem that confronts the French and Italian economies. This is the task of financing the huge import surplus which results from pressing needs for imported food, raw materials, and equipment, on the one hand, and from still reduced exporting capacity on the other. Although financing difficulties and world shortages did not permit fulfillment of original goals, considerable import surpluses, largely financed through United States aid, were achieved in 1946. The following table [table 4.4] presents estimates of the balances of payments of the two countries for that year.

TABLE 4.4 ESTIMATED FRENCH AND ITALIAN BALANCES OF PAYMENTS IN 1946 (IN MILLIONS OF DOLLARS)

| Item | France[a] | | Italy | |
|---|---|---|---|---|
| | Credits | Debits | Credits | Debits |
| Goods and services: | | | | |
| Estimated exports and imports (including freight)[b] | 550 | 2,540 | 400 | 850 |
| U.S. surplus property | — | 300 | — | 160 |
| Services | 150 | 170 | 25 | 20 |
| Total | 700 | 3,010 | 425 | 1,030 |

# TABLE 4.4 ESTIMATED FRENCH AND ITALIAN BALANCES OF PAYMENTS IN 1946 (IN MILLIONS OF DOLLARS) (*CONTINUED*)

| Item | France[a] Credits | France[a] Debits | Italy Credits | Italy Debits |
|---|---|---|---|---|
| Donations: | | | | |
| Interim U.S. supply program | — | | 58[c] | |
| UNRRA (including freight) | — | | 380 | |
| Private donations | 50 | | 130 | |
| Total | 50 | | 568 | |
| Credits utilized (net): | | | | |
| Lend-lease "pipeline" credit | 240 | | — | |
| Export-import bank loans | 621 | | 22 | |
| U.S. surplus property credits | 300 | | 160 | |
| Other credits | 96[d] | | — | |
| Total | 1,257 | | 182 | |
| Other accruals: | | | | |
| Reimbursement for net troop pay | | | 144[e] | |
| Total foreign aid | (1,307) | | (894) | |
| Net sales (or accruals) of gold and foreign assets[f] | 1,003 | — | — | 289 |
| Total credits and debits | 3,010 | 3,010 | 1,319 | 1,319 |

[a] Data for France and French Colonies.

[b] These figures are based on official estimates which differ substantially from the official customs statistics. The latter contain defects resulting, in Italy, from the multiplicity of exchange rates, in France, from valuation of imports at subsidized domestic prices, and in both countries from the still disrupted state of custom operations.

[c] Program financed through lend-lease appropriations to bridge the gap in essential supplies to Italy between the termination of the U.S. Army's civilian supply program late in 1945 and the start of UNRRA aid.

[d] France drew 106 million dollars on the 243 million credit granted by Canada in addition to the 40 million drawn in 1945, incurred debts of about 120 million under payments agreements, and received long-term and short-term investments of approximately 100 million dollars. On the other hand she repaid about 230 million dollars on foreign credits; of this sum 200 million was paid on the 600 million dollar post-liberation credit from the United Kingdom, the remainder of which was funded.

[e] Includes 4 million dollar reimbursement by Canada; remainder from the United States. Does not include 101 million made available in December 1946– January 1947 as counterpart of earlier U.S. military expenditures in Italy for purposes other than troop pay.

[f] Residual item—includes errors and omissions.

It is evident that foreign aid made a fundamental contribution toward balancing the French and Italian international accounts.

Total aid, in the form of grants, loans, or other devices, amounted to 1,307 million dollars for France and to 894 million for Italy. After account is taken of the share of other countries in the provision of UNRRA aid, private donations, and loans, the United States contribution to recovery in France and Italy during 1946 may be estimated at 1,200 and 720 million dollars, respectively. These figures are highly significant both for the two countries under review and for the United States. They amount to 40 and 70 per cent, respectively, of the total foreign requirements of France and Italy during 1946, and together they account for almost one-third of the total amount of gifts and loans made available to foreign countries by the United States during that year.

While financing the import surplus has been the dominant balance of payments problem for both countries, the table [table 4.4] also reveals substantial differences in the structure of their international accounts which may be summarized as follows:

(1)   Whereas French exports paid for only a little over one-fifth of imports, Italian exports accounted for almost half of imports.

(2)   Almost all of the foreign aid given to France took the form of interest-bearing and repayable loans, while the bulk of the assistance to Italy was provided through nonrepayable grants.

(3)   Most strikingly, whereas France had to supplement foreign aid by liquidating a large portion of her gold and foreign asset holdings, Italy appears to have accumulated substantial amounts of foreign exchange during 1946.

It should not be inferred from these differences, however, that Italy's international economic position is more favorable than that of France. In many respects France has undoubtedly made more progress toward international equilibrium. While the revival of Italian exports has indeed been remarkable, the need to export was very much greater in Italy than in France; at the same time, Italian imports had to be much more severely curtailed. France, being able to borrow abroad and to call upon her large gold and foreign asset holdings, could afford a broader and more constructive import program and the allocation of a larger fraction of domestic production to internal capital formation and the raising of consumption levels. Italy, being largely dependent upon foreign donations and having practically no external resources of her own, found it necessary to confine imports largely to subsistence requirements and to rebuild minimum working balances in gold and foreign exchange. Moreover, approximately one-third of the foreign exchange earned by Italy in 1946 represented inconvertible sterling balances which were accumulated only because the sterling area was unable to provide the products required by the Italian import program.

*Prospects for 1947.* In 1947 both France and Italy will continue to need outside aid to meet minimum requirements for food, raw materials, and industrial equipment, but the amount of such assistance, while considerable, is likely to be smaller than in 1946.

At the beginning of the year, France still had 574 million dollars available from the Export-Import Bank credit of 650 million extended in June 1946. Of this amount 450 million dollars was scheduled for disbursement in 1947, and further surplus property and similar credits are expected to be received from the United States during the year. The sum of 97 million dollars also remained available to France at the beginning of the year on its Canadian credit. In December 1946, Argentina granted France a new credit of 134 million dollars subject to the signing of a commercial agreement, and early in 1947 a private medium-term revolving credit equivalent to 50 million dollars was obtained in

London to finance the purchase of wool in the British Empire. Finally, France has applied for a 500 million dollar loan from the International Bank for Reconstruction and Development.

Italy received 101 million dollars in December 1946–January 1947 as reimbursement for earlier United States military lira expenditures for purposes other than troop pay, and further small amounts will accrue from this source. Approximately 130 million dollars remained available at the end of 1946 as the unfulfilled portion of the UNRRA program, and Italy is one of the six countries scheduled to receive post-UNRRA relief out of the 350 million dollar appropriation now under consideration by the Congress. On the understanding that funds will be forthcoming from this source to meet Italy's relief needs, the Export-Import Bank earmarked, in January 1947, 100 million dollars for loans to finance specific export-oriented branches of Italian industry. In addition, Italy may seek assistance from the International Bank of which she has recently become a member.

Transfers on credit terms of United States surplus vessels will provide considerable balance of payments relief for both countries by reducing their dollar outlays for freight. The United States Maritime Commission has approved the sale to France and Italy of 75 and 100 Liberty ships, respectively. By April 1947, all vessels contracted for had been delivered to France, and 50 to Italy.

As members of the International Monetary Fund, France and Italy may draw 131 million and 45 million dollars, respectively, during 1947 to meet short-term requirements, but neither country is likely to use these facilities to the full.

In France, liquidation of gold and foreign assets will continue to supplement foreign aid, but to a greatly reduced extent. The Government expects to obtain 405 million dollars from this source during 1947. In view of the reduced level of gold reserves, most of this amount will have to be derived from the sale of private foreign assets requisitioned in the course of 1946. Italy will probably spend a portion of her sterling balances, a part of which have recently been made convertible into dollars, but will seek to retain her other still inadequate external reserves accumulated during 1946.

If all these factors are taken into account, it appears unlikely that during 1947 total foreign aid and use of existing foreign reserves will exceed 1,600 million dollars for France and 600 million for Italy. On the other hand, both countries (and especially Italy) must strive to increase imports above the 1946 level if they are to attain lasting results in economic reconstruction. It is clear, therefore, that both countries must seek considerably increased current receipts through exports and a revival of revenue from tourist and other service items. This conclusion brings into sharp focus the problem of foreign trade and exchange.

## FOREIGN TRADE AND EXCHANGE

For both France and Italy significant changes have taken place since prewar days in the composition of trade, as shown by the following table [table 4.5].

The trade of both countries has been greatly affected by loss of the German market, particularly with regard to exports. For France this is reflected in the relative decrease in exports of raw materials, and more particularly in the drastic reduction of iron ore shipments to the Ruhr. In the case of Italy, exports of foodstuffs have been affected since Germany was one of the principal prewar markets for Italian fruits and vegetables.

The result for both countries is greater reliance on exports of manufactures, a development that, if permanent, may well render their foreign trade more sensitive to foreign competition and to fluctuations of demand.

TABLE 4.5 PERCENTAGE DISTRIBUTION OF FRENCH
AND ITALIAN FOREIGN TRADE BY COMMODITY GROUPS,
1938 AND 1946

|  | Imports | | Exports | |
|---|---|---|---|---|
|  | 1938 | 1946 | 1938 | 1946 |
| France[a] | | | | |
| Foodstuffs | 10 | 20 | 13 | 21 |
| Raw materials[b] | 71 | 50 | 39 | 20 |
| Finished products | 19 | 30 | 48 | 59 |
| Total | 100 | 100 | 100 | 100 |
| Italy | | | | |
| Foodstuffs | 13 | 33 | 32 | 22 |
| Raw materials[b] | 48 | 48 | 8 | 8 |
| Finished products | 39 | 19 | 60 | 70 |
| Total | 100 | 100 | 100 | 100 |

[a] Excluding trade with Colonies.
[b] Including semi-finished products.

The import statistics of both countries reflect the low level of domestic food production. For the two other commodity groups, the data show significant differences between the two countries: Italy, confronted by pressing needs for food and raw materials and obtaining her imports mainly through foreign relief, suffered a drastic reduction in imports of manufactured goods; France, on the other hand, was able to launch the Monnet Plan of Modernization and Equipment by importing considerable quantities of capital goods.

With respect to the distribution of imports and exports by countries, it is clear that the importance of the United States as a supplier has increased greatly, while Central and Eastern Europe have, at least for the present, lost much of their importance both as markets and as sources of supply. The latter development has affected Italy more than France because of her greater dependence on this area for both imports and exports. Italian exports have been redirected both to the United States and to Western and Northern Europe.

Although intra-European trade is being conducted within a framework of payments agreements calling for a high degree of bilateral balancing, an appreciable degree of multilateralism persisted in the trade structure of both countries. Trade between France and Italy became so unbalanced that toward the end of 1946 France was required to transfer to Italy 8 million dollars in gold. During 1946, both countries achieved significant export surpluses with Switzerland (France 32 million dollars and Italy 31 million[2]) and with Belgium (73 and 7 million dollars, respectively[3]). The Italian export surplus of approximately 100 million dollars with the sterling area has already been mentioned.

Because of price inflation and the unreliability of the 1946 value statistics, recourse to weighted volume indexes is necessary in order to obtain an approximate measure of the recovery of exports. Such indexes, exclusive of Colonial trade, have been estimated for 1946 at 38 for France and at 45 for Italy (1938 = 100). A comparison between these figures and the average level for 1946 of the production curves shown in the chart on page 79 [chart 4.1] shows that Italian exports appear to have recovered almost pari passu with industrial production, while the French export volume lagged behind industrial output.

*Exchange controls.* The success of the Italian export drive was facilitated by the exchange rate and exchange control policies followed by that government. Both countries started the year 1946 with newly and substantially devalued currencies, the franc having been reduced in value from 50 to 119 to the dollar in December 1945 and the lira from 100 to 225 to the dollar in January 1946. Exchange controls were not relaxed at the time of the devaluation, but in March 1946 the Italian Government introduced a major innovation by permitting exporters to sell 50 per cent of their receipts of "hard" foreign currencies on the open market in Italy, provided that the purchasers of the exchange used it within a specified period of time for the import of essential commodities. Italian traders, who had had some experience with a similar system in 1937–39, quickly organized a foreign exchange market where dollars, pound sterling, and Swiss francs were regularly traded at "free export rates." The free market value of the dollar has recently been quoted around 530 lire as compared with the official rate of 225 lire, so that the average return per dollar to the exporter has been 377 lire. This is tantamount to a devaluation of the lira by forty per cent for export transactions, and comparable treatment has recently been extended to tourist expenditures, emigrant remittances, and capital transfers. This additional devaluation as well as the incentive of obtaining relatively free disposition over foreign exchange resources gave a powerful stimulus to Italian exports and, in particular, contributed to the expansion of shipments to hard currency countries.

France has recently taken a very limited step in the same direction by permitting the textile and automotive industries to retain 10 per cent of their foreign exchange proceeds to pay for imports of industrial equipment. On the whole, however, France has tried to foster exports through priority allocations of raw materials and through direct allocations for export on the British model. Difficulties in enforcing these allocations have been encountered because of the attractive prices offered for the same goods in the domestic black market.

On the basis of what is known concerning import requirements and of available means of financing, it would appear that France must achieve a relatively much larger expansion of exports from the 1946 level than Italy. It is true that the first condition for increased exports is increased production. But much will depend on whether or not producers will find sufficient incentives for sending a large portion of their output abroad at competitive prices. This is recognized as an important prerequisite for fulfillment of the goals set by the Monnet Plan.

## PLANS AND GOALS

The Monnet Plan of Modernization and Equipment was published in December 1946 and adopted as the official program of the French Government in January 1947. But its outlines had been known for some time in advance, and had formed the basis for presentation of the French case in the loan negotiations with the United States last spring.

The Plan declares that, in view of prevailing low productivity in France, extensive re-equipment and modernization is necessary to prevent stagnation and restrictionism from spreading gradually throughout the French economy. The French public is exhorted to postpone certain consumption expenditures and submit to regulations now in order to achieve a greatly increased flow of consumer goods and restoration of economic freedoms once the investment plan has been carried out.

The Plan is the result of a cooperative effort on the part of French Government, industry, and labor. It does not detail a rigid program for every branch of economic activity for the next four years, but rather sets goals for such aggregate magnitudes as national income, investment, labor force, and required foreign aid. It provides specifically, however, for considerable expansion and modernization of the French internal transportation system and of five fundamental branches of French industry. In these industries it is planned to attain by 1950 the following percentage increases in production over 1938: coal, 37; electricity, 79; steel, 77; cement, 255; and agricultural machinery, 371 per cent. The execution of these programs is recognized to be dependent upon obtaining the necessary manpower through adoption of the 48-hour week, an active immigration policy, and transfers of French labor to industry from agriculture, government services, and the distributive trades.

With the exception of agricultural machinery, the branches of industry toward which the main effort of the Plan is to be directed are either nationalized (railways, coal mines, electricity) or highly concentrated (iron and steel, cement). This as well as the nationalization of the major commercial banks and insurance companies should facilitate the channelling of investment funds toward their planned uses.

Total net investment, inclusive of expenditures for reconstruction and deferred maintenance, is planned for the four years 1947–1950 at the equivalent to about 19 billion dollars, of which 3.7 billion is scheduled for 1947. This outlay is expected to lead to an increase in the national income from 25 billion dollars in 1947 to 31 billion in 1950. If this objective appears somewhat modest, it should be remembered that agriculture will continue to play an important part in the French economy and that its contribution to the national income cannot be increased significantly. Of the total proposed investment about three billion dollars is expected to be financed through foreign credits (two billion) and liquidation of foreign assets (one billion), while the remaining 16 billion is to be provided by domestic savings. At present, difficulties are faced in both directions. The needed foreign financing is not yet assured, while the internal investment program is endangered by the unwillingness to save that is characteristic of inflationary conditions, as well as by the competition of other government expenditures for available savings. The recent decision of Finance Minister Schuman[†] to reduce by 40 per cent the scheduled expenditures under the Monnet Plan, pending the balancing of the ordinary budget, illustrates the interdependence between the Plan and the achievement of monetary and financial stability. However, in spite of difficulties and possible departures from original schedules, the Monnet Plan will leave its mark on the economic structure of France and of Europe.

Planning on the part of the Italian Government has so far been confined largely to the advance preparation and submission to Allied agencies of detailed import requirements. These programs aim at a general increase in economic activity, but no comprehensive attempt has been made to recast Italy's industrial structure, which was seriously distorted by the self-sufficiency drive of the thirties. No decision has yet been taken with respect to nationalization of industry or to the future functions of the Institute of Industrial Reconstruction (IRI), the agency that owns a majority interest in many of Italy's leading banking and industrial enterprises. Workers' councils have functioned in many important Northern Italian factories since liberation, but their legal status remains undefined. A beginning of agrarian reform has been made by providing for allocation of uncultivated land to farmers and by introducing long overdue changes into the *mezzadria* (sharefarming) contract. But, on the whole, the solution of this, as well as many other problems, remains in abeyance.

It is well recognized that in Italy, which even before the war had one of the lowest standards of living in Europe, modernization of the economy and substantial raising of consumption

---

[†] Robert Schuman (1886–1963) was the French finance minister (1946), then prime minister (1947–1948), foreign minister (1948–1953), and minister of justice (1955–1956). As foreign minister he contributed to the founding of the European Council and the European Coal and Steel Community.

levels are essential long-run requirements for economic and social stability. But political deadlock, incomplete sovereignty, and the very magnitude of the problems left as the legacy of Fascism, have prevented the Italian Government from developing an integrated economic and social program.

Economic policy has thus been widely divergent in the two countries. In France parties bitterly opposed to each other in the political field have rallied around the Monnet Plan, doubtless with different ultimate aims in view, but with a unanimity and continuity that can hardly be explained by mere tactical considerations. It may be that the idea of a national economic goal appeals strongly to the French people because of the frustrating lack of direction from which they suffered during the interwar period. Italy, on the contrary, emerged cruelly disillusioned from a long period of excessive "dynamism," and the considerable progress achieved in Italian reconstruction has resulted largely from the confluence of individual ventures, with or without encouragement from the State.

Notwithstanding these differences in approach to the long-run problem of reconstruction, both countries now face largely similar tasks of achieving continued expansion of output, of halting the inflationary process, and of balancing their international accounts. The solution of these problems will require continued effort on the part of the peoples of both nations and continued cooperation from abroad.

### NOTES

1. See Robert W. Bean, "Results of Monetary Reforms in Western Europe," in the Bulletin for October 1946, pp. 1115–1122 [*Federal Reserve Bulletin* 32, no. 10 (October 1946), pp. 1115–1122].
2. According to Swiss trade statistics.
3. According to Belgian trade statistics.

# 5

# PUBLIC FINANCE, MONEY MARKETS, AND INFLATION IN FRANCE

The French inflation, which had assumed a threatening pace in the second half of 1946, was suddenly brought to a halt by the announcement of the "Blum experiment" in December. With its threefold attack on prices, on private credit inflation,[1] and on the deficit of the public finances, it succeeded in radically altering the psychological climate and produced substantial lowering of prices in the stock, gold, and foreign bank note markets, as well as in the markets of commodities that are apt to be hoarded as a hedge against inflation. The general price level, though not too responsive to the two successive decrees ordering price reductions of 5 per cent each, remained stable up to April.

These gains, however, could not be maintained in the face of unfavorable developments in the "real" sector of the economy. In spite of increasing coal and power availabilities, industrial production remained stagnant in the first five months at a level of about 88 per cent of the 1938 average. More important, the food supply situation worsened as a bad wheat harvest became

Confidential. *Review of Foreign Developments*, July 29, 1947.

a virtual certainty. From April to May, wholesale and retail prices suddenly rose by 12 and 6 per cent, respectively, as a result of an even sharper rise in the prices of agricultural commodities. These rises have been responsible—jointly with the exit of the Communists from the Government—for the strike wave of the past two months. It seemed as though France had reached the threshold of yet another inflationary upsurge caused by successive price and wage increases as well as by the increased budget deficit.

It may be hoped that this danger has been averted by the Government's successful resistance to the wage demands of the unions, and by a series of energetic financial measures (cf. pp. 104–106). Wage increases remained on a moderate level. After a short strike, railway workers were granted pay increases and bonuses averaging 12 per cent, and in private industry the Government permitted collective bargaining for the negotiation of "production bonuses" up to 7 francs an hour equivalent to wage increases up to 15 per cent. The bonuses are supposed to be justified by the increase in production since the middle of 1946 and by the consequent reduction in overhead expenses and are not to form the basis for price increases. Similar upward adjustments for civil servants also have been granted. If compared to the wage and salary increases of July 1946 that averaged 33 per cent and reached 44 per cent in the case of the coal miners, the present pattern of increases cannot be considered as a major inflationary breakthrough.

## THE FINANCIAL CRISIS OF JUNE

The increases granted were sufficient, however, to upset the balance of the ordinary budget that had been precariously achieved by Finance Ministers Philip and Schuman* over the preceding months through a series of cuts in expenditures. This setback together with the outbreak of social disturbances had the effect of reversing the four-months-old trend on the stock and (black) foreign exchange markets, and the prospect of an increased level of costs enhanced the desire for liquidity on the part of banks and business and led to partial non-renewal of Treasury bond subscriptions. Complaints about insufficiency of liquid funds had already become increasingly vocal as a result of the price cuts and restrictive credit policy carried out during the previous months.

Any prospects of long-term borrowing were further dimmed by these developments. An issue of railway bonds of 10 billion francs was placed only with difficulty even before the present crisis. Subscriptions to 2.5 per cent, three-year Reconstruction bonds which are modeled on the U.S. war bonds and were introduced in April, were unsatisfactory. Furthermore, the restrictive credit policy led to pressure on the market for government securities that could not be entirely met by the usual support from the Caisse des Depots et Consignations, the financial agency centralizing savings deposits.

This situation coincided with particularly heavy maturities of Treasury bonds in May and June amounting to 41 and 51 billion, respectively.[2] At the end of May the margin of available advances from the Bank of France to the Treasury, which had been increased by 40 billion in April through an accounting device,[3] amounted to only 36 billion francs.

Faced with renewed financial difficulties, the Government acted boldly. It may even be said that it "profited" from

---

* André Philip (1902–1970), already an interior minister under the French 1942 provisional government headed by General Charles de Gaulle, was finance minister in 1946 and 1947 in the Socialist-led governments of Félix Gouin, Léon Blum, and Paul Ramadier.

the threat of crisis in order to push through measures (such as the drastic reduction of subsidies and the renewal of the capital levy) which it would hardly have been able to enact in the normal course of affairs. Moreover, the Government chose wisely to have one big crisis rather than two separate ones, one now over the budget, the other somewhat later over the balance of payments. Although, because of the recently granted World Bank loan, there was no *immediate* necessity for further foreign financing, the Government in anticipation of larger needs in the fall asked [for] and obtained from Parliament the transfer of $250 million[4] worth of gold from the Bank of France to the Stabilization Fund. Should the gold transferred be actually sold, French gold holdings will be reduced to $445 million or to less than half of what was considered a safe minimum at the time of the Washington loan negotiations of 1946.

## SUCCESSIVE 1947 BUDGET ESTIMATES

In order to understand the financial measures that have been taken, the recent history of the French budget has to be briefly recalled. Both the Monnet Plan and M. Schuman's exhaustive *Financial Inventory* of December 1946 had preached the doctrine of equilibrium of the ordinary budget. Internal borrowing and extraordinary receipts—among which the most important were the countervalue in francs of foreign credits and of gold and foreign exchange liquidations—were to be reserved for the financing of the extraordinary or reconstruction budget which also included equipment outlay for nationalized enterprises and financial assistance to local governments.

Since preliminary estimates made early in 1947 showed a 110 billion deficit of the ordinary budget (550 billion receipts and 660 billion expenditures), reconstruction expenditures of 312 billion francs, and other outlays amounting to about 150 billion, it was decided to block 40 per cent of the reconstruction expenditures pending the balancing of the ordinary budget. It was indeed perfectly clear that the financing of this vast deficit expenditure of 572 billion could be achieved only by a massive injection of inflationary purchasing power.

In April, Schuman presented revised estimates in which the ordinary budget was shown in balance at a level of 590 billion francs, reconstruction expenditures at 187 (60 per cent of 312), and other outlays at 168 billion. Of the uncovered expenditure of 355 billion francs, 120 billion were expected to be realized through foreign exchange operations, and 80 billion through delay in cash expenditures by issuance of Credit National drafts to contractors and suppliers, leaving 155 billion to be raised by borrowing. At the time the contribution of genuine savings was expected to amount to 5 per cent of the estimated national income of 2,770 billion francs, or 135 billion. This rather bold assumption left only 20 billion expenditures to be accounted for.

Two months later, a new revision of the estimates was necessary. Expenditures had to be revised upward by 71 billion francs owing partly to the wage increases of railway workers and partly to some restoration of the earlier cuts in reconstruction expenditures. At the same time, the state of the money and capital markets led the finance minister to revise downward his estimate of the year's public borrowings by 45 billion francs to 90 billion. The prospect of increased imports, on the other hand, led to the expectation that franc receipts from foreign credits and gold liquidations would be higher by 10 billion francs than estimated. Total charges of the Treasury uncovered by either revenue or prospective borrowing amounted, therefore, to 126 billion francs.[5]

## NEW FINANCIAL MEASURES

The financial measures taken to cope with the situation were as follows:

(1)   Subsidies on bread, milk, and the transportation and postal systems were cancelled leaving only the basic industrial raw materials of coal and steel in a subsidized status. On the other hand, in order to mitigate the effects of this momentous decision on the classes of the population that would be particularly hurt by the resulting price increases, family allowances as well as pensions for the sick and the aged were raised. The net savings realized will amount to 44 billion francs.

(2)   New revenues will yield 75 billion francs. The most unexpected measure has been the increase by 25 per cent of the capital levy (solidarity tax) that had been instituted after the currency exchange of July 1945. The due date of the last quarter of the liability incurred under the tax was advanced from November to September and a "fifth quarter" is to become due in November. This measure aroused the opposition of the Right, but served to soften the Left's anger at the suppression of subsidies. Other revenue is to be obtained from increased excise taxes on tobacco, matches, alcohol, and gasoline; from increased application of the pay-as-you-go principle; from income assessments according to "outer signs of wealth";[6] and

from sales of government-owned industrial shares and of surplus military vehicles.

(3) Finally, 30 billion francs are to be obtained from a further compression of civilian and, in particular, military expenditures.

Total resources thus obtained amount to 150 billion francs and exceed, therefore, the Treasury's expected deficit by 24 billion francs—a safety margin for the general salary increase for civil servants that was voted in just this amount on July 16. As was pointed out above, however, the Treasury's receipts still include net estimated internal borrowings of 90 billion, and it is by no means certain that even this reduced target can be reached. The Treasury itself was apparently anything but certain on that count since it asked Parliament also for an increase by 100 billion francs of its authority to borrow directly from the Bank of France. How necessary were these additional facilities is clear from the fact that advances in the amount of 44 billion francs were used during the month of June, exhausting entirely the previous authorization of 100 billion and using up 8 billion of the new one hardly a week after its passage through Parliament.

In spite of ever-recurring financial difficulties, the developments of the last months have yielded the following noteworthy results:

(1) Improved expenditure control and gradual inclusion of certain formerly extrabudgetary categories of public expenditure into the ordinary and extraordinary budget voted by Parliament.

(2) Progress of economic decontrol as evidenced by the suppression of most subsidies and by the abolition of tobacco and gasoline rationing. Excise taxes on these two products have been raised so as to bring their prices to a point where supply and demand are equated.

(3)  Most important, achievement of the equilibrium of the *ordinary* budget owing to a sustained effort at reduction of expenditures and to raising of new revenues.

## PRIVATE VS. PUBLIC CREDIT NEEDS

The close interaction between private credit needs and the problems faced by the Treasury has recently been brought out very well in the first annual report of the National Credit Council, a supervisory and coordinating body that had been created by the Banking Law of December 2, 1945. The report provides breakdowns of bank credits by borrowers (business and government) and by lenders (Bank of France and commercial banks). The following table [table 5.1] shows how, for 1946 (in particular for the

#### TABLE 5.1 TOTAL CREDIT SUPPLY IN FRANCE, 1945–46

|  | Dec. 31, 1945 | | June 30, 1946 | | Dec. 31, 1946 | |
| --- | --- | --- | --- | --- | --- | --- |
|  | Billions of francs | Per cent | Billions of francs | Per cent | Billions of francs | Per cent |
| Total bank credits— by lenders: | | | | | | |
| Commercial banks | 340 | 87 | 421 | 84 | 474 | 79 |
| Bank of France | 52 | 13 | 80 | 16 | 126 | 21 |
| Total | 392 | 100 | 501 | 100 | 600 | 100 |
| Total bank credits— by borrowers: | | | | | | |
| Business | 118 | 30 | 181 | 36 | 305 | 51 |
| Government—total | (274) | (70) | (320) | (64) | (295) | (49) |
| Treasury bonds | 243 | 62 | 260 | 52 | 210 | 35 |
| Credit National drafts | 31 | 8 | 60 | 12 | 85 | 14 |
| Total | 392 | 100 | 501 | 100 | 600 | 100 |

second half of that year), the Bank of France financed a constantly increasing share of the total outstanding credits of the
banking system while a constantly decreasing portion of these
credits constituted a direct or indirect aid to the Treasury.

The credit expansion thus proceeded not by government
borrowing from the commercial banks, but, on the contrary,
through credits obtained by private industry and trade which
were largely financed by the Central Bank, either directly
through rediscounts or indirectly through non-renewals of Treasury bonds; the latter had to be refinanced in the form of direct
advances from the Bank of France to the Treasury. The decrease
of 50 billion [in] Treasury bonds in the second half of 1946 is
almost exactly matched by the increase in direct Bank of France
advances to the Treasury (from 13 to 68 billion francs) during
the same period. The increase in this item which is generally
regarded by the French public as the most important indicator
of the Treasury's position has, therefore, been caused less by the
budget deficit than by the inability of the commercial banks to
expand their lending to business enterprises without liquidating
to some extent the credit previously granted to the Treasury. A
similar situation has been responsible for the recent increase in
direct Bank of France advances.

What little expansion of government borrowing from the
banks there has been in 1946 has taken place through discounts of drafts in payment of contractors and suppliers. It has
already been mentioned that these drafts, underwritten by the
Credit National to make them eligible for rediscount at the
Bank of France, are expected to be a major source of deficit
financing during the current year. By a decree of February 27,
1946, the maturity of these drafts has been extended from 9
to 12 months and the settlement of public contracts through
drafts (rather than cash) has been made compulsory for the

full amount of the sums due rather than, as previously, for 75 per cent only.[7]

## CAPITAL MARKETS AND PRIVATE SAVINGS

Average levels of real income being quite low, savings out of current income are quite small under present conditions. In addition, as is to be expected in a period of inflationary pressures, great difficulties are experienced in channeling what private savings there are toward the investments planned by the State. Furthermore, the nationalization of important branches of French industry had the consequences that these branches could finance themselves only through fixed-income issues which were at a clear disadvantage with respect to variable-income securities because of the constant rise in prices.

In 1946, new bonds and shares were issued in the amount of 84 billion francs, half of which were bond issues of the semi-public Credit National and Credit Foncier; nationalized enterprises accounted for 9 billion francs; [and] the surprisingly large amount of 22 billion went to private consumers' goods industries.[8]

Available resources of the Caisse des Depots et Consignations, the agency centralizing the funds of savings banks and social security contributions and using them for underwriting government securities, increased by 64 billion francs, but of these 45 billion had to be used to support the market of government securities rather than for new subscriptions.

The *Report of the National Credit Council* presents an estimate of private capital formation by adding the 19 billion franc net increase in resources of the Caisse des Depots to the 84 billion new market issues. There is, however, some double counting between these two items since part of the increase in funds at the disposal of the Caisse doubtless went to subscribe to bond issues of such quasi-public bodies as the Credit National and the Credit Foncier. It appears likely, therefore, that private savings excluding changes in cash holdings have remained below 100 billion francs; they have amounted, therefore, to about 3 per cent of the national income of 2,770 billion francs. This result makes it quite improbable that it will be possible to reach in 1947 the Monnet Plan target of 9 per cent[9] of which the Government had expected at one point to obtain about one-half.

## FUTURE OF THE MONNET PLAN AND INFLATION

It seems clear, therefore, that, with present low levels of real income, private capital formation is incapable of contributing to the financing of the planned investment expenditure to the extent envisaged by the Monnet Plan. Realization of this fact has brought about three distinct developments:

(1) Objectives of the Plan are being scaled down, although no official indication of this has as yet been given except for the reduction of extraordinary government expenditures.

(2) Recent financial measures have, for the first time, brought forth the tendency to raise investment funds through taxation, i.e., by securing a surplus in the ordinary budget.[10] The proceeds from the 25 per cent increase in the solidarity tax and from certain other taxes have been specifically set aside for the financing of the extraordinary budget.

(3) Residual reconstruction expenditure, i.e., that part that is not covered by tax or extraordinary non-tax receipts (such as

franc proceeds from foreign loans and gold sales), is financed primarily by the banking system. This residual is the result of a constantly shifting compromise between the minimum requirements of the investment program and the maximum limits assigned to inflationary means of finance by an uneasy and experimental concept of "controlled inflation."

This threefold attack—slowing down of the investment program, financing of investment from a surplus in the ordinary budget, and a limited amount of inflationary finance—could provide the pattern for meeting the difficulties of the active reconstruction period provided a solution is found for two problems:

(1) *Agricultural output.* It was seen earlier that the latest inflationary spurt was due almost exclusively to a rise in farm prices reflecting unsatisfactory output and distribution of farm products. Increasing agricultural output is a preliminary condition if controlled inflation is not to degenerate into runaway inflation through constant increases of food prices and the consequent irrepressible demands for higher wages.

(2) *Exchange rate.* With internal prices and costs under slow but steady pressure, the present exchange rate already has become a barrier to French exports in several lines, including tourism. If it is correct, as is argued in the foregoing, that continuation of inflationary pressures is to be reckoned with for some time, the question of an adjustment in the rate is certain to become acute.

## NOTES

1. See this *Review*, January 28, 1947, p. 10 [republished in this volume as chapter 1; see p. 47, first paragraph].

2. These bonds were issued at the time of the 1945 exchange of currency which had led to a large shift from currency holdings to bank deposits and to their investment in government bonds by the banks.

3. By requiring the Bank to increase by 40 billion francs the permanent loan granted to the Government in countervalue of the right of note issue and by reducing the Treasury's advance account by the same amount.

4. Only 18 billion francs ($150 million) are to be transferred immediately, but authority is vested in the Government to transfer an additional 12 billion if necessary during the recess of Parliament.

5. $20 + 71 + 45 - 10 = 126$.

6. Widespread tax evasion by the "new rich" has made it necessary to resort to this time-honored expedient. Income presumptions are based on rent paid, the number of domestic personnel (a male servant leading to a presumption of twice that yielded by a female!), and on the horsepower of private cars owned.

7. Of a total of 98 billion Credit National drafts in circulation on December 31, 1946, 86 billion were held in the banking system and were distributed in approximately equal amounts between the commercial banks (44 billion) and the Bank of France (42 billion). Even if 100 per cent of the drafts were to be rediscounted, the Treasury would still obtain the advantage of having avoided to that extent an increase of its direct advances from the Bank of France with its attendant "psychological" consequences.

8. [Ministère de l'Économie Nationale], *Etudes et Conjoncture*, March–April 1947, p. 12.

9. Total investment envisaged by the Monnet Plan for 1947 is estimated at 17 per cent of national income to be raised in the following manner: 5 per cent through the franc proceeds of foreign loans and gold liquidations, 3 per cent through self-financing of business and farm enterprises, and 9 per cent through the capital market.

10. All taxation, ordinary and extraordinary, has so far been included in the ordinary budget.

# 6

# CREDIT RESTRICTIONS AND DEFLATION IN ITALY

October 1947 marked the high tide of Italian price inflation. After having approximately doubled within the
space of a year, wholesale prices fell steadily after
October and leveled off in March 1948 at 15–20 per cent below
the peak reached five months earlier. The cost of living decreased
by around 12 per cent. The fall in prices experienced during these
months was accompanied by many familiar symptoms of depression. Industrial production fell off in spite of constant or increasing raw material and energy supplies, the stock market crashed,
and important firms went through financial difficulties and often
avoided bankruptcy only by subsidies from the Treasury.

The reversal of the inflationary movement in October 1947
has been most commonly associated with the quantitative credit
restrictions which were issued by Minister of the Budget Einaudi in August 1947 and which became effective on October 1.
As of that date all banks were to set aside an amount equal to 20
per cent of their deposits in excess of ten times their capital or an
amount equal to 15 per cent of their total deposits, whichever was
smaller. These amounts were either to be invested in government
or government-guaranteed securities for deposit at the Bank of

Italy, or to be held in an interest-bearing blocked account at the Bank of Italy or the Treasury.[1] Furthermore, 40 per cent of any net increment in deposits after October 1 was to be set aside in a similar fashion until the reserves thus created reached 25 per cent of total deposits for each bank.

It is recognized that a number of other factors have at the same time exerted a downward pressure on prices, such as the payment of the first installment of the capital levy voted in May 1947, the bumper olive crop, slaughter of livestock following the drought, and a considerable volume of franco valuta imports[2] of sugar, meat, and fats. The virtual assurance of continuity of American aid as the Interim Aid and European Recovery Programs took shape also had a significant psychological reaction.

Nevertheless, the establishment of primary and secondary reserve requirements remains among the prime causes of the October reversal because of both their real and their psychological impact. In spite of official warnings, bank credit expansion had become an increasingly important factor in the inflationary process, as is brought out clearly by the following table [table 6.1].

TABLE 6.1 ASSETS OF ITALIAN BANKS, 1944–47
(IN BILLIONS OF LIRE AND PER CENT OF TOTAL ASSETS)

|  | Dec. 1944 | Dec. 1945 | Sept. 1946 | Sept. 1947 |
|---|---|---|---|---|
| Cash assets and reserves | 140.5 | 189.4 | 243.9 | 212.7 |
|  | 42% | 35% | 27% | 14% |
| Securities | 88.9 | 136.4 | 205.8 | 252.5 |
|  | 27% | 26% | 23% | 17% |
| Other assets | 105.2 | 209.2 | 448.2 | 1,045.2 |
|  | 31% | 39% | 50 % | 69% |
| Total | 334.6 | 535.0 | 897.9 | 1,510.4 |
|  | 100% | 100% | 100% | 100% |

Source: Bulletin of the Bank of Italy.

The "Other assets" in this table consist almost exclusively of loans to business and individuals. Some absolute and relative expansion of this category was of course to be expected, with the resurgence of economic activity after liberation. The increase, however, became alarmingly rapid in the year beginning September 1946. It forced the liquidity of the banks down to a very low point and, by forcing them to withdraw reserves held with the Treasury and the Bank of Italy, created difficulties for the financing of the budget deficit. As usual, it is difficult to appraise to what extent bank loans permitted speculative hoarding of commodities at various stages of production, but in the absence of effective inventory controls there can be little doubt that a portion of the loans was so employed. In any event, the expansion of bank credit far outstripped the increase in industrial activity which from September 1946 to September 1947 increased by approximately 20 per cent.

The need for bank credit restrictions was therefore real both to contain inflation and to avoid large-scale Treasury recourse to direct advances from the Bank of Italy.

The new reserve requirements enacted by Einaudi were not calculated to bring about an actual contraction of credit on the part of the banking system as a whole: the application of the new requirements resulted in the freezing of an amount (112 billion lire) which was approximately equal to that already held by the banks with the Bank of Italy and the Treasury in cash or securities (97 and 18 billion, respectively). This freezing of a large fraction of the already scant liquid resources of the banks could not fail, however, to have a profound influence on their credit policy and on economic conditions in general. In the first place, many individual banks did not hold sufficient reserves, in cash or securities, and in their case the new requirements resulted in an actual liquidation of credit commitments. Secondly, the banks whose reserve position was adequate had considered the reserves which had been frozen as part of their available funds and immediately strove to build up excess reserves by making access to credit more difficult. Finally, a good deal of economic activity, particularly in the fields of reconstruction and investment, was predicated not merely on a constant, but on an *expanding* flow of credit and would therefore have been hurt even though the total volume of bank credit had remained unchanged.

The credit restrictions (in conjunction with the simultaneous payment of the first installment of the capital levy) resulted in a severe shortage of cash. Several large firms in the North experienced difficulties in meeting their payrolls. Einaudi's advice to them was to liquidate the large hoards of raw materials, foreign exchange, and extraneous assets (real estate, industrial shares, etc.) which they had acquired during the preceding inflationary phase. The fall in commodity prices, particularly in the black market, followed. The fall in foreign exchange and stock market prices which had started as early as June received new impetus. The stock markets were particularly affected as loans for purchasing or carrying securities were the first to be curtailed. Furthermore, new issues of securities which had become the only source, the Treasury apart, of fresh funds for industry were absorbed only with great difficulties by the market. The general index for variable-income securities was halved between September and February.

The psychological reactions of the credit restrictions reinforced their "physical" impact. A phenomenon that is well known from experience with rationing was noticed: loans which were of little urgency but could not be refused by the banks were applied for even though they were not needed, thus further reducing the volume of credit for meeting real needs.[3] Furthermore, a certain distrust toward the banks developed and resulted in a reluctance to deposit and even in scattered withdrawals. Officially encouraged expectations of a continued price fall led to postponements of purchases and thereby to further downward pressures.

The stage was thus ideally set for the starting of a deflationary movement, particularly in the industries producing capital goods. To make the situation more critical, wages not only failed to decrease, but continued to increase because of their automatic but lagging connection with the cost of living. But it was precisely because the danger of an abrupt collapse of large parts of Italian industrial activity became suddenly so real that the Government started compensatory spending on a large scale: almost immediately upon the onset of the crisis the Treasury came to the rescue of a number of threatened branches and firms, mostly in the sector of heavy industry. A 50 billion lire fund was set up for the reconversion and modernization of the mechanical industries; the capital of the IRI (Istituto per la Ricostruzione Industriale) was increased by 8 billion lire; subsidies were granted to domestic coal, lignite, sulphur, and silk producers; [and] special credit facilities and subsidies were given to artisans, small and medium-sized industries, as well as for the industrialization of Southern Italy.

In view of these developments, it has been observed that the Italian Government became involved in the contradiction of having its minister of industry undo what had been done by its minister of the budget. It is certainly curious to notice how Einaudi's "orthodox" policy actually led to more State intervention in, and greater State control of, Italian economic life. But aside from this point, the combination of deflation with expansionary measures in specifically selected fields was a logical economic policy for Italy to follow after the violent inflation it had undergone. Initially, the "open" postwar inflation in Italy (as in France) probably permitted reconstruction to proceed more rapidly than might have been possible under conditions of monetary stability.

But as the pace of the inflation quickened, an increasing portion of the investment (hoarding of inventories and foreign exchange, non-essential building, expansion of the distributive trades) was wasteful and often competed successfully with genuine reconstruction and modernization activities. It thus became actually easier *and possibly tempting* to carry on these activities in a deflationary environment, i.e., in a situation where the universal scramble for raw materials, skilled labor, and foreign exchange resources would give place to a relative abundance. In Italy the temporary recession had another consequence which may prove beneficial in the long run: it exposed the profound maladjustments in Italy's industrial structure which had remained hidden as long as prices rose.

The deflationary movement might have been expected to flatten out in January/February 1948. In December, the note circulation increased by 108 billion lire or by 16 per cent as a result of heavy year-end payments combined with stationary revenue. In January, Einaudi revised the prospective budget deficit upward, from the originally planned 300 billion lire to 500–600 billion, i.e., an amount similar to fiscal year 1946–47. At the same time the banks had rebuilt a margin of liquidity; toward the end of January, they had accumulated 50 billion lire in excess reserves. In February, interest rates for loans to brokers and dealers collapsed from 9.50 to 1 per cent. Furthermore, the Government took a series of measures designed to revive business and investment activity: the payment of the first installment of the progressive (as distinct from the proportional) capital levy was postponed from January until June, the progressive tax on dividends was abolished and business firms were permitted to use part of their profits for the revaluation of their assets on a more realistic basis.

In spite of these developments, industrial activity continued to decline; in January it had decreased by 15 per cent from the peak reached in October even though the seasonal decline in electric power availabilities had been very slight during the winter. On the stock markets, new heavy losses were suffered in February. The reason for the continued listlessness of economic activity was, of course, the feeling of insecurity created by the approaching elections.* Private investment activity came practically to a standstill and some precautionary capital flight was noticed.

In view of the outcome of the elections, there will be great need to be watchful lest an investment boom caused by the return of confidence unleash a new inflationary upsurge.

The Italian experience of the last six months—which is the closest approximation yet to the long-awaited postwar cyclical downturn—serves to illustrate a number of more or less familiar propositions:

(1)   It is always possible to stop an inflation if there is a will to do so; bank credit restrictions have an important part to play in the halting of the inflationary process.

(2)   It is almost impossible to arrest a violent inflationary process without provoking a deflation.

(3)   While moderate inflation is compatible with, and may even assist the carrying out of, planned investment activities, such activities are likely to fare better under mildly deflationary conditions than during a violent inflationary process which results mainly in wasteful and speculative investment.

(4)   Deflation is still feared more than inflation. In Italy, the latter was left to proceed for years before bringing forth energetic

---

* On April 18 and 19, 1948, the first postwar elections for the Italian Parliament were held with the Cristian Democratic Party acquiring the relative majority of seats with almost 49 percent of the votes and a defeat of the Popular Democratic Front (Socialist and Communist Parties) with 31 percent of the electorate.

measures designed to combat it; while at the first sign of deflation, the alarm of public opinion was considerable and governmental action was immediately and powerfully forthcoming.

## NOTES

1. Previously, Italian banks were subject to the same reserve requirements to the extent of the excess of their deposits above twenty, or, since 1946, above thirty times their capital. In practice, however, this regulation which dated from 1926 was not enforced and was ineffective in view of the lag of the banks' capital accounts behind the expansion of deposits.
2. I.e., imports financed by privately held foreign assets; see this *Review*, May 6, 1947 [republished in this volume as chapter 3].
3. A black market for credit with interest rates up to 15 and 20 per cent also developed as a consequence of this situation.

# II

# THE MARSHALL PLAN AND THE END OF DISCRIMINATION

# 7

# TRADE STRUCTURE OF THE "MARSHALL PLAN COUNTRIES"

An appraisal of the possible beneficial effects of multi-lateral clearing and similar schemes as well as of their prospective dollar costs must rest on an examination of the structure of European trade. The statistics required for that purpose are available for 1938 in the League of Nations publication *The Network of World Trade*. For 1946 the European Division of the Department of Commerce has assembled and organized a considerable amount of data which show only a few minor gaps as far as the "Marshall Plan countries" are concerned.[1]

Trade statistics of several countries present particular difficulties because of incorrect valuations, multiple or depreciating exchange rates, and laxity of the Customs. Adjustments for these shortcomings have been made, so far as possible. In particular, the trade statistics of Greece, Austria, France, and Italy had to be recomputed. Because of the remaining gaps and the uncertain nature of some of the adjustments made, the 1946 figures as given in the following cannot claim to be more than an indication of the orders of magnitude involved.

---

Confidential. *Review of Foreign Developments*, August 12, 1947.

124

THE MARSHALL PLAN

# I. SHARE OF THE MUTUAL TRADE OF THE "MARSHALL PLAN COUNTRIES" IN THEIR TOTAL TRADE

Since the "Marshall Plan countries" as a group have a considerable import surplus with the outside world the sum of their imports from and exports to each other[2] yield a much higher ratio when related to exports than when related to imports. In 1938, the average proportion occupied by imports from other countries of the group in total imports of these countries was 39 per cent including Germany and 29 per cent excluding Germany; the corresponding percentages for exports were 51 per cent and 39 per cent.

No complete German statistics are available for 1946; since German foreign trade in that year was very small, it has been considered advisable to exclude German trade altogether. The intertrade of the "Marshall Plan countries" in 1946 amounted to 28 per cent of their total imports and to 43 per cent of their total exports.

These figures show both the importance and the resilience of the intertrade of the group of countries under consideration. This is all the more remarkable as the group includes all those European countries whose trade is largely oriented to transoceanic countries rather than to the Continent.

The proportion of intertrade in the total trade handled by the group is necessarily smaller than the above percentages; in order to obtain this proportion total intertrade must be related to (1) intertrade plus (2) imports from countries outside the group plus (3) exports to countries outside the group, whereas previously intertrade was related to either (1) + (2) or (1) + (3). The results are as follows:

In 1938, the share of intertrade in the total flow of trade conducted by the group was 28 per cent including Germany in the group, and 20 per cent excluding Germany. In 1946, without Germany, the intertrade amounted to 21 per cent of total trade. The constancy of the percentages from 1938 to 1946 is again surprising, especially in view of the greatly increased importance of imports from the United States for almost all countries under consideration.

## II. MULTILATERAL BALANCING AND NET BALANCES IN THE INTERTRADE OF THE "MARSHALL PLAN COUNTRIES"

The intertrade of each of the "Marshall Plan countries" with all the other countries of the group has been subdivided into three categories:

1. Trade that can be compensated bilaterally
2. Trade that can be compensated multilaterally
3. Net balance of trade of the country with the rest of the group.[3]

Adding up the data for all countries the following result is obtained [see table 7.1].

The result may come as a surprise to those who took too literally the often-heard complaints that intra-European trade is

TABLE 7.1 INTERTRADE OF
"MARSHALL PLAN COUNTRIES"

|  | Bilaterally compensable trade (per cent) | Multilaterally compensable trade (per cent) | Net trade balances (per cent) | Total Per cent | Total Millions of $ |
|---|---|---|---|---|---|
| 1938 | 82 | 7 | 11 | 100 | 4,820 |
| 1946 | 69 | 10 | 21 | 100 | 3,780 |

confined to the "strait jacket" of bilateral payments agreements. The amount of net balances and the opportunities for multilateral offsetting of balances have increased materially since 1938. The country that has contributed most to this development is the United Kingdom, the British net export surplus to the other countries of the group amounting to over two-thirds[4] of the total export surpluses. In 1946, Great Britain had thus more than taken over the role played in 1938 by Germany which then accounted for about 60 per cent of the total net export surpluses in the group (while Great Britain then played a similar role as a net importer).

The most important net importers in 1946 were the Netherlands ($157 million), France ($139 million), Belgium ($136 million), and Denmark ($116 million), accounting together for approximately two-thirds of the total net import surpluses of the group. In the course of 1947 certain shifts in the relative positions within the group have taken place: Italy has probably changed from a net exporter to a net importer position, while France is becoming a net exporter to the group. It is interesting to note that Switzerland has been on balance a net importer.

The column "Multilaterally compensable trade" shows the trade that *could have been* multilaterally balanced rather than trade which in fact was so balanced. Since in many cases no multilateral payment mechanism was available, much of the multilaterally compensable trade created financing problems just as though it represented net balances.

If machinery for settling multilateral balances had been available in 1946, the financing of net balances would have required about $800 million. Assuming that the countries concerned would have financed their own net balances to the extent of 10 per cent of the total flow of intertrade, the amounts of dollars to be injected into the system would have amounted to little over $400 million. On the same assumption of self-financing, but without machinery for settling multilateral balances, the dollar needs would have been almost twice this figure [see Appendix table I and Appendix table II].

#### APPENDIX TABLE I BILATERALISM, MULTILATERALISM, AND NET TRADE BALANCES IN THE INTERTRADE OF "MARSHALL PLAN COUNTRIES" (IN MILLIONS OF DOLLARS), 1938

| | Bilaterally compensable trade | Multilaterally compensable trade | Net trade balances[a] | Total |
|---|---|---|---|---|
| Austria | 172 | 18 | (−)12 | 202 |
| Belgium-Luxembourg | 762 | 4 | (+)83 | 849 |
| France | 700 | 102 | (+)23 | 825 |
| Germany | 1,633 | 1 | (+)306 | 1,940 |
| Italy | 422 | 24 | (−)58 | 504 |
| Netherlands | 586 | 148 | (−)44 | 778 |
| Sweden | 556 | 76 | (−)39 | 671 |
| Switzerland | 316 | 46 | (−)50 | 412 |
| Denmark | 471 | 87 | (+)22 | 580 |
| Greece | 112 | 4 | (−)15 | 131 |
| Norway | 285 | 13 | (−)65 | 363 |
| Portugal | 62 | 2 | (−)30 | 94 |
| Turkey | 140 | 22 | (−)5 | 167 |
| Eire | 220 | 14 | (−)12 | 246 |
| United Kingdom | 1,436 | 152 | (−)289 | 1,877 |
| All Countries | 7,873 | 713 | 1,053 | 9,639 |
| Total Intertrade[b] | 3,936 | 357 | 527 | 4,820 |

[a] Import and export surpluses are indicated by minus and plus signs, respectively. Summation is made regardless of sign.

[b] The figures for "Total Intertrade" are one-half of those for "All Countries"; the latter figures contain twice the amount of the actual flow of trade since every movement of goods is recorded in both imports and exports.

## APPENDIX TABLE II BILATERALISM, MULTILATERALISM, AND NET TRADE BALANCES IN THE INTERTRADE OF "MARSHALL PLAN COUNTRIES" (IN MILLIONS OF DOLLARS), 1946

|  | Bilaterally compensable trade | Multilaterally compensable trade | Net trade balances[a] | Total |
|---|---|---|---|---|
| Austria | 25 | 5 | (–)71 | 101 |
| Belgium-Luxembourg | 622 | 130 | (–)136 | 888 |
| France | 643 | 194 | (–)139 | 976 |
| Germany | — | — | — | — |
| Italy | 171 | 10 | (+)81 | 262 |
| Netherlands | 432 | 10 | (–)156 | 598 |
| Sweden | 505 | 59 | (+)76 | 640 |
| Switzerland | 524 | 80 | (–)19 | 623 |
| Denmark | 477 | 27 | (–)119 | 623 |
| Greece | 5 | 18 | (–)80 | 103 |
| Norway | 260 | 49 | (–)51 | 360 |
| Portugal | 112 | 16 | (–)11 | 139 |
| Turkey | 88 | — | (+)69 | 157 |
| Eire | 270 | 26 | (+)4 | 300 |
| United Kingdom | 1,109 | 130 | (+)553 | 1,792 |
| All Countries | 5,243 | 754 | 1,564 | 7,561 |
| Total Intertrade[b] | 2,621 | 377 | 782 | 3,780 |

[a] See footnote a to appendix table I.
[b] See footnote b to appendix table I.

## NOTES

1. Appreciation is expressed to Mr. Fred Strauss, Chief of the European Division, Department of Commerce, for placing these data at our disposal.

2. Imports and exports within a group of countries must of necessity be equal, except for inaccuracies in the statistics and the differences arising from f.o.b. [free on board] valuation of exports and c.i.f. [cost, insurance, freight] valuation of imports. Since in 1938 the difference between total exports and imports was small relative to total trade, no adjustment was made for that year.

3. The method can best be made clear by an example. Suppose a country has the following trade with two countries, A and B,

|   | Imports | Exports |
|---|---------|---------|
| A | 100 | 50 |
| B | *70* | *90* |
|   | 170 | 140 |

then the three categories are obtained as follows:

1) Bilaterally compensable trade with A = 2 × 50, with B = 2 × 70; total = 240.
2) Multilaterally compensable trade = twice the amount of that bilateral trade balance whose sign is opposite to the sign of the total trade balance: 2 × (90 − 70) = 40.
3) Net balance: 170 − 140 = 30.

The sum of the three items (240 + 40 + 30) equals total trade of 310 (i.e., 170 + 140).

4. For this and the following figures, see the table[s] in the appendix showing trade by countries [sic].

# 8

# INFLATION AND BALANCE OF PAYMENTS DEFICIT

T wo theses on the "dollar shortage," one relating to its cause and the other to its cure, have gained wide acceptance over the past year. The former maintains that the balance of payments difficulties of many countries are largely due to domestic inflation, the latter that the principle of non-discrimination cannot be applied as long as the world remains short of dollars. The following note offers some comments on the first of these problems. The second problem will be discussed in the next issue of this *Review*.*

During the first two postwar years, the need for balance of payments assistance of European countries was generally explained in terms of the structural changes in the world economy which were brought about by World War II. The great need for reconstruction and the low level of production in Europe, the loss of invisible income from overseas, and the disruption of traditional trade relations of Western Europe with both Eastern Europe and the Far East—all these were held, and no

Confidential. *Review of Foreign Developments*, August 24, 1948.

* See "Dollar Shortage and Discrimination," published in the September 7, 1948, issue of *Review of Foreign Developments*, republished in this volume as chapter 9.

doubt justly, to provide a sufficient explanation for the need of large-scale aid from the United States. When, however, in 1947 European recovery suffered a relapse, and balance of payments equilibrium seemed farther away than ever, "monetary" phenomena were given increasing weight at the expense of the "real" structural factors. The development of the terms of trade was widely discussed; devaluation was no longer entirely brushed aside as an untimely and blunt instrument; and the connection between domestic inflation and external imbalance was increasingly stressed. The latter, in particular, is the central theme of the latest annual BIS [Bank for International Settlements] report which acknowledges that the economic policies of several European governments display an increasing awareness of this connection.

The causal link between inflation, whether open or repressed, and foreign exchange shortages is easily understood. In the case of open inflation, the rise in domestic prices soon makes it unprofitable to export and profitable to import as long as exchange rates remain pegged.[1] In the case of repressed inflation, the pressure of redundant internal purchasing power brings about a diversion of both factors of production and output from export industries to domestic nonpriority uses.

This reasoning is appealing inasmuch as it seems to offer a shortcut to the solution of balance of payments difficulties; it is obviously easier to "disinflate" or to stop an open inflationary process than to bring about basic readjustments of industrial structure and of trade patterns.

There certainly is a good deal of validity in the "monetary" explanations of the foreign exchange shortage, but it would be dangerous to rely on "disinflation" alone for securing external equilibrium. The relaxed tension of domestic demand, the greater availability of labor, and the symptoms of depression in nonessential activities, all of which characterize at present the economic situation in a number of European countries, are merely presenting these countries with an opportunity to carry out such readjustments in their productive structure as may help to render them eventually independent of foreign aid. If this opportunity is not seized, there will be either economic stagnation offering no hope for ever emerging from the condition of external imbalance or a growing public demand for indiscriminate "reflation" which would reproduce the situation prior to "disinflation."[2]

The need for caution in drawing conclusions from the connection between inflation and balance of payments deficit becomes even more apparent when it is realized that *the causal relationship runs both ways.* In the postwar situation, foreign aid was not so much a consequence of internal inflation as vice versa: internal inflation was given a powerful stimulus by reconstruction and investment activities which in turn were rendered possible only by the large volume of raw material and equipment imports financed by U.S. grants or loans. No doubt, these imports do eventually result in an increased flow of consumers' goods. In the short run, however, foreign aid shipments other than food and consumers' goods in general can exert, paradoxically, an inflationary effect on the recipient countries. This is true in particular when the net imports, because of their "bottleneck" nature, permit use of large quantities of hitherto unused domestic labor and raw materials in reconstruction and investment activities while individual savings are still at very low levels. In fully employed economies, additional investment resulting from "reconstruction imports" will attract already employed domestic factors of production and will therefore result in an upward pressure on wages and prices.[3]

The possible inflationary effect of certain categories of foreign aid shipments on the economies of the recipient countries creates a difficult problem of policy. To press for monetary stability on the one hand, and for inclusion of a maximum amount of so-called "recovery items" in shipments financed through U.S. aid on the other, may mean advocating deflationary and inflationary measures at the same time. Should monetary stability be achieved primarily by a reduction in investment activity, the absorption of "recovery items" on the scale which prevailed during the inflationary phase would become impossible. Such inability to absorb recovery imports[4] is a danger signal since it denotes economic stagnation and failure to proceed with the capital formation which is essential to the achievement of equilibrium in the long run. If disinflation is brought about and is maintained by a reduction in essential investment expenditures, the cure may be worse than the disease; if, on the contrary, it is caused by a curtailment of expenditures for non-essential investment and consumption, and if the resources thus released are gradually channeled into export industries and essential investments, disinflation can indeed make a considerable contribution to the economic rehabilitation of the areas now dependent on aid from the United States.

## NOTES

1. It may be noted that the existence of a fixed rate of exchange is a limitation on the "openness" of the inflation. During the ideally "open" German inflation of the 'twenties there never developed a foreign exchange shortage, one reason being that the fall in the foreign value of the mark in general kept ahead of the increase in domestic prices.

2. See on this problem in the United Kingdom, "Retreat from Austerity," *The Banker*, July 1948, pp. 12–15.

3. It may be pointed out that, similarly, U.S. net exports of raw materials and machinery can have, in the short run, an anti-inflationary effect on

the U.S. economy. For the shipment of these goods abroad may result in the postponement of capital expansion projects which might otherwise have materialized; it also makes it impossible for these goods to compete for complementary and already otherwise employed factors of production (labor and materials) through which they would be put to use in the American economy. This anti-inflationary effect of U.S. net exports on the domestic economy is the logical counterpart to their inflationary effect on the foreign economies, but in the present situation the actual significance of the former effect is no doubt far smaller than that of the latter and is certainly outweighed for the United States by the aggregate inflationary impact of our foreign aid program.

4. The Italian Government has had considerable difficulties in recent months in disposing domestically of the coal it had imported under the Interim Aid Program.

# 9

## DOLLAR SHORTAGE
## AND DISCRIMINATION[1]

I n an interesting series of articles on "The World and the Dollar" the London *Economist* came recently once more to the
conclusion that discrimination against American goods is an
essential tool of commercial policy if Europe and the world are
to achieve recovery and economic independence.[2] The "admirable doctrine" of nondiscrimination must be shelved, according
to the author of the series, as long as the world does not have as
many dollars as it would like to spend.

This thesis is in the process of becoming widely accepted. The
United States made substantial concessions to it in agreeing to
the "scarce currency" clause of the Bretton Woods Agreements
on the International Monetary Fund and to Article 23 ("Exceptions to the Rule of Nondiscrimination") of the ITO [Interna-
tional Trade Organization] Charter. The advocation of closer
European union by the United States has been interpreted as
the final admission that the "admirable doctrine" could not be
maintained, let alone applied, in the present situation.

The examples cited to support the case for discrimination appear quite convincing at first sight. Why should Britain

---

restrict the purchase of books from Australia and of tobacco from Kenya simply because the dollar shortage forces it to limit book and tobacco imports from the United States?[3] Why should Canada ban chocolate imports from France only because the dollar shortage forces it to prohibit imports of American candy bars?[4] Why, in other words, should the restrictive effects of the dollar shortage be allowed to affect, and possibly paralyze, trade among the non-dollar countries?

In reviewing this argument we shall not discuss here the general case for or against discrimination. We shall rather meet the argument on its own ground, i.e., we shall examine only how likely it is that discrimination is an effective device in dealing with the dollar shortage. It is the contention of this note that a consistent policy of discrimination is likely to impede structural changes in trade patterns which are necessary for the overcoming of the present condition of imbalance in international economic relations. This may be made clear in the following manner:

(1)  Suppose that in the second example cited above Switzerland (a more likely source of chocolate imports for Canada) is substituted for France. Then, it will be seen immediately, the argument that it would be senseless for Canada to ban chocolate imports from Switzerland along with those from the United States does not hold any longer. For any export surplus that Canada is able to secure with Switzerland through a reduction in imports would be readily convertible into dollars and would pro tanto reduce Canada's dollar deficit.

(2)  Let us now return to the original example with France as the third country. A Canadian export surplus with France is not convertible into dollars and does not therefore make any immediate contribution to the easing of Canada's dollar position. But surely Canada will not indefinitely accumulate

French francs. It will either be successful in pressing the French for imports more essential than chocolate, or it will have to make a determined attempt to redirect part of its exports from France to the United States. In both cases, its dollar position is likely to be improved.

(3) But, it will be argued, Canada is not likely to achieve an export surplus at all as the result of its nondiscriminatory import cuts because France by pursuing the same policy will have reduced its purchases of, say, books from Canada along with those from the United States. The consequence of dollar shortage plus nondiscrimination is then the stifling of trade among France and Canada. This may well be true, but it may be asked whether the consequence of this particular reduction in mutual trade would not be beneficial in the longer run. For the reduction in intertrade between France and Canada makes export surpluses available in both countries which may be redirected to the Western Hemisphere; and in case such redirection is not possible the resources released by the reduction in intertrade could be devoted to the production of goods which would find an outlet in the dollar area or which might replace goods previously imported from that area.

It is generally recognized that the solution of the "dollar problem" will require far-reaching readjustments of trade patterns and, in particular, an expansion of Europe's sales and a reduction of its purchases in the Western Hemisphere. But it is one thing to state this necessity and another to provide sufficient incentives and penalties to bring the readjustment about. If the whole burden of the readjustment is thrown on the bilateral relationships between the United States and the dollar-poor countries, while all other trade relationships are carefully insulated from the effect of the dollar shortage, the elasticity of the trading system and its capacity for readjustment are greatly reduced. It is a fallacy to assume that because currencies are largely inconvertible, no multilateral adjustment of a given bilateral trade relationship in disequilibrium is possible at all. This adjustment is merely more laborious than under conditions of currency convertibility since it requires the reshuffling of exports and of resources. Especially under conditions of full employment, it is hard to see how equilibrium can at all be reestablished without such reshuffling.

The preceding argument may be considered from a somewhat different angle: suppose that there are excellent opportunities for mutually beneficial and balanced trade between two countries which cannot be taken advantage of because of the rule of nondiscrimination, both countries being unable to afford buying from the United States the goods which they want to buy from each other. As long as it is impossible to shift resources, a strong argument may be made for a discriminatory policy. Such instances should, however, be justified on an ad hoc basis rather than be sanctioned in advance by the principle of discrimination against U.S. goods. If this principle were applied systematically and all non-U.S. trade were to proceed on an artificially sheltered basis, the result would indeed be a growth of that trade, possibly even on a balanced basis, while the dollar problem would likely remain as critical as ever. Such a situation would, of course, provide the dollar-short countries with an excellent opportunity for pointing out that since they have achieved growing and balanced trade with all countries except the United States, the fault must obviously lie with the United States which "does not make enough dollars available," "does not behave like a mature creditor country," etc., and has therefore to take the responsibility for the shortage by providing further loans and grants.

It is not intimated here that discrimination is being advocated with this design in mind. The partisans of discrimination live much more in the past than in the future. The origin of the doctrine is the experience of the 'thirties when it would have been most important to isolate as much as possible the effect of the sudden halving of American imports of goods and services. Rather than to permit the propagation of the depression by deflation, devaluation or nondiscriminatory import cuts, it has been pointed out that the countries affected by a depression starting in another area ought to take domestic compensatory measures combined with discriminatory exchange controls.[5] The problem is not to circumscribe and to offset the effects of an American depression, but to let the dollar shortage have its full effect in producing a diversion of exports to hard currency areas, and in general to shake loose and readjust old and new trade patterns so as to permit a progressive reduction in U.S. foreign aid shipments. The advocates of discrimination are fighting the last war, and if they win out, the present war against the dollar shortage may well be lost.

The preceding argument stresses the dangers of a policy based on the belief that the scarcity of dollars makes a systematic policy of discrimination necessary. In itself, however, the opposite policy is certainly not sufficient to make a contribution to the cure of the dollar shortage. The effect of nondiscrimination on trade may be roughly compared to the effect of disinflation on production:[6] by freeing resources, both make possible their redirection into patterns which will reduce the dependence of Europe on outside aid. The actual implementation of this redirection is a task which requires that the opportunities offered by disinflation and nondiscrimination be seized upon by intelligent planning and deliberate policy.

## NOTES

1. For a previous note on the dollar shortage, see this *Review*, August 24, 1948 [republished in this volume as chapter 8].

2. *The Economist*, June 26, 1948, pp. 1051–1052; July 3, 1948, pp. 4–5; July 10, 1948, pp. 44–46 ["Dollar Shortage for Ever," *The Economist*, June 26, 1948, Vol. 154, Issue 5470, pp. 1051–1052; "Dollars—An American Problem," *The Economist*, July 3, 1948, Vol. 155, Issue 5471, pp. 4–5; "The Need for Discrimination," *The Economist*, July 10, 1948, Vol. 155, Issue 5472, pp. 44–46].

3. Thomas Balogh, "The Problem of the British Balance of Payments," *Bulletin of the Oxford Institute of Statistics*, Vol. IX (July 1947), p. 222.

4. "The Need for Discrimination," *The Economist*, July 10, 1948, p. 45.

5. Robert Triffin, *National Central Banking and the International Economy*, Postwar Economic Studies no. 7, Board of Governors, Federal Reserve System [in Lloyd A. Metzler, Robert Triffin, and Gottfried Haberler, *International Monetary Policies*, Postwar Economic Studies, no. 7, September 1947, Washington, DC: Board of Governors of the Federal Reserve System, pp. 46–81]. That the origin of the doctrine of discrimination lies in the preoccupation with a depression induced by a foreign country appears quite clearly from the League of Nations report, *Economic Stability in the Postwar World* (1945, pp. 245–247) quoted by Triffin.

6. See this *Review*, August 24, 1948 [republished in this volume as chapter 8].

# 10

# THE OEEC *INTERIM REPORT* ON THE EUROPEAN RECOVERY PROGRAM—A SUMMARY

he *Interim Report* published by the Organization for European Economic Cooperation on December 30, 1948, constitutes a first preliminary report on the long-term programs and prospects of the E.R.P. participating countries. This summary was prepared for use by ECA in connection with its presentation of its second-year program to Congress. A critical appraisal of the long-term program is planned for a subsequent article in this *Review*).

The European Recovery Program [ERP] is based on the belief that, with an adequate amount of aid from the U.S., the participating countries will become independent of extraordinary outside assistance at the end of a period set at approximately 4 years. From the beginning of the ERP an effort was therefore made to draw up long term programs of action for the future individual participating countries and for the ERP area as a whole. These programs were to give a measure of the magnitude of the task ahead, of the U.S. aid required to fulfill it; and of the pattern of production, consumption, and trade necessary for assuring self-support after the termination of the aid program.

Confidential. *Review of Foreign Developments*, February 8, 1949.

The first effort at visualizing the long term goal of the ERP was made by the Committee of European Economic Cooperation (CEEC) in 1947. The countries that had convened in Paris to formulate a joint recovery program, attempted to forecast their industrial and agricultural production goals and their balance of payments for every year from 1948 to 1951. The CEEC drew together the country estimates. In view of the shortness of the time available and of the novelty of the task, these programs were only rough outlines. The CEEC, in drawing them together, lacked the power to amend them substantially in the light of any inconsistencies which it would discover among them. The work accomplished did, however, have its usefulness for it confirmed the conviction that the goal of eventual self-support could be reached provided a strenuous effort was made to expand production and exports. Furthermore, the experience gained from this first attempt proved very useful when a second attempt at long term forecasting was undertaken.

From the beginning of ECA and OEEC operations, it was realized that an approximate idea as to the desirable future pattern of development of the European economy was essential for the making of every day policy decisions. High priority was therefore given to the preparation of a new set of long term programs far more comprehensive in scope than those that were submitted to the CEEC. Instructions were sent by OEEC on the preparation of the long term program in the summer of 1948 together with instructions for the 1949–50 program. These instructions directed the participating countries to provide a general statement setting out their plans of action by means of which they intended to maintain their economy in 1952–53 without extra-ordinary external assistance. Specifically the individual countries were asked to submit a description of the targets for industrial and agricultural production; of the amount of investment required to carry out these targets; of the financial policy to be followed to make financing of this investment consistent with monetary stability; of the standard of living that will be reached; of the balance-of-payments position that will result in 1952–53 from these programs; and of the conditions necessary for their achievement.

The OEEC has prepared an *Interim Report on the Long Term Program* which draws together and analyzes the programs of the participating countries. As specifically stated in the report it does not present an integrated program for the ERP area as a whole with all internal inconsistencies removed. Rather, it sets itself the preliminary task of setting out the results of the country programs, of examining them critically, and of pointing up the major problems and difficulties arising from the overall picture obtained. At the same time, the report indicates the direction in which the European countries will have to look for a solution of these difficulties.

In the following a short summary is given of the main features of the interim report. Some emphasis will be laid on the comments and criticisms of OEEC. This ought not to give the impression that the OEEC has nothing good to say about the country submissions, but obviously the criticisms made by OEEC provide ECA and the U.S. Government with a particularly useful starting point for its own evaluation and for the formulation of its own policies.

## A. PRODUCTION

### 1. Industry

Excepting Western Germany whose output is still abnormally low, the average increase in total industrial production planned by the participating countries amounts to about 25 per cent over the next 4 years. The planned increase above prewar for all countries amounts to 30 per cent. The following table [table 10.1] shows output goals for key products.

### TABLE 10.1 PRODUCTION ALREADY ATTAINED AND DEVELOPMENT SCHEMES IN VARIOUS INDUSTRIES (1935-38 = 100)

| Metropolitan territories | 1947 | 1948–1949 programme | 1949–1950 programme | 1952–1953 programme |
|---|---|---|---|---|
| Coal | 80 | 91 | 97 | 111 |
| Electricity | 148 | 166 | 180 | 222 |
| Crude oil (throughput)[a] | 98 | 174 | 231 | 480 |
| Steel (raw) | 69 | 102 | 115 | 129[b] |
| Steel (finished) | 74 | 107 | 121 | 140[b] |
| Aluminum | 89 | 120 | 141 | 210 |
| Nitrogenous fertilizers | 113 | 149 | 177 | 239 |
| Potash | 96 | 123 | 136 | 176 |
| Soluble phosphates | 101 | 136 | 174 | 196 |
| Textiles (total consumption of fibres) | 84 | 99 | 108 | 122 |
| Machine tools | 73 | 85 | 105 | 139 |
| Equipment including machine tools | — | 115 | 125 | 145 |
| Motor vehicles (commercial) | 108 | 152 | 155 | 180 |
| Motor vehicles (private passenger) | 49 | 67 | — | 116 |

*Note:* This table, and most of the subsequent tables in the report relating to OEEC countries, do not include figures for Switzerland.

[a] This item reflects the large increase in refining capacity which is planned. The increased crude oil throughput is accompanied by a reduction of imports of refined petroleum products.

[b] Omitting the Bizone the figures become: Raw Steel 158, Finished Steel 171.

OEEC comments in particular on the following points:

(a)  The combined four-year program provides for more than dou-
     bling the prewar consumption of oil, while hard coal consump-
     tion is due for an increase of only 13 per cent above prewar.
     While the OEEC Report recognizes the need for increased
     motor transport, it is critical of large-scale substitution of oil
     for coal.

(b)  Investment in electrical power generating equipment is
     planned in the amount of $2 billion for the four-year period.
     The OEEC Report acknowledges the importance of achieving
     an increase in generating capacity, but points to the necessity
     of curtailing other investment projects if an outlay of this mag-
     nitude is to be achieved.

(c)  The planned advance in textile production does not seem to
     have taken sufficiently into account reduced marketing pos-
     sibilities as a result of industrialization. Provision for textile
     equipment is considered over-generous.

(d)  As a result of various raw material or plant shortages, doubt is
     expressed as to the possibility of achieving the indicated out-
     put goals for steel, non-ferrous metals except aluminum, sul-
     phuric acid, and woolen textiles.

## 2. Agriculture

The national agricultural programs add up to a rate of increase
of about 15 per cent with respect to 1935–38. This is lower than
the progress planned for industrial production with respect
to prewar, but in view of the lag of agricultural behind industrial recovery in the postwar period, a considerable improvement in agricultural output is planned for the next 4 years.

The following table [table 10.2] shows production goals for the whole ERP area.

The increase in production above prewar is mainly due to the considerable expansion programs of France, the U.K. and Turkey. All other countries plan to return substantially to the prewar level of harvests with the exception of high yield crops such as potatoes and sugar beets for which expansion of 33 per cent is contemplated. As to livestock, cattle and sheep are expected to increase about 10 per cent above present levels while a 70 per cent increase is planned for pigs.

Large increases in food production are foreseen for the overseas territories, with most stress being laid on vegetable oil, sugar and rice. Development of agriculture is to be pushed principally

TABLE 10.2 OUTPUT OF MISCELLANEOUS AGRICULTURAL PRODUCTS AND LIVESTOCK NUMBERS (1935–38 = 100)

|  | 1947–1948 | 1948–1949 programme | 1949–1950 programme | 1952–1953 programme |
|---|---|---|---|---|
| Bread grains | 60 | 93 | 97 | 114 |
| Coarse grains | 82 | 95 | 101 | 116 |
| Potatoes | 93 | 125 | 116 | 131 |
| Sugar | 81 | 111 | 112 | 134 |
| Oils and fats | 77 | 80 | 92 | 115 |
| Meat | 67 | 70 | 78 | 106 |
| Milk | 76 | 84 | 91 | 111 |
| Timber | 93 | 100 | 100 | 95 |
| Cattle | 98 | 98 | 101 | 110 |
| Sheep | 88 | 90 | 93 | 101 |
| Pigs | 60 | 64 | 76 | 109 |
| Poultry | 81 | 90 | 98 | 112 |
| Farm horses | 92 | 91 | 90 | 90 |

by additional mechanization, particularly in France and the U.K., and by almost doubling the application of fertilizers with respect to prewar. OEEC's comments on the agricultural programs are the following:

(a) The French plan of turning France into a large-scale agricultural exporter of bread grains and meat to other European countries is considered as of fundamental importance to the participating countries because of the dollar saving of about $200 million it will make possible. The report injects a note of caution, however, by stating that "its success depends on mechanization, the availability of manpower, a very substantial increase in the use of fertilizers, and the adoption of modern agricultural techniques by a large agricultural population composed largely of small farmers."

(b) European productive facilities for agricultural machinery should be better utilized through standardization, regular provision of spare parts and similar methods.

(c) In spite of increased mechanization and application of fertilizers, the report is somewhat skeptical as to the possibility of improving agricultural yields to the extent envisaged.

(d) Attention is called to the importance of pest and crop disease control and to the potential contribution of agricultural education and advisory services. The desirability of providing incentives to agricultural output by guaranteeing markets, particularly in conjunction with the expansion of agricultural production in the overseas territories, is also emphasized.

(e) In view of stationary timber production in Western Europe and the uncertainty surrounding the volume of timber imports from Eastern Europe, "further attention needs to be paid to the economy in the use of timber, to a greater use of steel in replacing timber, and to the provision of other raw materials for pulping."

(f)   With respect to agricultural development in the overseas ter-
      ritories, attention is directed to the advisability of developing
      large-scale production of corn, millets and other coarse grains
      to replace imports from the Western Hemisphere. Stress is also
      to be placed on the cultivation of cocoa, which is an important
      "dollar earner," and of rice and other indigenous foods to obvi-
      ate the needs of imports into the overseas territories from the
      Western Hemisphere.

## 3. Transportation

The shipbuilding program of the participating countries calls
for bringing the combined merchant fleet almost back to prewar. Construction of tankers is given priority over dry cargo.
With respect to present total tonnage the program implies an
increase of 20 per cent, which is fully endorsed by the OEEC
report in view of its potential contribution to European balance
of payments.

Rail transportation is not expected to be expanded substantially. The effort of the participating countries will consist mainly
in increasing efficiency and electrification of existing lines. With
respect to the latter, the report points to the considerable cost of
the electrification projects as an offset to the economy in coal
which is achieved.

## 4. Manpower and Productivity

With the exception of Italy and Western Germany where unemployment is expected to remain a problem, all country programs
provide for full employment of the laboring force. They do not,

however, envisage an absorption of immigrants on a large scale. The OEEC report is not satisfied with this reluctance on their part and "intends to discuss this problem further, since it appears that there may be countries where programs can be more easily achieved by absorbing some of the surplus manpower available in other countries."

Output per man hour during the next 4 years is scheduled to increase by 15 per cent. The OEEC report is doubtful of the prospects of achieving this goal and discusses longer hours and an increase of the labor force employed in the vital sectors of the economy as substitutes.

## B. BALANCE OF PAYMENTS WITH THE OUTSIDE WORLD

The risk of different countries' projects being inconsistent with each other is much greater in the field of trade than in that of production. For instance, it is only to be expected that France will plan to export in 1952–53 to Belgium a different amount from what Belgium independently expects to import from France during the same period. For this reason, the OEEC report, which has only scattered (though valuable) comment to offer with respect to the production targets, really comes into its own in the chapter on trade and balance of payments. It is here that the need to reconsider basic policies of the participating countries is discovered as a result of a thorough examination of the aggregate country programs.

In adding up the projected imports and exports of the participating countries to the outside world, the following picture is obtained [table 10.3].

## TABLE 10.3 SOURCES OF OEEC COUNTRIES' IMPORTS FROM OUTSIDE WORLD AND DIRECTION OF OEEC COUNTRIES' EXPORTS TO OUTSIDE WORLD (EXCLUDING DEPENDENT OVERSEAS TERRITORIES) (IN BILLIONS OF DOLLARS [1948–49 PRICES])

| | 1938 | | 1947 | | 1952–1953 programme | |
|---|---|---|---|---|---|---|
| | Imports | Exports | Imports | Exports | Imports | Exports |
| North & Central America | 4.1 | 1.45 | 7.3 | 1.05 | 3.8 | 2.1 |
| South America | 1.7 | 1.0 | 1.7 | 0.75 | 2.1 | 2.0 |
| Non-participating sterling area | 2.9 | 1.9 | 2.0 | 2.0 | 3.3 | 3.1 |
| Eastern Europe[a] | 3.0 | 2.5 | 0.9 | 0.75 | 2.2 | 2.0 |
| Other countries | 1.3 | 1.1 | 0.6 | 0.85 | 1.4 | 1.4 |
| Total | 13.0 | 7.95 | 12.5 % of 1938 | 5.4 | 12.8 | 10.6 |
| North & Central America | 100 | 100 | 179 | 72 | 93 | 146 |
| South America | 100 | 100 | 97 | 73 | 122 | 192 |
| Non-participating sterling Area | 100 | 100 | 69 | 104 | 116 | 165 |
| Eastern Europe[2] | 100 | 100 | 30 | 30 | 73[b] | 80 |
| Other countries | 100 | 100 | 46 | 77 | 108 | 127 |
| Total | 100 | 100 | 96 | 68 | 99 | 133 |

[a] It has been assumed that in 1938, 35 percent of the exports of participating countries to Germany went to Eastern Germany. Exports of Western Germany to Eastern Europe have been assumed to be 70 percent of total German exports to Eastern Europe. No allowance has been made for interzonal trade. On this basis planned exports to Eastern Europe in 1952–53 represent 30 percent of the 1938 volume. Calculations on other equally plausible assumptions suggest, however, that they may represent one-third more than the 1938 volume.

[b] The inclusion of Eastern Germany in Eastern Europe makes it difficult to compare imports in pre-war and post-war years. It has been assumed that, in 1938, 30 per cent of the imports of the participating countries from Germany came from Eastern Germany. Imports of Western Germany from Eastern Europe have been assumed to be 65 per cent of total German imports from Eastern Europe. No allowance has been made for interzonal trade.

The principal contribution to the "viability" of the participating countries in 1952–53 is to come from increased exports via increased production. A further contribution is to derive from the invisible items, especially shipping services and tourist trade, which are expected to result in a total net surplus of $1.2 billion in 1952–53. This compares with a surplus of $2.0 billion in 1938, but the progress is considerable with respect to 1947 when invisible balance of the participating countries was negative to the extent of $750 million. The report underlines the ambitious character of the target for invisibles, but reserves its main criticism for the aggregate import and export targets revealed by the country programs.

The participating countries plan to hold total imports approximately constant; while imports from North American sources are to be reduced, purchases from non-dollar sources (including South America) are to be expanded substantially. This is the first point with which the OEEC report takes serious issue. In its opinion, availabilities in these areas have been overestimated to the extent of about $1 billion out of a total import program of $12.8 billion. The commodities concerned are mainly cotton and non-ferrous metals from South America, wool from the sterling area, grain and timber from Eastern Europe and fats and oils from the Far East. As a result of these probable shortfalls, either the import program would have to be curtailed or the dollar deficit of the ERP area will not decrease as scheduled because of the continuation of imports of these commodities from North America.

OEEC's criticism of the export goals is even more serious. Combined exports have been projected for 1952–53 at 133 per cent of 1938 and at 194 per cent of 1947. In relation to prewar the planned expansion of exports is particularly marked in relation to South America and the sterling area. With respect to the 1947 performance, more than doubling of export volume is hoped for in relation to North America and South America and Eastern Europe.

After a searching analysis of potential markets, the report comes to the conclusion that, *should present policies be continued*, total exports in 1952 to the outside world are likely to be over $2 billion smaller than the estimated $10.6 billion. This pessimistic conclusion still allows for an expansion of exports by nearly 57 per cent above the 1947 experience and by over 7 per cent above the prewar level. The reasons for the lower figures projected by OEEC are essentially industrialization in the non-participating sterling area and South America; the commercial ties that those areas have developed over the past ten years with non-European suppliers; and, in general, the stagnation which has marked, over the past thirty-five years, the volume of world trade in manu-factures. Should OEEC's forecast be correct, the balance-of-payments equilibrium in 1952–53 could be achieved only by a cut of 25 per cent in the proposed import program.

But the OEEC report does not resign itself to this bleak prospect. Having come to its pessimistic conclusions, it discards the assumption (continuation of present policies) on the basis of which the conclusion was reached. This means that "drastic changes in present policies are made," that "European goods will become competitive in every sense," that "There is an immediate drive" to re-establish and widen trade ties. Even if these policies are carried out, the OEEC still foresees a balance-of-payments gap of about $1.5 billion in 1952–53. But the magnitude of the problem will have changed decisively. A reduction of 10–15 per cent will be painful but no longer represents an unmanageable task fraught with great social and political dangers.

In the final section, which is permeated by a remarkable sense of the urgency and the magnitude of the task ahead, the OEEC report indicates the measures that are required for a solution. The European countries are requested to take action in three fields:

1.  Development of new sources of supply, particularly in overseas territories and resumption of imports from Eastern Europe.
2.  Economy in imports from the outside world. This is necessary in view of OEEC analysis of world availabilities as well as because of the limitation of the export drive even under the more optimistic assumptions. In particular, European agricultural production is believed capable of further expansion and the planned import increases of oil, textiles, copper, and timber are again criticized.
3.  The main reliance is to be placed on a vigorous drive to increase earnings. An aggressive sales policy is to be adopted throughout the world and a cut in the terms of trade must be taken to assure its success. This trend implies a condemnation on the part of OEEC of any attempts to solve balance-of-payments problems through monopolistic and discriminatory manipulation of the terms of trade. If the proper policies are adopted the report is not pessimistic about prospects of European sales in the U.S. It points out that Western European exports of manufactured goods to the United States are only 1 per cent of the total U.S. market for manufactures whereas other markets are already largely supplied by Western European exporters.

The report also makes a strong plea for exploring all possibilities for the earning of dollars in third markets. Here again the report is much more optimistic than most previous analyses of the subject. The developments during 1948 indicate that this optimism may be justified. During the first 9 months of 1948, Australia, New Zealand, India, Pakistan, Ceylon, Burma, South Rhodesia and Iraq achieved a trade surplus of $44 million with the United States and Canada as against a deficit of $428 million in 1948. The report repeatedly stresses the necessity of starting the export drive immediately in the interest of re-establishing trade ties. Any further delay would be permanently harmful to the prospect of European recovery because potential foreign customers are evermore looking to their own industries or to industries in third markets to replace European products.

Finally, the report emphasizes the necessity of a far greater measure of European cooperation than has been achieved. Measures which would enlarge the European market will result in cost cutting, which is essential to the export drive, and in a more efficient utilization of resources in the participating area as a whole. In the subsequent chapter on cooperation, particular stress is laid in this connection on the necessity to coordinate investment plans so as to prevent duplication and errors of location. It is recognized that investment plans cannot be coordinated meaningfully in the absence of a valid and stable system of exchange rates and a measure of comparative price stability throughout the participating countries. For this, as well as for many other reasons, a strong case must be made for cooperation in the financial and monetary fields as well as in production and trade policies.

## C. INTRA-EUROPEAN TRADE AND PAYMENTS

The participating countries have planned to expand their inter-trade by about 50 per cent from 1947 to 1952–53. This expansion would bring the volume of this trade back to its prewar level. As far as intra-European trade is concerned, exports for one participating country are imports for another; since the OEEC countries are in general endeavoring to expand exports while restricting imports, the failure of this trade to expand above prewar levels is easily explained and possibly justified. Nobody wishes to foster intra-European trade in isolation and at the possible expense of European exports to the outside world.

Far more preoccupying are the inconsistencies which are revealed among the plans of the individual countries. The report shows that these discrepancies are due not only to random errors, naturally to be expected when 17 countries draw up independent estimates of their inter-trade, but also, in at least two instances, to mutually incompatible economic policies.

In their trade with the other Continental countries, the Benelux countries and the Bizone expect to have a surplus of $257 and $209 million, respectively, while the other Continental participating countries only plan on a net deficit of $52 million. The surplus of Belgium and the Bizone figure importantly in the plans of these two countries for eventual self-support since they expect to finance the largest part of their remaining dollar deficit through their earnings in intra-European trade. These plans may run into serious difficulties; for with the one exception of Sweden, the other Continental countries do not expect to earn dollars in the Western Hemisphere in excess of their imports from it.

The second problem relates to trade between the Continental countries and the sterling area. The U.K. which, before the war, was a large scale net importer from the continent now plans a small surplus for 1952–53; it expects the continent to finance independently its traditional large scale purchases in the rest of the sterling area and plans to use part of its own surplus with the sterling area for the financing of its remaining dollar deficit. This policy, if successfully carried out, would make it possible for Continental countries to earn, as in the prewar period, sufficient sterling for financing their deficit with the rest of the sterling area (as planned, e.g., by France) or for covering their dollar deficit (as planned, e.g., by Denmark). The U.K. has indicated its willingness to make reasonable adjustments in its plans, but insists on achieving its triple aim of balance with the dollar area, continuation of some debt redemption, and resumption of some overseas investment.

The underlying difficulty in both problems is the impoverishment of Europe which causes most countries to restrict imports of non-essential and luxury goods from other participants. In view of the importance of these goods for Europe's exports drive in general, the OEEC report takes a stand against excessive stifling of this trade even among European countries. A solution should be found, rather, through an expansion of the production of essential commodities in the participating countries for export to other participants. It appears that the colonial development plans and France's intention to become an agricultural exporting country have not been fully taken into account by the import plans of the European countries.

In any event, the difficulties of arriving at an all round satisfactory pattern of intra-European trade and the need for balance in dollar accounts should not drive Western Europe into unnecessary bilateralization. The OEEC report recommends following up the payments scheme by a gradual relaxation of exchange controls and trade restrictions.

## D. INVESTMENT, STABILITY, AND CONSUMPTION

The gross national product of almost all participating countries is expected to be higher in 1952–53 than in 1938. On the whole, the increase assumed by the countries appears to be of the order of 20 per cent as compared with 1938 and approximately 35 per cent as compared with 1947. In view of the previously mentioned necessary balance-of-payments adjustments, the OEEC puts the probable increase with respect to 1938 at no more than 10 to 15 per cent. The contemplated increases in national income and in output are to be made possible by a continuous process of investment which in most countries is expected to absorb in 1952–53 as much as 20 per cent of the total production. This high percentage immediately poses the problem of monetary stability.

At the present time and throughout the aid program, American aid makes possible a much larger investment effort than would otherwise be compatible with monetary stability. The additional investment deriving from foreign aid will, however, decrease as the ECA program advances and will have to be replaced by domestic forms of savings if investment is to be maintained at a high level. The participating countries do not expect that individual savings (including sometimes depreciation allowances) will amount to more than from 8 to 13 per cent of national income. The remainder of the investment task will have to be accomplished either by corporate savings or by a surplus in the budget. The OEEC report has some interesting comments on the limitations of the latter policy; taxation is not necessarily an addition to savings since it may absorb incomes that would otherwise have been saved rather than spent; high levels of taxation may be damaging to incentives; and in some countries taxes are considered an integral part of the cost of living, and with wages geared to the latter, taxation cannot fulfill its task of curtailing income and expenditure.

Inflation results from too high an investment program in relation to government expenditures and to the level below which living standards should not or cannot be compressed. The OEEC report paints a full picture of the internal and external distortions resulting from inflation, whether open or suppressed. It recognizes the value of specific price and rationing and controls certain circumstances; but it comes to the conclusion that, in the coming years, the major part in the fight against inflation must be played by overall fiscal, monetary, and investment policy. Fiscal reform is in order in several countries. The report is less positive with respect to the possibilities of cutting budgetary expenditures, mainly because of the uncertainties of the international situation.

When fiscal reform is a long term task and when consumption levels cannot be cut, the only course remaining open to fight inflation is the reduction of investment expenditures. On this alternative the OEEC report has the following comments:

> The most urgent need of Western Europe today is an increase and a modernization of its capital equipment, the greater competitive power that such modernization will give, and the higher standards of life that may eventually flow from the greater investment. To cut down the plans of investment is to accept defeat. There will always be those in any country to whom such a course, with the immediate easements that it appears to offer, seems welcome. But there is no satisfactory long-term solution other than increased productivity. None the less, there may be circumstances in which the recognition that the task proposed is beyond a country's physical capacities may be inescapable. It may be better to proceed in an orderly fashion with a limited investment programme, than to see a larger planned programme frustrated and delayed because inflation prevents adequate resources from becoming available. A cruel dilemma may thus confront certain countries.

The OEEC will undertake a more detailed examination of the individual investment programs. It appears even now that the planned expansion of oil refining and of textile production might result in a wasteful duplication of resources. The investment programs also have to be re-examined in the light of OEEC's judgment about the limitations of material supplies from the outside world.

Consumption levels vary widely from one European country to the other, both in absolute terms and in relation to prewar. On the average it is estimated that consumption was in 1948 still about 20 per cent below prewar. A return to substantially the prewar level is aimed at by the country programs for 1952–53. The OEEC report takes the more realistic view that a level of consumption in 1952–53 of from 5 to 10 per cent above that of 1948 may be all that is consistent with independence of external aid. In line with this general suggestion, the report invites the participating countries to reconsider their food consumption plans which call for substantial increases in meat consumption and to continue the emphasis on bread grains.

## E. COOPERATION

The interim report on the long term program is in itself the highest expression of the cooperation that has been achieved so far by the participating countries. The last chapter of the report roughly outlines further progress that the organization expects to achieve.

First place is given to the coordination of investment policies and plans. The obstacles interfering with this task are numerous: inflation, monetary instability and artificial exchange rates makes cost comparisons difficult and the control which the various governments have over the amount and description of investments varies widely from country to country. Nevertheless, mutual consultation is essential if the limited resources available are to be used to the best advantage of the ERP area as a whole.

A similar effort of coordination must be undertaken with respect to current production. In this field, much useful groundwork is already being laid by the technical committees of the OEEC.

A considerable cooperative effort must be accomplished with respect to employment, manpower and migration policy. The unemployment problems of Italy and Germany cannot be solved by action of these countries alone.

Standardization and other technical projects are being extended in view of their potential contribution to increased productivity.

Finally, the report mentions its continuing work toward the liberalization of trade and payments, and reports on the ways at further progress for the Customs Union Study Group.

# 11

# INTERNATIONAL ASPECTS
# OF A RECESSION

The present paper is concerned with the possibility of an international recession and with its implications for the "dollar shortage." In its first part, the stability of foreign economies will be examined, with particular reference to those of Western Europe. The second part deals with the probable consequences of a downturn for international economic equilibrium.

## I. THE STABILITY OF
## FOREIGN ECONOMIES

Up to the middle of 1949, signs of a recession are fewer and less conclusive in foreign countries than in the United States. More and more countries, however, appear to achieve stabilization regardless of whether they have been suffering from the "open" or the "repressed" variety of inflation and also regardless of the kinds and the degree of control under which their economies have been functioning.

Confidential. *Review of Foreign Developments*, June 7, 1949.

Incentives to invest have been particularly strong in all war devastated countries not only because of the large backlogs of consumer demand and the need for reequipment in capital goods, but because relatively small amounts of investment (repairs of houses, railroads, replacement of damaged or outworn machinery) were sure to yield an exceptionally quick and high return. Once this abnormal demand for investment comes to an end, a rather severe readjustment ought to be expected. This type of readjustment did take place in 1947–48 in Italy where the completion of the most urgent repairs coincided with restrictionist monetary policies which killed the speculative, inflation-induced type of investment. The other marked instance of a postwar recession is Belgium[1] where war destruction had not been important and where the Government followed a policy of giving primary attention to the filling of consumers' demands.

Spotty evidence of slackening consumer buying is available in France, Germany, the Netherlands, and the United Kingdom. Investment pressures have eased considerably in Sweden and Switzerland, and a number of large-scale reconstruction and reequipment programs particularly in the field of transportation (shipbuilding in England, railways in France and Italy, and truck production in Western Europe in general), are nearing completion.

In many countries the public authorities have elaborated investment plans which so far they have had the greatest difficulty in financing without inflation and which, therefore, might be expected to prevent any tendency toward a depression. It is by no means certain, however, that everything will work out in this way. Many European countries have now made a considerable fiscal effort to create the savings necessary to offset the planned investment. But this investment, to a very large extent, is carried out by the private entrepreneur. At some point, it may simply not be forthcoming in the volume expected and then, provision having been made for it by budget surpluses, selectively restrictive bank credit policies, etc., there would be an ideal setting for a deflation. What needs to be pointed out, therefore, is that the present semi-planned economies of Western Europe have by no means achieved a reliable coordination of savings and investment decisions. Of course, in the past inflation-ridden years, investment projects have repeatedly been subjected to cuts which would presumably be restored as demand recedes. But the feeling of security induced by this consideration may well prove to be illusory, for an entrepreneur who very much wanted to undertake an expansion of his plant a year ago may feel quite differently about such a project when the inflation around him has subsided or turned into deflation.

Even the nationalized industries cannot be entirely relied upon to undertake investment programs when a recession has started to set in. In the first place, these industries have already invested at a very high rate during the recent inflationary phase, so that all that might be expected from them is the continuation of the present rate. Moreover, the managers of these industries have been told so insistently over the past years that they should use ordinary business judgment and criteria that, at least during the initial phase of a recession, they may well postpone investments when business in general adopts a wait-and-see attitude.

Another uncertainty affecting business activity in European countries is the level of individual savings. The general inflationary climate and the uncertainty about the prospective level of private savings has led, in a number of countries, to an extremely limited reliance on personal savings as an offset to the planned level of investment. All the other forms of savings, such as corporate savings and budget surpluses, seemed far superior in that they were more enforceable, i.e., they were less forecasts which may or may not become true, than targets which can consciously be aimed at by economic policy.

Thus, in France the "inflationary gap" was calculated in 1947–48 on the assumption of zero personal savings. In Great Britain, the current estimate of private savings for 1949 is 200 million pounds but this consists, to the extent of 214 million, of direct taxes on capital. In countries like Norway and the Netherlands the national accounts were actually drawn up on the assumption that there would be a certain amount of net dissaving by private individuals.

It goes without saying that a zero or negative level of personal savings is an anomaly caused by exceptional backlog demands or by inflation. When the backlog demands are filled, when the inflation is stopped and excess liquid holdings have been reduced, a sudden reappearance of private savings on a substantial scale is possible; it is quite likely to take the official planners by surprise.

What policy will or should European countries follow when they are faced, despite planning for full employment, by a recession resulting from overestimates of private investment and underestimates of private savings? As long as inflationary tendencies prevailed, the task of the authorities was clear enough, though by no means easy to carry out. The weapons to be used were the familiar ones of restrictive fiscal and monetary policy, supplemented if necessary or advisable, by the use of negative or veto controls over private investment.

Novel problems arise, on the other hand, when individuals are suddenly found to save again, and when private investment ceases pushing incessantly against the limits which have been assigned to it in the total investment program, but starts to fall short of these limits. For a number of reasons it appears unlikely that foreign countries in general, and those of Western Europe in particular, will be able or ready immediately to counteract such developments. In the first place, a mere reversal of the policies followed during the inflationary phase, such as, e.g., the lifting of credit and investment controls, may be ineffective in reviving demand. Secondly, in countries where inflations have been protracted and violent, the authorities may prefer to err on the side of disinflation, at least for a while. This may be sound policy also because such inflations presumably have given rise to considerable misdirection of resources which ought to be corrected. Finally, and most important, the trend toward recession brings almost automatically a certain improvement in the foreign exchange position of the countries concerned and their authorities will therefore hesitate to take "compensatory" measures which are likely to re-create the same degree of dollar shortage as existed prior to the onset of the adjustment process. Clearly, the loosening up of the labor market and of resources in general ought to be taken advantage of in order to carry out a reorientation toward export industries (or toward activities providing domestic substitutes for imports).

Economic policy therefore will not be concerned solely with the restoration of a sufficient aggregate of effective demand. Balance of payments preoccupations will probably rule out indiscriminate "reflation" with its reliance on the automatic working of the multiplier but rather will point to the necessity of specific direction of the re-expansion process. But the official investment planning seems to be efficient mainly in expanding the so-called basic sectors of the economy (energy, transportation, iron and steel). With the exception of some large-scale industries, such as petroleum refineries and shipbuilding, the official planners do not seem to have been very successful in planning directly for the expansion of exports[,]not to speak of their direction. This may be a field where exchange rate adjustments, which would render exporting attractive to business, could play a useful role not only in immediately producing greater balance of payments equilibrium, but also in generating and guiding a new investment wave.

The present uncertainties about the future course of business activity in European countries makes it necessary to reexamine ECA policy concerning counterpart funds. Hitherto the United States power over the use of these funds was used primarily to fight inflation either directly by withholding them from current spending or by making release dependent on effective anti-inflationary action. With deflationary tendencies outweighing inflationery [sic] pressures a reversal would consist in stopping debt retirement programs which are followed in a number of countries and in supplementing releases by additional expansionary action by the foreign governments. But in view of the undesirability of a policy of indiscriminate reflation, such a simple about-face would in general not be adequate; it will be necessary for the ECA to make sure that spending of counterpart funds does not promote short-run recovery from recession at the expense of impeding longer-run recovery from the dollar shortage.

## II. INTERNATIONAL REPERCUSSIONS OF A RECESSION

In examining the implications of a recession for international balance of payments equilibrium we shall assume at first that a downturn occurs only in the United States while other countries continue to enjoy a high level of economic activity.

## Effects of a Recession in the United States Only

This is almost a classical case by this time, for most discussions about appropriate post-war international economic policy have taken this situation as their starting point. It generally was assumed that a fall in U.S. demand would produce balance of payments difficulties abroad, and an international equivalent to the theory of internal compensatory fiscal and monetary policies was elaborated by such writers as [Ragnar] Nurske and [Robert] Triffin.* In such a situation, it was propounded, it would be wrong for the affected countries to "play the rules of the gold standard game" and to contract money and incomes. On the contrary, international currency reserves ought to be freely spent and the contractive domestic effect of the outflow properly counteracted so as to avoid spreading the deflation and intensifying it in the United States.

Unfortunately this type of analysis is not too relevant to the present situation, because the starting point is so strikingly different from what it was assumed to be in the earlier analyses.

Here, as in several other areas of economic policy, we have already for several years been acting as though we were fighting a depression. For by maintaining a large export surplus we were bolstering domestic income; moreover, our export surplus is now

---

* Ragnar Nurkse (1907–1959), an Estonian Canadian economist, worked for the Economic Intelligence Service of the League of Nations from 1934 to 1945. In 1945, he moved to Columbia University. In the postwar years, Nurkse was a pioneer of development economics, supporting the theory of "balanced growth," the principal target of Hirschman's criticism in his 1958 book, *The Strategy of Economic Development* (New Haven, CT: Yale University Press). Robert Triffin (1911–1993) was a Belgian American economist who worked for the Federal Reserve (1942–1946), the IMF (1946–1948), and the OEEC (1948–1951), before becoming a professor of economics at Yale University. Triffin was a critic of the Bretton Woods System; his critique is known as the Triffin dilemma or Triffin paradox.

financed very largely by government aid, and since we generally authorize the release of the local currency counterpart of our aid, the offsetting policy recommended by Nurkse is already in effect.

In this situation a reduction in U.S. demand would still mean, of course, less U.S. foreign purchases at lower prices, but it would also mean cheaper foreign purchases in the United States. Assuming that the foreign country's volume of imports is controlled either directly or through exchange rate adjustment, the dollar savings accruing to it from the fall in import prices could well exceed the loss sustained by the fall in the price *and* volume of its exports. This is the direct result of our starting point, i.e. the large U.S. export surplus. When we start from a position of balance there can be little doubt that a depression in a leading trading country will create balance of payments problems for the other countries; but if that country maintains a considerable export surplus at the time a recession sets in, the same proposition does not necessarily hold.

This reasoning applies in particular to the countries participating in the European Recovery Program which in 1948 still exported to the United States only about one fourth of their purchases in this country. As a result of their unbalanced trade position, the rise in world prices since the war has meant for them—quite apart from any deterioration in the terms of trade—a larger absolute dollar gap. A decline in dollar prices would correspondingly improve their position and they probably would still retain a net gain even though the volume of their exports to the dollar area were to be somewhat reduced.

The unstabilizing impact of a U.S. recession is therefore likely to be felt mainly in those countries that do not receive substantial amounts of aid from the United States. These countries, however, are quite unlikely, under present circumstances, to apply the policy of freely spending their dollar reserves. Over the past years, all countries have become conscious of the dollar problem and of the desirability to husband their dollar resources. A country that sees its dollar deficit increase in the wake of an American slump would immediately take defensive measures. [Charles P.] Kindleberger[†] argued several years ago that increased dollar earnings of foreign countries may give rise to an even greater increase in current dollar payments. In the present situation the inverse reaction could occur: for every dollar lost as a result of a shrinkage of the American market, the foreign country may well retrench its purchases in an amount larger than one dollar. Such a process could occur even if at first, the affected country decides on an immediate retaliatory import cut that is no more than equivalent to the loss in exports; for a secondary reduction in imports may take place as a result of the decline in incomes that would follow upon reduced economic activity in industries dependent on American raw materials and equipment.[2]

In conclusion it is clear that the countries which are most likely to suffer from an American recession are those that receive their dollars primarily through trade channels rather than in the form of U.S. aid. It would seem, therefore, that, in the event of a continuation of present business trends, we would have a special responsibility with respect to these countries. Moreover, it may be in our own interest to see to it that immediate curtailment of their imports from the United States in retaliation for decreased exports to the United States is avoided or minimized.

The continued existence of sizeable foreign aid programs is a substantial safeguard against an international spread and

---

[†] Charles P. Kindleberger (1910–2003) was an American economist. He worked for the Federal Reserve Bank of New York (1936–1939) and the Board of Governors of the Federal Reserve System (1940–1942). As an officer of the Department of State he participated in the design and launch of the Marshall Plan. In 1948, Kindleberger became a professor at the Massachusetts Institute of Technology.

deepening of a recession at this time just as the abrupt end of private U.S. lending at the onset of the Great Depression had then an important intensifying effect. However, there are certain limitations to the extent to which we may rely on the foreign aid outlays as a stabilizing factor.

In the first place, the emphasis on the real or commodity aspect of our aid tends to provoke curtailments of the dollar amount of aid made available when prices fall. Secondly, it is already apparent that a recession in the United States may bring about a decreased willingness to maintain our foreign aid programs although at least a slowing down of the progressive reduction in these programs may be called for from an objective point of view. If it is assumed, of course, that the Federal Budget ought to be in balance under all circumstances then it is possible to argue, as has been done during the recent Congressional debate, that our foreign aid programs are not inflationary—the contention of last year—but deflationary since they make necessary a greater tax burden than would be required otherwise. This argument would be particularly strong if it is found that the recipient countries do not actually spend all of the aid received, but accumulate an important fraction of it in the form of additional reserves. To tax the American consumer in order to permit foreign Central Banks to hold idle dollar balances would indeed be purely deflationary action. This combination of circumstances actually occurred with respect to several countries during the past months. But, normally, a great deal of confidence can be placed both in the difficulties of maintaining the Federal Budget in balance during the recession and in the eagerness of foreign countries to prove their need for aid by promptly using it for the purchase of American goods.

At best, however, our foreign aid outlays will serve to cushion a domestic recession and to inhibit its propagation. The fact that the United States is entering into a period of domestic readjustment with a still huge export surplus which it alone sustains by its aid programs, automatically rules out any large-scale reliance on foreign transactions actively to restore our domestic position. In order to be able to carry out any "beggar-my neighbor" type of policy, we would first have to make additional gifts to our neighbors. Actually we are pushing ahead with plans to reduce foreign aid appropriations progressively and this policy serves to place almost exclusive reliance on domestic rather than international policies in the active combatting of a depression.

## Effects of a Recession in Foreign Countries

It was found in the preceding section, that under present circumstances a recession arising only in the United States would have less unbalancing effects on foreign economies than was generally believed. If it is assumed that simultaneously there is some disinflation in foreign countries the conclusion follows that the dollar shortage will almost certainly be alleviated.

For the purpose of this analysis it would be tempting to distinguish two components of the dollar shortage: a "monetary" one which would designate the external consequences of the condition of open or repressed inflation which has characterized European, South American and other economies since the war; and, secondly, a "structural" component which would express the needs for temporary outside financing required to attain a certain level of productivity while maintaining a socially necessary standard of living. Unfortunately the line of distinction between the components cannot be drawn with any precision. Inflation brings in its train a special balance of payments drain caused by capital flight, by wasteful investment, and by failure to export;

but it is impossible to tell how big this burden is in relation to the total deficit. Moreover, it is likely that a prolonged inflation cannot be stopped without provoking a downturn and without thereby doing away with part of the "structural" component of the dollar shortage, in addition to the monetary one.

In such a situation the need for aid dollars will probably decrease suddenly and situations may arise in which a foreign country is actually unable to absorb foreign aid in the amounts available.

Conditioned as we already are to a general dollar shortage, such inability to absorb aid almost strikes us as something against nature, but it is of course not any more perverse than the inability of an economy to make reasonably full use of its manpower and machinery. A very striking example of this kind of situation has been given by Italy which has accumulated in the form of additional reserves of gold and foreign exchange close to one half of the aid received over the past year. This has been done indirectly, of course (i.e. by not using the dollar proceeds of its exports), since ERP dollars are necessarily tied to commodity imports, even though not to imports from the United States. The accumulation of reserves has been largely the result of the stabilization of the Italian internal situation combined with the adoption of a more realistic exchange rate than prevailed elsewhere in Europe.

Similar instances of inability to absorb aid and of accumulation of foreign exchange reserves have been encountered in other countries where symptoms of a recession have appeared, i.e. Germany and Belgium. There has also been a failure on the part of many OEEC countries to utilize substantial amounts of intra-European aid in the form of drawing rights under the Payments Scheme.

Such failure to utilize aid brings us face to face with the fact that our basis for apportioning aid still is the dollar shortage as conclusively demonstrated by foreign countries themselves rather than their need as established on the basis of valid and unambiguous criteria, defining the "structural" component of the dollar shortage. Vis-a-vis foreign countries receiving aid from us, we are in a position similar to that of the national planning authorities vis-a-vis the private investors: we can tell a country that it is over-extending its resources with respect to the financing that we can make available while we would find it difficult to push it into absorbing more dollars than it does.[3] Every reduction in the *use* of dollars by a particular country we are almost bound to interpret as proof that we had overestimated actual needs. A generalized recession would force us to do more thinking than hitherto on defining *need* for aid, a task that had been taken care of so far for us by physical shortages, inflationary pressures, and social unrest.

The Italian example also serves to show that our view of a gradual and regular tapering off of the need for aid may be based on the assumption of a world where planning is perfect and business cycles are non-existent. After the immediate reconstruction period when war damage is largely repaired, when pipelines are refilled, when some of the most important deferred demands in both consumption and investment are satisfied, and when the monetary overhang has been worked off in one day or another, many foreign economies are likely to pass through a period of adjustment during which their needs for foreign aid may be smaller than in a subsequent period when a new cycle of investment is undertaken. But the very fact that we have not made any provision for cyclical changes in the need for aid may help in the overcoming of foreign recessions. For the accumulation of dollars on the part of a foreign country experiencing a recession and the realization that it may well face a cut in aid if the accumulation continues may yet cause it to throw caution overboard and to undertake vigorous anti-deflationary action.

Thus it becomes possible to distinguish three postwar stages in the interaction between internal and external disequilibrium. It cannot be denied that to a certain extent during the immediate postwar period an inflation carried with it a dollar premium.[4] In a second period, as the volume of our aid shrank, anti-inflationary policies gained in attractiveness since they permitted foreign countries to absorb the decrease in our aid with a minimum of internal stresses. In a third period the competition for the dollars made available by us may yet become a powerful factor in avoiding any prolonged recession of foreign economies. This would be a new and possibly quite valuable mechanism: so far every country that in a depression made faster progress than the rest toward recovery was penalized by experiencing a strain in its balance of payments and a loss in reserves. Now, with the resulting deficit being made good by dollars contributed by the United States out of a limited amount of aid, the penalization would be changed into a reward.

## The Devaluation Issue

It may be in order to add a few words on the devaluation issue in the light of the foregoing remarks. The case against devaluation in the postwar period rested primarily on the following arguments:

1. Devaluation will not decrease imports since imports are already held in check by direct controls.
2. Devaluation will not increase exports (a) because the elasticity of supply is very low, and (b) because prices do not impede exports the only competitive element in obtaining orders being prompt delivery.

3. Devaluation will be upsetting for any degree of internal stabilization that may have been achieved because it may result, either through the influence of the rising prices for imports or through psychological influences, in a general rise in prices which will make for claims for higher wages, etc.

This mere listing shows that the situation has sufficiently changed to render most of the arguments against exchange rate devaluation obsolete. While the effect of devaluation on imports may still not be decisive because of the existing quantitative controls, the effect on exports cannot be doubted. Price is again a compelling consideration. Furthermore, [although] countries do not yet wish to insulate themselves against a fall in the U.S. price level, they need [to] be less concerned than previously about a devaluation imperiling internal stabilization both because of their own progress in achieving stability and because of the fall in the U.S. price level.

Today, the only valid consideration militating against an exchange rate adjustment would be the contention that sufficient progress is already being made toward external balance at existing exchange rates. The opponents of devaluation will, therefore, tend to prove today the contrary of what they proved yesterday; while the principal argument so far has been that devaluation would not improve the balance of payments, today concern will be voiced about devaluation helping *too much*, deepening the depression in the United States and curing the dollar shortage at precisely that cost in real income which it was the intention of the Marshall Plan to avoid. As we have seen there is a distinct possibility that a serious recession would do that. But excessive effectiveness of devaluation alone, i.e. unaccompanied by a cyclical downward movement abroad, could always be corrected by combining it with a considerable relaxation of existing quantitative import controls. Moreover, [if] devaluation takes place in the midst of a recession, it is apt to have a pump-priming effect and by initiating a new cycle of investment it may well create an additional balance of payments strain, as happened in a number of instances during the Great Depression.

## NOTES

1. See this *Review*, April 12, 1949 [Robert Solomon, "Recession in Belgium," *Review of Foreign Developments*, April 12, 1949].

2. This explanation of the inverse "Kindleberger effect" is quite different from that used by Kindleberger in his original argument. Here it is assumed that imports from the United States are non-competitive for the foreign economy, that on the contrary they are important in sustaining production and investment in the receiving country. A cut in those imports is likely to be followed by a contraction in economic activity and incomes that, whatever the repercussions of the drop in incomes earned in export industries, may lead to a further curtailment of purchases in the United States. I believe that by reversing this argument one obtains a rationalization of the original Kindleberger effect that is logically unassailable and more realistic than reasoning in terms of the multiplier and negative propensities to save.

3. We have come remarkably close to doing this recently with the message of Mr. [Paul G.] Hoffman to Mr. [James D.] Zellerbach, ECA mission chief in Italy, commending the Italian Government for its achievement of financial and monetary stability, but urging it at the same time to undertake and encourage an "aggressive" investment effort.

4. It is not implied that foreign countries have wilfully engineered inflation in order to become "eligible" for U.S. aid. An inflation is far too much fraught with social and political dangers for it to be provoked lightly by any government. Insofar as inflations have resulted from positive action, rather than from omissions, on the part of national governments, they have been due to overambitious investment and development programs, rather than from any conscious attempt to capture a larger share of U.S. aid than would have been obtained otherwise.

# 12

# THE U.S. RECESSION AND
# THE DOLLAR POSITION OF
# THE OEEC COUNTRIES

## ALBERT O. HIRSCHMAN AND BARBARA HINRICHS

n an earlier article[1] it was argued that a slight recession of
the American economy would not necessarily prove upsetting for the balances of payments of those countries that rely
heavily on American aid in the financing of their import surplus.
It seemed a priori probable that a U.S. recession would result,
for countries with large initial excess of imports over exports, in
larger dollar savings on the import side (as a result of declines in
U.S. prices) than in dollar losses on the export side (as a result of
decreased U.S. purchases). The British crisis may seem to belie
this thesis; and the Snoy-Marjolin report on the division of
ECA aid in 1949–50 maintains that the fall in dollar earnings of
OEEC countries as a group during 1949 has been much larger
than any dollar savings resulting from the fall in the prices of
American exports. Calculations based on U.S. foreign trade data
show that this statement is correct for the United Kingdom and
the sterling area, but does not hold for the Continental OEEC
countries. Even for the United Kingdom and the sterling area
the net loss incurred as a result of the excess dollar losses over
dollar savings in the course of the recent readjustment amounts
to only a fraction of the actual loss in gold and dollar reserves.

---

Confidential. *Review of Foreign Developments*, September 27, 1949.

Suppose that the United States exports $10 billion during a base year and that the unit value of its exports drops by an average of 10 percent during the next year, then $9 billion will buy the same volume of goods in this year as $10 billion did the year before. The savings accruing to foreign countries due to price declines in the United States amounts therefore to $1 billion. This figure can then be compared to the actual dollar losses incurred by foreign countries as a result of both the decline in the prices of goods they export to the United States and the lowered volume of their sales. This procedure is prompted by the consideration that the fall in export and import prices and the fall in the foreign countries export volume are direct and unavoidable consequences of the U.S. recession while the foreign countries have it within their power to prevent the volume of their imports from the United States from rising in reaction to the fall in U.S. prices.

The most significant result of Table I below [table 12.1] is the striking difference in behavior between the sterling area and the Continental OEEC countries. While the sterling area's dollar losses in the second quarter exceeded its dollar savings the opposite held for the Continental OEEC countries and their dependencies: the savings accruing to these countries as a result even of the relatively small price declines in the United States were sufficient to wipe out any decrease in dollar earnings that occurred between 1948 and 1949.

This difference is explained mainly by two considerations: first the sterling area earned its own way to a much larger extent than the Continental OEEC countries. In 1948 the sterling area covered 70 percent of its imports from the United States by its exports to the United States, whereas this ratio stood at only 20 percent for the Continental OEEC countries. The Chinese proverb: "Who sleeps on the floor cannot fall from his bed" thus applied to these countries. Unlike the sterling area countries, the

## TABLE 12.1 DOLLAR SAVINGS AND LOSSES IN TRADE OF OEEC COUNTRIES WITH THE UNITED STATES (IN MILLIONS OF DOLLARS)

|  | Sterling area | Continental OEEC countries[a] | Total |
|---|---|---|---|
| Second quarter of 1949 (annual rate compared to 1948) |  |  |  |
| Dollar savings accruing to foreign countries as result of price declines of U.S. exports[b] | 104 | 188 | 292 |
| Dollar losses (decrease in U.S. imports) | 252 | 30 | 282 |
| Net savings or losses (–) | –148 | 158 | 10 |
| Second quarter of 1949 compared to 2nd quarter of 1948 (annual rates) |  |  |  |
| Dollar savings accruing to foreign countries as result of price declines of U. S. exports[2] | 133 | 256 | 389 |
| Dollar losses (decrease in U.S. imports)[2] | 260 | –88 | 172 |
| New savings or losses (–) | – 127 | 344 | 217 |

[a] Including dependent overseas territories, excluding Switzerland.

[b] Calculated by applying the decline in the unit value index for *total* U.S. exports to the value of U.S. exports in the base period. Up to the second quarter of 1949 the index had declined by 5.2 percent from the average of 1948, and by 6.7 percent from the second quarter of 1948.

Continental OEEC countries were likely to reap almost the full benefit of any U.S. price declines since they did not stand to lose much sales volume to the United States. On the contrary—and this is the second explanation of the difference between sterling

area and Continental OEEC countries—for some of them, sales
to the United States had remained at so low a level in 1948 that
they could expand them even during our domestic readjustment. This is typically true of all countries in which recovery had
lagged such as Germany, Austria, Greece, and Indonesia (See
Table II [table 12.2]). Turkey and the Netherlands also were able
to increase their sales to the United States in 1949. The decrease
of U.S. purchases from countries like France, Italy, Belgium, and
Sweden was sufficient to offset these gains in the comparison
of the second quarter of 1949 with the average of 1948, but not
in that with the second quarter of 1948. For this comparison the
table thus actually reveals a net gain (in place of a loss) which,
together with the dollar savings due to U.S. price declines, adds
up to a sizeable improvement in the dollar position of the Continental OEEC countries. But even those European countries
whose exports to the United States declined from the second
quarter of 1948 to the second quarter of 1949 gained on balance
as a result of the decline in U.S. prices. The only notable exception to this rule is Sweden whose exports of wood pulp were hit
particularly hard.

For the United Kingdom and the sterling area the situation
is the reverse. In both comparisons the "losses" exceed the "savings" and the net loss for the second quarter of 1949 amounts for
both comparisons to between $30 and $40 million on a quarterly
basis. In spite of the fact that much has been made of the decline
in prices and U.S. purchases of sterling area products the contribution of the United Kingdom to this loss is larger than that
of the rest of the sterling area. In any event, the aggregate loss
is small if compared to the actual gold and dollar loss of $260
million sustained by British reserves during the same period.
The explanation of the major part of this drain must be sought,
not in the effects of the recession in the United States, but in

## TABLE 12.2 DOLLAR SAVINGS AND LOSSES IN TRADE OF OEEC COUNTRIES WITH THE UNITED STATES (IN MILLIONS OF DOLLARS)

| Countries | Second quarter of 1949 (annual rate) compared to 1948 | | | Second quarter of 1949 compared to second quarter of 1948 (annual rates) | | |
|---|---|---|---|---|---|---|
| | Dollar savings[a] | Dollar losses[b] | Net savings or losses (−) | Dollar savings[a] | Dollar losses[b] | Net Savings or losses (−) |
| U.K. | 33.8 | 117.9 | −84.1 | 34.8 | 125.2 | −90.4 |
| Other sterling area | 70.0 | 134.0 | −64.0 | 95.6 | 134.0 | −38.4 |
| Sterling area | 103.8 | 251.9 | −148.1 | 130.4 | 259.2 | −128.8 |
| Austria | 7.6 | 0.4 | 7.2 | 10.0 | −2.0 | 12.0 |
| Belgium-Lux. | 16.2 | 16.4 | −0.2 | 15.6 | 15.6 | 0 |
| Belgian Congo | 2.6 | 16.9 | −14.3 | 3.6 | 2.0 | 1.6 |
| Denmark | 2.8 | 1.6 | 1.2 | 3.2 | 0.4 | 2.8 |
| France | 31.0 | 21.7 | 9.3 | 47.2 | −23.2 | 70.4 |
| French colonies | 6.7 | 2.7 | 4.0 | 9.6 | −7.2 | 16.8 |
| Germany | 45.4 | −15.9 | 61.3 | 63.6 | −27.2 | 90.8 |
| Greece | 12.4 | −5.9 | 18.3 | 14.8 | −10.0 | 24.8 |
| Italy | 21.8 | 36.6 | −14.8 | 31.6 | 36.4 | −4.8 |
| Netherlands | 16.4 | −17.8 | 34.2 | 20.4 | −27.6 | 48.0 |
| Indonesia | 4.8 | −55.9 | 60.7 | 6.4 | −72.0 | 78.4 |
| Norway | 4.4 | 4.8 | −0.4 | 4.4 | −5.2 | 9.6 |
| Portugal | 4.0 | 8.4 | −4.4 | 5.2 | 5.2 | 0 |
| Sweden | 6.2 | 45.5 | −39.3 | 10.0 | 55.2 | −45.2 |
| Turkey | 5.3 | −29.5 | 34.8 | 9.2 | −28.4 | 37.6 |
| Continental OEEC countries[c] | 187.6 | 30.0 | 157.6 | 254.8 | −88.0 | 342.8 |
| Combined OEEC and sterling area | 291.4 | −281.9 | 9.5 | 385.2 | 171.2 | 214.0 |

[a] Dollar savings on U.S. exports due to U.S. price declines. For method of calculation, see footnote b to table 12.1.

[b] Decrease or increase (−) in U.S. imports.

[c] Excluding Switzerland.

capital movements and in an exceptional increase in sterling area imports from the dollar area.

In general, it is clear that the "dollar savings" calculated by us on the assumption that the volume of imports from the United States would remain constant in the face of U.S. price declines, are highly theoretical. Rather than decrease in proportion to the fall of the unit value index, U.S. exports to both sterling area and Continental OEEC countries showed considerable increases from 1948 to the second quarter. Thus between the second quarter 1948 and the second quarter 1949 U.S. exports increased by $89 million to the sterling area, and by $30 million to the Continental OEEC countries. This was not, of course, an automatic reaction of an elastic demand of foreign countries for U.S. imports. It is largely explained by the slow start of ECA procurement during 1948 and its acceleration during the second half of the 1948–49 fiscal year. To some extent, the easing supply situation in this country may also have led to an exceptional rise of U.S. exports as a result of shorter delivery dates and of the exportation of scarce items previously reserved for the domestic market. The increase in the volume of imports from the United States thus explains why sterling area gold losses have been so much larger than indicated by our figures and why the Continental OEEC countries have not added considerably to their reserves. Nevertheless, the data shown here on net dollar savings or losses are meaningful since they isolate the effect of the U.S. recession on the dollar position of the OEEC area from other factors that, to a large extent, have operated independently.

In summary, immediate dollar losses were suffered in the course of 1949 by foreign countries as a result of decreased foreign purchases by the United States. But these losses could have been virtually cancelled, for the combined sterling and OEEC areas, by the savings accruing to these countries as a result of reduced U.S. prices. The disturbing feature about the development of U.S. foreign trade in 1949 was therefore not so much its impact on the immediate dollar position of foreign countries as the long-run implications of the premature halt in the expansion of U.S. imports for an eventual solution of the dollar problem.

### NOTE

1. See this *Review*, June 7, 1949 [republished in this volume as chapter 11].

# III

# EUROPEAN INTEGRATION AND THE WAY BACK TO MULTILATERALISM

# 13

## THE NEW INTRA-EUROPEAN PAYMENTS SCHEME

A fter a prolonged, many-cornered deadlock, a compromise agreement on a new Intra-European Payments
Scheme was reached on June 30, expiration date of the
scheme hitherto in force.

### PRINCIPAL FEATURES OF
### THE NEW SCHEME

(1)  As heretofore the OEEC countries are going to estimate their
balance of payments position with each other; this essential
preliminary work has been largely completed, but can presumably be made final only when the country allocation of ECA
funds for 1949/50 has been decided.

(2)  The countries with estimated surpluses on current account
will extend grants ("drawing rights") to the deficit countries
by placing at the latters' disposal a corresponding amount of
local currencies deposited in counterpart to ECA aid. ECA

Confidential. *Review of Foreign Developments*, July 19, 1949.

allocations will continue to be split into "basic" and "conditional" aid, with the conditional portion corresponding to the drawing rights extended by the intra-European creditors to the intra-European debtors.

(3) So far, the drawing rights granted by a creditor to a debtor could be used only within that particular bilateral trading relationship. This continues to hold for 75 per cent of the drawing rights under the new payments scheme. With an important qualification which will be explained below, the remaining 25 per cent will now be usable anywhere within the OEEC area.[1]

(4) The transferable portion of the drawing rights is to be fully backed by ECA dollars. This means that a country to which the drawing rights are transferred will be able to obtain full dollar compensation for its unscheduled export surplus toward other European countries. The dollars will presumably be held in a pool by ECA; but the amounts which are likely to be involved are so small that the scheduled creditor countries, out of whose ECA allocation the pool would presumably be constituted, may not find it too objectionable to contract a direct gold or dollar obligation to those countries to which drawing rights will be transferred.

(5) Belgium holds a very special position under the new scheme, because of the fact that its intra-European surplus is far in excess of its dollar deficit. Its estimated dollar deficit for 1949/50 amounts to $200 million while its intra-OEEC surplus has been estimated at $450–500 million. Were Belgium to receive conditional ECA aid to the full amount of its intra-European surplus, a substantial accumulation of dollar reserves would result. Under the scheme, however, Belgium has committed itself to extend long-term (25 years, 2 1/2 per cent) credits as ECA grants it conditional aid over and above $200 million: the first $125 million of financing above this figure are to be formed

by Belgian credits and drawing rights (backed by ECA conditional aid) in equal shares; whereas Belgium will contribute only one-third in credits to the next $75 million of intra-European financing. Any further financing of the Belgian export surplus could come about only through transfers of drawing rights from other creditors and such drawing rights would be fully backed by ECA dollars; but a ceiling of $40 million has been set for those transfers.[2] The purpose of this ceiling is to limit both the accumulation of dollars on the part of Belgium and the potential dollar losses of the other OEEC countries, in particular the United Kingdom. Altogether, Belgium will extend credits up to $87.5 (62.5 + 25) million and will be able to accumulate dollar reserves up to $152.5 (62.5 + 50 + 40) million.

## DISCUSSION

The new scheme represents a considerable retreat of ECA from its original objectives of full intra-European transferability of drawing rights and of a substantial amount of dollar convertibility, i.e., the right for the holder of drawing rights to exchange them in full or in part for ECA dollars if he so chooses. From the outset of the negotiations, the United Kingdom took a vigorous stand against convertibility and opposed transferability insofar as transfer of drawing rights would expose the original grantor to the loss of conditional aid dollars. The British position stiffened further during the last phases of the discussion as a result of the supervening drain on British hard currency reserves. A by no means negligible portion of this drain consisted of British gold transfers to Belgium ($22 million in the first and $44 million in the second quarter of 1949) as well as of smaller transfers to Switzerland and the Bizone.

*Convertibility.* In advocating convertibility of drawing rights from the outset, i.e., the liberty of intra-European debtors to exchange the drawing rights for dollars as of the moment the drawing rights are granted, ECA probably asked for too much. Under present conditions most drawing rights may well have been thus exchanged by the debtors thereby forcing intra-European trade back into bilateral balance. But it would have been highly desirable to obtain a provision permitting the intra-European debtors to convert into dollars a portion of any drawing rights *unutilized* at the end of a given period. This would have given them some incentive to reduce their intra-European deficit.

*Transferability.* Transferability of drawing rights within the OEEC area is considerably whittled down and hamstrung in the new Agreement if compared to original ECA objectives although some advance from the exclusively bilateral character of the 1948/49 scheme has been achieved. Assuming intra-OEEC trade to expand somewhat from last year's level (about \$7 billion excluding Switzerland) and drawing rights to remain at last year's level (\$810 million) it can be estimated that only about 2 to 3 per cent of total intra-OEEC trade will be affected by the transferability provisions. But even this very limited degree of transferability that has been introduced is further curtailed by the special provisions affecting Belgium:

(a)     transfer of drawing rights *to* Belgium are limited by the \$40 million ceiling;

(b)     transfers of drawing rights *away from* Belgium to other OEEC countries are made unlikely by the fact that the transferable portion of drawing rights granted by Belgium will be utilized in conjunction with drawings on the Belgian credits that are being made available. By exercising their right to transfer these drawing rights Belgium's debtors would therefore deprive themselves of the opportunity to utilize credits granted by Belgium.

Transferability of drawing rights has a double objective. One is to make possible a correction of errors in forecasting the bilateral surpluses and deficits. In this respect, the transferability of 25 per cent of the drawing rights may be of real value since it may be sufficient to take care of all but the more glaring misjudgments.[3]

The other, more important function of transferability of drawing rights is the introduction of more competition among European suppliers.[4] It is with respect to this function that the new scheme does not seem to hold much promise. For competition and pressure on prices to make themselves felt in the grantor country it is not necessary for the recipient of drawing rights actually to transfer them, but it is essential that he be given the possibility of bargaining with the grantor country armed with the weapon of transferability. As the new scheme stands, this weapon will be available to the debtors only for the last quarter of their forecast deficits or, on the basis of the figures given above, for the last fortieth of their estimated purchases in the creditor countries. Since, in addition, the new scheme contains no provisions rewarding the debtor for non-utilization of drawing rights, the new scheme will suffer essentially from the same defect as the old one: it invites the debtor to utilize the major part of his drawing rights at all cost, regardless of the prices asked by the creditors. It can only be hoped that the current change in world economic conditions will accomplish what the new mechanism of the payments scheme cannot possibly hope to achieve by itself.

*Dollar backing of transferable drawing rights.* An important point of discussion closely connected with the issue of transferability was the question whether, and to what extent, transferred drawing rights should be "backed" by dollars, i.e., whether a transfer of drawing rights from the original grantor to another country should result in a corresponding loss of conditional aid to the former or, possibly, in some extension of credit on the part of the latter. The British point of view was that transferability of drawing rights should not be tied to transfers of conditional aid dollars. The British held that—just as direct convertibility of drawing rights into dollars at the option of the debtor—such an arrangement would have highly restrictive effects both on the readiness of the creditors to extend drawing rights and on their subsequent commercial policies. Belgium, on the other hand, held out for full dollar backing of the transferable portion of the drawing rights—and won, but only after the British had succeeded in sharply reducing both the portion of drawing rights that can be transferred in general, and in particular the amount that could be transferred to Belgium. According to press comments, ECA has won at least one point in securing full dollar backing for transferable drawing rights. Actually, the objective of ultimate dollar balance of Europe requires that the payments scheme should not become a device making it just as easy for some European countries to earn additional dollars in Europe as in the United States.[5] This, however, is precisely the result of the adopted principle of full dollar backing of transferable drawing rights. In order to make additional exports to other OEEC countries less attractive to, say, Sweden, than additional exports to the United States it would have been desirable to require Sweden to finance a portion of its unscheduled exports to Europe by credits and to obtain dollar payment only for the remainder, rather than for the full amount of drawing rights transferred to it. At present, however, this defect of the scheme is not very important because of the small degree of transferability achieved.

*Belgium's special position.* The one undisputable virtue of the new scheme is that it has provided for new Belgian credits. In view of Belgium's stubborn resistance to any such suggestions in the past, this is a welcome development. The price paid for it in the scheme is the permission given to Belgium to earn dollars far in excess of its actual dollar deficit. The resulting accumulation of dollars by Belgium will have to be financed (indirectly) through the ECA appropriation, so that the net volume of goods currently available to the OEEC countries through ECA aid will be diminished by this amount. If, however, the OEEC countries other than Belgium are considered as one group and the U.S. and Belgium as another, the arrangement is seen in a more favorable light. The OEEC-minus-Belgium countries will be compensated for the loss in dollar commodities by an equivalent amount of Belgian goods and will furthermore receive Belgian credits which might not have been forthcoming without the additional ECA dollar aid to Belgium.

There is some question, however, about the full validity of this argument. Belgium might have been forced to extend intra-European credits in any event by its continuing domestic marketing difficulties which are no doubt in part responsible for the magnitude of the estimated Belgian intra-European surplus.

## CONCLUSION

Three lessons seem to emerge from the negotiations of the new Intra-European Payments Scheme and their outcome:

(1) The scheme that has resulted from months of discussion is still essentially bilateral in character, and the failure to have achieved substantial advances towards increased competition

and multilateralism will lend increased significance to the other attacks on the European problem presently under consideration: liberalization of commercial policies and exchange rate adjustments.

(2) ECA's weakness in the negotiations was due in part to the effect of the "conditional aid" system in strengthening the bargaining position of the intra-European creditors; with the wisdom of hindsight, one might say that an offshore purchase system for financing intra-European balances would have had a welcome effect in strengthening the bargaining positions of both the intra-European debtors and ECA.

(3) More fundamentally, the nature of the final compromise can be ascribed to the fact that ECA had to bargain with every one of the main participants in the scheme and was forced to make concessions each time so that the sum of the concessions was, in the end, considerable. If ECA had been confronted by a unified OEEC viewpoint, the resulting compromise would probably have been closer to its initial position. From a narrowly Machiavellian point of view it has sometimes been argued that the United States has no interest in the emergence of a unified European area. Actually, the current experience demonstrates that, as long as we are dealing with the European area as a whole, our interests can only be served by a consolidation of that area which would assure us equality in negotiations in place of our present position as a minority participant.

## NOTES

1. The status of Switzerland in the new scheme remains to be determined. Switzerland has requested to be eligible as a "transferee" for the transferable portion of drawing rights.

2. Belgium will extend credits only to the Netherlands, the United Kingdom, and France. As the allocation of conditional aid to Belgium over and above the first $200 million is tied to the simultaneous utilization of credits, it appears that the whole second $200 million tranche of intra-European financing made available by Belgium is reserved to the above three countries. The drawings of the other countries will have to be accommodated by the first $200 million and by possible transfers of drawing rights to Belgium that can be contained within the $40 million limit. In this connection some technical questions will be raised:

(1) What will happen if some of these other countries do not utilize their drawing rights while France, the United Kingdom, and the Netherlands have already utilized their portions of the first $200 million tranche? Will then Belgium have to start giving credit to these three countries before the first $200 million drawing rights are exhausted?

(2) How is the allocation of the $40 million maximum amount of allowable transfers to be administered? Is it going to be made available on a "first come, first served" basis or according to some rationing scheme?

3. It must be remembered, however, that forecasts of balances among countries with a large and comparatively well balanced inter-trade are subject to a considerable margin of error. Often an error of 10 per cent in estimating gross payments from one country to another will be sufficient to change the sign of the estimated balance.

4. Since most net debtor countries are also creditors in relation to some countries and since drawing rights are fixed on a bilateral basis, competition will take place not only among the net creditor countries. Furthermore, the net debtor countries will be able to compete for the drawing rights originally allocated to the net creditors.

5. This point is made specifically in the statement of Mr. [Paul G.] Hoffman on the Payments Plan, released to the press on July 7, 1949.

# 14

## PROPOSAL FOR A EUROPEAN MONETARY AUTHORITY

A "Reserve Bank for Europe" was one of the specific subjects included for further study by the financial subcommittee of the European Assembly during the recent session of that body; the present paper is a first exploration of the issues raised by this proposal.

Immediate scepticism is generally expressed when the advocates of closer European integration speak of the desirability of a "common European currency." It is quite correct, as *The Economist* pointed out recently, that a common currency requires, among other things, the abandonment of fiscal sovereignty and is, therefore, inconceivable in the absence of political federation.

Confidential. Albert O. Hirschman Papers (MC #160), box 65, folder 7, Federal Reserve Correspondence and Papers, 1948–1951, November 2, 1949. This introductory note by the ECA economist Harold van Buren Cleveland appears on the front page of the document: "The attached memorandum was prepared by Mr. Albert O. Hirschman of the Federal Reserve Board in response to an informal request. Because it is a competent review of some of the problems encountered in finding a method for coordinating fiscal and monetary policies among the participating countries, it is being circulated in Program Coordination and Fiscal and Trade Policy for study and comment. The views expressed in the memorandum are the author's and not necessarily those of the Board."

The question cannot be disposed of in this summary fashion, however. While it may be impossible to tear down the economic and fiscal attributes of national sovereignty by direct assault, it may be possible to coordinate these attributes and to build, as a recent ECA study puts it, new institutions in the "interstices" of the national prerogatives.

In particular the familiar argument against the "common currency" idea must be critically examined on three grounds:

(1)   In the first place, it is not true that the present sovereignty of the OEEC countries in the pursuit of domestic monetary and fiscal policies is unbounded. In the *Convention for European Economic Cooperation* these countries have specifically committed themselves to achieve and maintain domestic financial and monetary stability; more specific commitments were made by countries such as France and Italy which experienced particular difficulties in this respect. It would be a logical step forward from this general commitment to set up an institution empowered to enforce and police it.

(2)   At present there exist two principal and sufficiently distinct functions of European national monetary authorities. First, domestic monetary and fiscal policy; secondly, administration of foreign exchange reserves and of exchange control. With respect to the second function the Western European countries are already today subject to common direction by the OEEC to a considerable extent. The dollars received from ECA which are an important fraction of their total dollar resources, are subdivided among the individual countries through a collective agreement reached within the OEEC. It is not altogether revolutionary, then, to think of further steps in this direction such as partial surrenders of foreign exchange reserves or earnings to a common pool.

(3) Finally it ought to be realized that even probability of failure to achieve greater European unification through institutional innovations in the economic field is no valid argument against them if our avowed aim is political unification. For the failure of the partial attempts undertaken in the economic area without the underpinning of a solid political structure will serve the useful purpose of bringing the Western European countries to realize that decisive political acts are prerequisites for further advances along the road of economic cooperation.

These considerations suggest that it is at least worthwhile to examine our subject more closely. Clearly it is futile to ask whether we are for or against a "common currency" for Europe; the question is rather whether it is possible to think of forms of monetary and financial organization for Europe that do not ask for the impossible, yet which would result in a closely knit European monetary and financial structure. We shall discuss this question by examining the functions of a hypothetical European Monetary Authority [EMA], thus avoiding the terms "common currency" and "Reserve Bank" which prejudge the issue from the outset.

## I. INTERNAL FUNCTIONS

In the field of internal monetary and fiscal policy there is clearly a wide range of graduated possibilities. The range extends from the federal state with its own budget, currency, and central bank to a body with purely advisory functions toward national governments and central banks. I shall attempt to sketch here a maximum solution subject to the constraints of the existing political structure. While this solution is itself a half-way house in many respects, it probably can be reached only in successive stages (see below, Section V).

## (1) Monetary and Credit Policy

There is to be established a European Monetary Authority which must be consulted on all questions affecting the cost, the availability, and the volume of credit. It has veto power over all decisions taken in this field by national monetary authorities. The whole monetary and credit policy of each country must be reviewed by it once a year and more often if necessary. Under certain safeguards it also has the power to order action by national monetary authorities.

With respect to the current instruments of monetary policy these general principles would be applied as follows:

(a) Discount rate policy.

The discount rates are set by the national banks, but are subject to approval by EMA; to make it possible for EMA to keep the rates under constant review it could be provided that the rates have to be set every three months whether or not a change is made.

(b) Reserve requirements.

Same as discount rate.

(c) Open market policy.

The EMA is to have a representative holding veto power within the national bodies making open market policy and is to have access to all the information available.

(d) Qualitative credit controls.

General regulations are subject to approval; periodic inspections must be provided for because of the latitude which the general regulations will normally leave to administrative discretion.

(e) Capital issues control.

Same as open market policy.

The powers here proposed for the EMA are wide; but they do not require any change of present institutions. EMA would simply be grafted on to the present national banking and monetary structures. Some standardization of controls, procedures, and statistics may be desirable so that EMA may be able to base its decisions on comparable data; but the present lack of uniformity renders EMA's task merely somewhat more difficult than it would otherwise be. The achievement of greater comparability of the national structures can confidently be left to time once the new agency is established.

In short, according to the preceding outline, EMA is to have all powers of a central bank save that to issue money; there is no provision for a common currency in our scheme. In what sense does this lack detract from the efficacy of the scheme?

Our basic assumption is that EMA will have to operate within the present political framework, in which national governments draw up national budgets and rely occasionally on national central banks for help in deficit financing. It appears that within this framework there would be no place for a supra-national bank of issue but only for a close coordination of national monetary policies of the kind indicated here. If the national central banks hold, as they generally do, the right to rediscount, to buy securities, and to advance funds to the governments there can arise a need for autonomous lending powers to be held by EMA only in three cases.

(a)    First, EMA could appropriate certain lending powers of the national central banks; thus it is conceivable for EMA to take over the power of the national central banks to make direct advances to the national governments. Such a step, however, would not necessarily fulfill the objective of securing EMA control over national fiscal policies (see below); in any event, it probably goes farther in the direction of Utopia than this project is intended to go. There are probably no lending functions that could not properly continue to be exercised by the national central banks under the supervision and control of EMA.

(b)    Secondly, one may think of lending operations undertaken to further European integration and for which local currency funds are not at present made available by the existing commercial or central banks. Such operations however, would clearly be of a medium or long-term nature and should therefore more appropriately be the function of an institution specializing in this field.

(c)    Finally, the EMA could play a role in filling certain foreign exchange needs of the member countries. This subject is discussed below.

The creation of a European bank of issue would be called for only if and when a regular federal European government comes into being. Even then it would not be essential if EMA's powers over the national central banks are extended so as to approximate those held by the board of governors over the federal reserve banks.

## (2) Fiscal Policy

Supra-national control of national fiscal policies presents a far more difficult problem than control over monetary policy since fiscal policy is a governmental function subject to the vote of national legislatures. By its active powers in the monetary field, EMA will make it difficult for the national governments to pursue irresponsible fiscal policies. But this indirect restraint could fail to bring about the desired result and it is one-sided since it is operative primarily in the event of an *inflation* brought about by improper budgetary policies. It would, therefore, be desirable to give EMA at least a direct investigative and advisory function along the following lines:

The cooperating European nations are to enter a convention in which the aims of their fiscal policies are spelled out in some detail: this convention will also set up EMA as its guardian; it will empower it to conduct investigations and to present findings. But in general, EMA will only be called upon to pass a general judgment on the budget; its findings may be, for example, that the budget of a member country is too large or too small, or too much or too little out of balance; it could also list possible means of correcting the situation but should not impose a specific course of action.

A general approach of this type appears the only practical one at present. It would be quite impossible for a supra-national body to "meddle" in national affairs to the point of objecting to (or of promoting) a particular expenditure or of asking for the introduction or abolition of a particular tax.

But the general approach also appears superior to attempts at gaining control of national fiscal policies by control of a particular segment of the public finances such as, e.g. the counterpart of ECA aid. In the first place if EMA's authority were limited to disposition of counterpart, its fiscal powers would be scheduled to decrease rapidly. Secondly, authority over counterpart releases has proven to be a relatively effective controlling device only in the case of a few countries with a budget deficit and a relatively inelastic banking system.

A similar comment applies to attempts at controlling fiscal policies by giving EMA exclusive authority to make, or to permit national central banks to make, direct advances to the national treasuries. These types of controls would exclude from their sphere all countries that do not run a deficit or whose governments finance themselves by borrowing from the commercial banks rather than from the central banks. Further, both types of controls (over counterpart and over central bank advances) would be likely to impart to EMA's policies a deflationary bias.

## II. EXTERNAL FUNCTIONS

## (1) Centralization of Foreign Exchange Earnings and Reserves

Should the cooperating countries transfer their foreign exchange reserves and earnings to the central authority? Intermediate solutions are naturally possible in the sense that one may think of partial rather than total transfers.

As long as the allocation of foreign exchange is subject to administrative control, an integral or even partial transfer to EMA of foreign exchange *earnings* would be an extremely bold step. Not only does it appear entirely unlikely to be taken within the present political structure, but it would probably confront EMA with insuperable difficulties of operation. Either one country's earnings will all remain earmarked for import into that country and in that case the pooling of the exchange earnings would be largely meaningless; or country A's dollar exports would finance, through the pool arrangement and through administrative decision of the EMA, country B's dollar imports. The latter eventuality would, however, appear intolerable to most European countries. The allocation of current foreign exchange receipts is one of the most powerful determinants of standards of living and of investment activity. The best way to doom any

204 &#8450; EUROPEAN INTEGRATION AND MULTILATERALISM

move toward European unity is to conjure up the vision of an equalization of the Swedish and Italian standards of living.

It may therefore be best to leave the disposition of current foreign exchange earnings in the hands of the national exchange control authorities, subject, however, to such supervision of exchange rates and exchange controls by EMA as to prevent dissipation of scarce foreign exchange resources. EMA's task in this field is not to supersede the national import plans by a master plan of its own, but to guide the member countries through its power over internal monetary, exchange rate, and exchange control policies toward a situation in which administrative import controls and compulsory surrender of foreign exchange earnings can be dispensed with. Once import licensing has been abolished, EMA could more easily be empowered to appropriate from the national central banks the usual central bank functions with respect to foreign exchange operations.

The case is somewhat different with respect to *reserves*. These are not ordinarily needed to import food and raw materials, but serve as shock-absorbers in the case of balance of payments accidents. Should these reserves be transferred to EMA? Here again we have to guard against over-enthusiasm. The current move toward greater liberalization of trade and payments presupposes free access of the national governments to their reserves. If all reserves were to be transferred to a common fund, resort to which would no doubt be circumscribed by a set of rules, then a much stricter effort to balance currently [sic] foreign exchange payments and receipts would become necessary.

Nevertheless, some pooling of reserves appears very desirable for a number of reasons. Under present dollar shortage conditions, such pooling would be the most striking expression of the will to cooperate on the part of the member countries. Even though pooling could only be partial at present, it ought to be established from the outset as one of the prime functions and objectives of the EMA. This consideration also makes it important to set a schedule that will determine further contributions to the pool at later dates: a formula might be established calling for surrenders of reserves once every year. Such a formula would take into account the initial level of the reserves (in relation to the needs of the individual countries) and their increase or decrease during the current year.

Reserve pooling appears also desirable because it would improve the prospects for obtaining Congressional authorization for making stabilization loans and grants. Such stabilization moneys would then appear as a counterpart for a tangible effort at European cooperation—the United States would, as it were, match the hard currency funds contributed to EMA by its own members. Such stabilization moneys should be made available directly to EMA or should become available to the national central banks only upon authorization by EMA. This treatment of stabilization loans or grants is justified by their purpose, which consists in providing further backing for, and to induce greater confidence in European currencies. It has rightly been said that stabilization loans are successful to the extent they are not used. They are not intended to be spent and should be utilized only in exceptional circumstances. For that reason, it would be reasonable to let them be administered by EMA thus interposing one more obstacle to their use by national monetary authorities.

EMA would thus hold a secondary reserve for the cooperating countries as a group. Its purpose would be:

(1)  to support member currencies in case of need;

(2)  to provide financing for net balances in intra-European trade;

(3)  in general to enhance EMA's authority in its dealings with the member countries.

Clearly, drawings on EMA's gold and dollar holdings would have to be coordinated with drawings on the International Monetary Fund. One obvious step would be for the European countries to request drawings on the Fund only after this has been approved by EMA; a much farther-going measure would be for the European countries to pool their quotas in the Fund and to let EMA do the drawing for them.

## (2) Exchange Rates

Coordination of the powers of the Monetary Fund with those to be given to EMA is all important in the case of exchange rates. The structure so far described, (coordination of domestic monetary and fiscal policies) should rule out the necessity of frequent changes of exchange rates of one member country vis-a-vis the other. Nevertheless such changes cannot be ruled out. The main emphasis is currently to be placed on the creation of a European area within which trade and payments are freed from restrictions. This freeing can only be a gradual process and at each new step unforeseen reactions of the flow of trade (and of capital) may make some exchange rate adjustment within the group of European countries necessary or advisable. As the monetary arrangements approximate the common currency stage, exchange rate movements of individual currencies within the European area ought to become less and less frequent.

The second type of exchange rate adjustment is that of the whole group together vis-a-vis the dollar. Such adjustments may continue to be necessary even after there is no more need for exchange rate adjustments within the group.

For both types of adjustments EMA should be given full responsibility. It should be called upon to approve any change

in exchange rates proposed by the individual country, but, unlike
the Fund, should also be empowered to propose such a change
itself. The initiative for the second type of exchange rate adjustment should rest exclusively with EMA.

## (3) Exchange Controls

Although it was argued above that EMA could not possibly pre-
tend to substitute its own judgment to the national exchange
control authorities in the allocation of foreign exchange, EMA
should be given certain functions of control and supervision of
national exchange control administration.

The principle may be established that EMA must give its
approval:

(a)  whenever a member country wishes to enact new or strengthen
     existing exchange restrictions vis-a-vis other members;

(b)  whenever a member country wishes to strengthen or *relax*
     exchange restrictions vis-a-vis non-member countries.

In addition, EMA ought to have wide powers of inspection of
national exchange control administration.

## III. SERVICE FUNCTIONS

For the success of EMA it would be extremely important to
endow it with a number of service functions that would make
it an agency that can be useful to its members, in tangible ways,
besides continually interfering in their affairs. For this reason and
to avoid further duplication of international agencies, it would

appear appropriate to let the Bank for International Settlements be absorbed by the European Monetary Authority. At present, the BIS performs a number of functions which are useful to the European countries, the most conspicuous service rendered being the technical administration of the Intra-European Payments Scheme. Transfer of these functions to the EMA, through absorption of the BIS, would be of particular significance if steps in the direction of true multilateral clearing can soon be made. A European Clearing Union operated by the EMA would be a close parallel to the Interdistrict Settlement Fund operated for the federal reserve banks by the Federal Reserve Board.

In addition EMA should immediately undertake intensive research into the banking and money market structures of its member countries so as to be able to suggest measures that will insure greater freedom and rationality in the movement of funds within the European area. It is extremely important that EMA display considerable initiative in this field; for its ultimate fate will depend on the question whether the goodwill created by the services rendered by EMA to the European community and to the individual member countries will appear to outweigh the ill-will that is bound to be generated by EMA's necessary interferences with individual countries' affairs.

## IV. NOTE ON ADMINISTRATION

The European Monetary Authority should have a board of governors constituted by the national finance ministers and the national central bank governors. In addition, the European Assembly should nominate a number of outstanding Europeans with knowledge of financial and economic affairs to serve as governors of the institution. These persons would not represent any one country but the interests of the European area as a whole. The board would vote by majority rule.

## V. THE PROBLEM OF STAGES

It is clear that the structure here described will not become reality overnight. Furthermore, it represents itself a halfway house in many respects. There have been many governments without a central bank, but the experience here proposed of a central monetary authority without a central government remains to be made.

The proposal derives precisely from the fact that it seems easier in the present situation to secure some surrender of sovereignty in the economic than in the purely political field. Within the economic sphere in turn, the surrender appears easier to obtain with respect to monetary than with respect to fiscal policies. Nevertheless, even this partial surrender of economic sovereignty will probably have to come in stages, some of which are implicit in the preceding discussion. Thus a pooling of reserves should be timed so as to coincide with the request for stabilization funds. The control of EMA over internal monetary policies of its members need be less strict as long as the exchange rates of the members are not stabilized vis-a-vis each other. Also, departures from the majority voting rule could be permitted during an initial period.

# 15

# LIBERALIZATION OF
# THE ECA DOLLAR

## Introductory Note

T here are two distinct aspects of any proposed liberalization of the ECA dollar. One deals with establishing the
maximum possible freedom to spend the ECA dollar
wherever and for whatever commodity is deemed desirable by
the recipient country or its citizens. The second aspect deals
with the freedom to spend or not to spend the ECA dollar, i.e.,
with the freedom to accumulate ECA aid, directly or indirectly,
in the form of monetary reserves.

The following paper by Miss Lichtenberg shows the
many ways in which the first freedom is currently hamstrung
and, in conclusion, points to the various possible avenues of
liberalization.

The second freedom so far has been greatly limited for two
reasons: first, since ECA aid is tied to procurement authorizations, it must be spent. This compulsion to spend could
be remedied directly by giving the Economic Cooperation

Restricted. *Review of Foreign Developments*, January 3, 1950.

Hirschman's paper served as an introduction to two other papers, one
by Caroline Lichtenberg ("Restrictions on the Use of the ECA Dollar") and another by
Samuel I. Katz and Gretchen H. Fowler ("U.S. Foreign Trade in the Postwar Period").

Administrator authority to disburse, as free dollars, a portion of ECA funds rather than as dollars tied to procurement authorizations. Secondly, even though ECA aid can be accumulated indirectly, through the non-spending of free dollars earned by European exports, such accumulations could not be considered desirable by the European countries as long as need (defined by balance-of-payments forecasts) remained the criterion for ECA aid. For, under these conditions, an accumulation of reserves necessarily led countries to fear that their aid would be cut since such accumulation could readily be interpreted by ECA as proof of reduced need for aid. In order to appease these fears, it is not necessary, however, that ECA attempt in advance to detail the sums that will accrue over the remaining life of the program to each country, a procedure which would be incompatible with the system of annual appropriations. It would be sufficient for ECA to announce that whatever the total amount of aid that may be voted by Congress, the percentage distribution of the aid among the recipients would be considered as presumptively fixed. This procedure has already been recommended by the OEEC and has been accepted by ECA for the distribution of aid in the next fiscal year subject, of course, to the Administrator's right of final review of allocations. This right, however, is likely to be exercised only in cases of violations by a recipient country of obligations assumed under the Recovery Program or in absolutely clear cases of *force majeure*.

A consistent program of liberalization of the ECA dollar would consist of the following steps (the last of which has already been taken):

1. Lift and ease to the maximum possible extent the current statutory and administrative restrictions on the spending of the ECA dollar under the system of procurement authorizations.

2. Give statutory permission to the Administrator to disburse a certain portion of ECA funds as free dollars.

3. Establish the principle that the percentage breakdown of country allocations is to be considered as fixed subject to ECA's right of final review in specific instances.[1]

While conceptually distinct, these three aspects of any program of liberalization of the ECA dollar must be pursued jointly. It is statistically obvious that the reliability of the balance-of-payments deficits decreases along with the deficits themselves: for, with a given margin of error, affecting gross payments and gross receipts, the resulting margin of error affecting the difference between payments and receipts is the greater the more receipts approximate payments. Economic reasoning also leads us to conclude that progress toward viability increases the uncertainty about both the exact size and the commodity composition of the narrowing deficit. This is due to the progressive elimination of bottlenecks, to the gradual disappearance of "must" programs with the progress of reconstruction and re-equipment, to the increasing range of substitution of non-dollar for dollar goods, and to the possibility of spectacular advances of exports as supply problems are solved.

These considerations lead us to doubt that there is as clear and unbridgeable distinction between assistance for balance-of-payments purposes and assistance for the building up of monetary reserves as has commonly been supposed. Once it is recognized that a narrow balance-of-payments deficit is by definition an unstable one, it is clear that any assistance given to finance that deficit can easily remain unused and may therefore in effect become an aid to the stabilization of the country's currency. The assistance made available by the United States during the second phase of the European Recovery Program is still essentially meant to finance balance-of-payments deficits; but there is an increasing chance—and hope—that this assistance may be converted in fact in aid to stabilization. Such assistance is, therefore, a transition to the concept of stabilization credits. It is the nature of such credits that they are given in the fundamental expectation that they will not be spent by the recipients, but that they can nevertheless be converted into balance-of-payments assistance under certain exceptional and unforeseen circumstances.

If it is correct to assume that the European Recovery Program now moves into a phase intermediate between pure balance-of-payments assistance and assistance for stabilization purposes, then it is doubly important that the ECA dollar be "liberalized" by freeing its spending from many of the restrictions surrounding it at present and by allaying all fears that failure to spend it well result in cutbacks in aid.

## NOTE

1. Adoption by ECA of the third step will in effect permit a country to accumulate dollars without the risk of seeing its aid reduced, but adoption of the second step still remains desirable to ensure maximum flexibility.

# 16

## EUROPEAN PAYMENTS
## UNION—A POSSIBLE BASIS
## FOR AGREEMENT

Both the Economic Cooperation Administration and the Organization for European Economic Cooperation have recently concentrated considerable effort on the elaboration of a plan to make European currencies transferable among each other. Since the spring of 1949, the OEEC has made a series of attempts to break down directly the barriers to a freer intra-European flow of goods and services. Increasingly, however, it was felt that the existing bilateral pattern of intra-European payments, which in general does not permit a country to offset a deficit in one direction by a surplus in another, bears a share of responsibility for the continuance of many trade restrictions. Mainly for this reason, the move toward a progressive elimination of quantitative restrictions in intra-European trade would be considerably strengthened by a payments system providing for multilateral compensation of balances within the European area. The ECA attaches considerable importance to the establishment of such a system, in substitution for the current, essentially bilateral Intra-European Payments Scheme, and is ready to supply its hard-currency needs by setting aside a substantial portion of the 1950/51 appropriation for this purpose.

Restricted. *Review of Foreign Developments*, February 28, 1950.

Plans for such a system, known as a European Payments Union, were discussed early this year in technical committees of the OEEC with the active participation of the ECA. Considerable progress was made in spelling out the principal issues on which agreement had to be reached before a workable plan could be devised. During the January session of the OEEC Council, however, the British chancellor of the exchequer* voiced a number of important doubts and reservations with respect to the proposal.[1] A measure of agreement on basic principles of a European Payments Union was reached eventually and was incorporated into the *Second Interim Report of the OEEC*.[2] Nevertheless, considerable difficulties remain in devising a plan that will be acceptable to all interested parties.

The following paper attempts to set forth some of the issues that are still sources of difficulty in reaching any general agreement, and speculates as to possible ways in which these difficulties might be resolved. Although the discussion around the European Payments Union is many-cornered and although the points of view of the United Kingdom and of the United States are by no means the two that are farthest apart, the writer finds it helpful to start out by listing the basic conditions which the British and the U.S. governments are likely to attach to any such agreement.

The U.S. government will probably insist that the EPU fulfill the following requirements:

1. It must result in full and automatic multilateral clearing of balances, due regard being given to pre-existing obligations and claims between pairs of participating countries.

---

* Sir Stafford Cripps (1889–1952), British Labor Party politician and former U.K. ambassador to Russia (1940–1942), served under the Attlee government first as the president of the Board of Trade (1945–1947) and then as the chancellor of the exchequer (1947–1950).

2. After exhaustion of multilateral drawing rights and of "swing" credit margins, net balances resulting from the clearing must be settled partly in gold, in order to avoid the formation of a high-cost, soft-currency area and in order to provide debtors with adequate incentives to avoid excessive imbalance.

3. Since the payments arrangements are useful only insofar as they contribute to a freer movement of trade in Europe, these arrangements must not lead to greater freedom to impose or strengthen restrictive measures than would exist without them.

The fundamental British reservations in connection with the payments union may be formulated as follows:

1. A European Payments Union cannot be permitted to interfere either with sterling's role as an international currency and or with its use as monetary reserve by a number of countries.

2. The Union should not increase the likelihood of gold and dollar losses by the U.K.

3. Whenever the clearing arrangement threatens to lead to substantial gold losses by the United Kingdom, the latter must be permitted to reintroduce any previously lifted quantitative restrictions.

From these two sets of principles a series of practical issues have arisen which may be catalogued in the following way:

1. Is the United Kingdom going to preserve its presently held right not to settle in gold or dollars any amounts of sterling accumulated by the European members of the transferable account area, such as Italy, Sweden, the Netherlands, etc?

2. What is going to happen to the sterling balances accumulated by the other European countries and held by them in the

expectation that they are readily available for the financing of any import surplus with the sterling area?

3. How are transfers of sterling from the rest of the sterling area to Continental countries to be treated?

4. Under what conditions will it be permissible to combat gold losses to the Payments Union by the imposition of quantitative restrictions?

In the following we shall take up each question in turn and shall try to sketch answers which, taken together, might prove acceptable both to the United Kingdom and to the United States.

## I. CEILING ON CREDIT FACILITIES EXTENDED TO THE U.K. BY THE EPU MEMBERS AS A GROUP

On this point the U.S. attitude is likely to be quite firm. Without an overall ceiling on credit facilities the U.K. could run import surpluses with countries like Italy which do not require any form of settlement, while possibly drawing gold from the EPU in settlement for credits earned with countries that do not hold sterling balances. In this way the EPU would become a one-way street for Britain. Multilateral compensation, insofar as the U.K. is concerned, would be severely limited and the system would contain no adequate incentives for Britain to avoid excessive imbalance, in fact there would be a premium on certain types of imbalance.

If it is to be more than an occasional member in compensation operations requiring the express approval of all affected parties, the U.K. ought, therefore, to be subject in this respect to the rules prevailing for all other members. Fractional gold payments should begin after exhaustion of a "swing" and of possible multilateral drawing rights granted to cover "structural" deficits. In the case of the U.K., there will be some question whether the swing should be calculated on the basis of the intra-European trade of the U.K. only or of the whole sterling area. A case may well be made for the latter and in this eventuality the swing accorded (and to be accorded by) the U.K., though limited, would be considerable.[3]

In what respect will the establishment of an overall "gold point" for the U.K. in its relations with the other EPU members as a group affect the use of sterling as an international currency? It is possible that, as a result of losing the unlimited overdraft facilities enjoyed so far with the European members of the transferable account area (Italy, Sweden, etc.), the U.K. will want to make these countries revert to bilateral account status. The only practical result of this action, however, would be to prevent the automatic transfer of sterling for current transactions from the few non-European members of the transferable account area (e.g. Egypt). It is unlikely, therefore, that such an action on the part of the U.K. would be very effective in stemming sterling accumulations by the European countries in question. We shall return later to the problem raised by transfers of sterling from the rest of the sterling area to the Continental members of the EPU. It is sufficient here to show that a restriction of the transferable account area would likely be either unnecessary or inadequate in dealing with the situation resulting from sterling accumulations by European countries which give rise to gold obligations on the part of the U.K. (The history of U.K.–Belgian payments relations sufficiently illustrates this point.)

There is no doubt that the establishment of an overall ceiling on overdraft facilities might result in gold losses to the U.K.

which it would not incur under present circumstances. This would mean, therefore, a violation of one of the basic conditions which the British have insisted upon. Any resulting British opposition to the Payments Union ought, however, to be neutralized by the arrangements with respect to existing intra-European sterling balances which are discussed in the next section.

## II. EXISTING STERLING BALANCES

The problem of building the sterling balances accumulated by several European countries into the EPU mechanism affects both British interests and the interests of the countries that have accumulated sterling in the past years.

The problem permits two opposite solutions which appear equally unsatisfactory and impractical: one would be to require the United Kingdom and the European holders of sterling to freeze, fund, or settle somehow the existing sterling balances and to enter into the clearing union with a clean slate. Clearly, this would be unacceptable to the countries which are large-scale holders of sterling because such an arrangement would deprive them of their present ability to finance an import surplus with the sterling area. It would also be unacceptable to the United Kingdom which would be apprehensive over the loss of confidence in sterling that would result from such an arrangement.

At the other extreme, there is the possibility of allowing current holders of sterling to keep it as an "existing resource." In view of the size of some of the accumulations, such a course would be tantamount to the exclusion of sterling from the clearing mechanism to a considerable extent. Not only would it materially restrict the area of multilateral compensation, but it would also have quite inequitable results—for instance a country holding sterling balances could have an overall deficit with the other ERP countries and yet be entitled to gold payments from the European Payments Union if it had a credit toward the non-sterling countries along with a larger debit toward the sterling area.

A solution, lying somewhere in the middle between these two extremes could be found by *transferring to the EPU* sterling balances presently held by European central banks. As a result, countries that have accumulated sterling would acquire a corresponding credit position in their EPU account which would be matched by a debit of the United Kingdom's account. These credits and debits would be as fully multilateral as all EPU accounts. The U.K. could not object to this operation on the grounds that it would reduce the standing of sterling as an international currency. The transaction would, indeed, enhance the standing of sterling since the sterling balances held by European countries would have been converted into a more widely usable currency. Neither would the *uses* of sterling as an international currency be affected. Individual traders would continue to deal in sterling and any conversion of sterling into EPU credits would be exclusively reserved to central banks. The U.K. might, however, object to the operation both because its liability would be increased through multilateralization and, as already discussed, because of the end of the unlimited over-draft facilities previously enjoyed.

To obtain U.K. agreement a number of provisions entailing *compensating advantages for the United Kingdom* may be considered:

1. Since the transfer of sterling balances to the European Clearing Union would increase both the value of these balances to the holder, e.g. Italy, and the weight of the U.K.'s obligation resulting from them, it might be considered equitable to request

from Italy, and to grant the U.K., a cancellation or a funding of a portion of the balances. The funding could take the form of setting up two EPU accounts, one of which would be currently available whereas the other would be blocked, for the U.K. and for Italy. The balances held in the blocked accounts would then be scheduled to pass into the current accounts in accordance with a pre-determined time schedule. However, there is no doubt that it will be extremely difficult to negotiate such agreements.

It is also conceivable to block, in the way just described, part of the U.K. debit while leaving Italy's credit untouched. Under these conditions, however, a full drawing down by Italy of its credit while part of the corresponding U.K. debit is blocked, would result in gold losses by the EPU and in credit extension by third EPU countries. In fact, such a development would mean a temporary taking over of part of the European sterling balances by the combined resources of the EPU and its members other than the U.K.

2. Alternatively, one might consider a simple device which would permit the U.K. to receive gold from the EPU before full reimbursement of the U.K.'s EPU debit. Let us assume that transfer of the sterling balances to the EPU would leave the U.K. with an intra-European debit balance of 100 while its normal "swing" margin would amount to 30 in each direction. Under those conditions the U.K. would have its "swing" margin on the debit side increased to 130, so that it would have to start making gold payments after having incurred an *additional* debit of 30. However, it could start receiving gold only after having accumulated intra-European credits in the amount of 130. To eliminate or reduce this asymmetry it could be decided that the U.K. is to receive partial gold payment for its intra-European credits after having accumulated European credits in an amount smaller than 130 (but not smaller than 30). From that point on, a U.K.

export surplus with the EPU countries would serve only in part to reduce further the U.K. debit with the payments union; the balance would accrue to the U.K. in the form of gold.

Such a provision could no doubt result in gold losses to the EPU, but these losses could be limited by applying a converse provision to the holders of EPU credits originating in sterling balances. In other words, provision could be made for permitting the present holders of sterling balances to draw down only a portion of these balances during a given period. If their total debit position during a period is larger than this portion they might be required to make a partial gold payment for the excess and would draw down their credits with the EPU for the balance of the excess.[4]

3. Finally provision may be made for reducing or funding the U.K.'s indebtedness to the payments union whenever the credit position of the former holders of sterling balances is reduced, whether or not this reduction comes about as a result of an export surplus of the U.K. Under such a provision the U.K.'s debit resulting from the transfer of Italy's sterling balances would be scaled down in the event of, say, an Italian import surplus with Belgium.

The rationale for this action would be that, with such a development in Italy's trade, Italy's claim to receive a compensation for its past export surplus to the United Kingdom would have been satisfied. Under our assumptions, Belgium would become a creditor and would be entitled to some receipts of gold or dollars after exhaustion of its swing margin.

This device again would mean that part of the U.K.'s debit could be taken over jointly by the EPU and the resources of its non-U.K. members. The difference between this device and the one discussed under (1) above is merely that here the cancellation or funding of the U.K. debit would take place only if and when the development of trade has shown that the U.K. is not called upon to satisfy Italy's claim to an import surplus. While attractive on this ground, the proposal is beset with considerable technical difficulties.

The above devices, used singly or in combination, should prove quite attractive to the United Kingdom for they would result in a reduction or a staggering of British liabilities and, under some combination of circumstances, in gold payments to the United Kingdom before full reimbursement of its present liabilities. All of these devices entail the possibility of gold losses to the EPU.[5] But a contribution from ECA for this purpose might be highly constructive—possibly more so than the one originally contemplated with the purpose of bridging the gap between debtors' gold payments and creditors' gold receipts.

Further, the use of such devices would not constitute privileged treatment for the United Kingdom at the expense of others. We have seen that because of existing arrangements with respect to sterling the U.K., upon becoming a full-fledged member of the EPU, would definitely have to give up certain rights presently held and used. Therefore, arrangements such as those we have discussed above would not mean the granting of special new advantages, but merely a compensation for the loss of advantages currently enjoyed by the U.K.

## III. TRANSFERS OF STERLING FROM REST OF STERLING AREA

The chancellor's memorandum to the OEEC Council[6] maintains that a problem similar to that of the European accumulations of sterling, exists with respect to transfers of sterling from the rest of the sterling area to the accounts of Continental countries. According to the memorandum, it would not be just to require the United Kingdom to settle its bilateral deficits partly in gold while its bilateral surpluses might be offset by equivalent deficits of the sterling area countries. This argument seems to overlook the fact that, as long as the U.K. administers the central reserve pool for the sterling area as a whole, it must bear a share of responsibility for balance of payments developments in the sterling area. When in 1949 much of the gold and dollar drain was found to originate in excessive dollar imports of the sterling area countries, the U.K. was able to bring pressure on the self-governing dominions to share in the cuts of dollar imports.

A similar action would be indicated and would no doubt be possible should the U.K. find at some future time that it is losing gold to the EPU as a result largely of adverse balance of payments developments of the sterling area countries vis-a-vis Continental Europe. As mentioned above, the responsibility of the U.K. for the whole trade of the sterling area with Europe could be taken account of by having the U.K. quota based on the figures relating to total sterling area trade with Europe rather than on U.K. trade alone.

## IV. FREEDOM TO IMPOSE QUANTITATIVE RESTRICTIONS

The dispute on the freedom to establish QR's [quantitative restrictions] in the case of gold losses to the EPU should not be insoluble. It must be realized that the establishment of multilateral clearing itself will do away with many QR's that so far were necessary to guarantee *bilateral* balance. Therefore the establishment of multilateral clearing, even if unaccompanied by any commitment concerning the *future* recourse to QR's, is likely to result in a decreased need for and, therefore, in less *current* use of QR's. This is indeed the main reason for which both global multilateralism and regional multilateral clearing schemes have been advocated.

It, therefore, would be needless perfectionism to jeopardize agreement on the EPU by a dispute on this matter. Several countries are likely to insist that a clause permitting them to impose additional QR's in case of gold losses to the EPU be written into the EPU convention. Given the present lack of coordination of national monetary and fiscal policies, resort to QR's simply cannot be outlawed if there are to be gold payments by debtors.

It is of course desirable to circumscribe the use of QR's. Thus it ought to be possible to stipulate that QR's should be resorted to only in the event of persistent and substantial gold losses. Further, an attempt might be made to permit only QR's applying to the other EPU countries as a group and to outlaw bilateral ones. Finally provision should be made for consultation prior to the imposition of QR's.

When all of this will have been done, however, the frequency of the resort to QR's will still depend essentially on the progress of the European countries toward balanced payments and toward coordination of monetary and fiscal policies.

It might also be noted that in view of the relatively small influence which the U.K. exercises over the internal policies of the self-governing dominions, pressure by the U.K. on these countries will generally take the form of exhortation to cut imports rather than of advice on such specifically internal measures as monetary and fiscal policies.

*Summary.* An agreement with the U.K. on the EPU might contain the following elements:

The U.K. agrees to the establishment of an over-all limit to its over-draft facilities with respect to *all* EPU members as a group;

beyond this limit partial gold payments are to begin. In addition, the U.K. agrees to the transfer of existing European sterling balances to the EPU accounts.

To obtain agreement on these points, the United Kingdom could be offered special benefits such as reduction or partial funding of balances, or arrangements that would permit the U.K. to receive gold payments for intra-European credits before full reimbursement of its EPU debit.

If existing arrangements with respect to the current use of sterling are to be maintained, the U.K. account with the EPU will necessarily be affected by, and the U.K. must be in some degree responsible for, the transactions that take place between the rest of the sterling area and Continental Europe; but, in compensation, the U.K.'s quota and therefore its overdraft facilities might be based on the trade of the sterling area as a whole with the other ERP countries.

Since multilateral clearing will lessen the need for QR's, its establishment itself is a positive step in the direction of *trade* liberalization whether or not accompanied by an explicit commitment not to reintroduce QR's in the case of gold losses to the EPU. An effort should be made to obtain reasonable assurances on this point, but undue emphasis should not be placed on it, since everything in this sphere will depend not on present commitments, but on the progress of European countries toward balanced payments and on the future growth of European unification.

## NOTES

1. OEEC Council, *European Payments Union*, Memorandum by the Chancellor of the Exchequer of the United Kingdom, Paris, January 27, 1950, c(50)30 (restricted).

2. [OEEC,] *Second [Interim] Report of the OEEC*, Paris 1950, pp. 224–232.

3. In this connection, it would seem that an entirely unnecessary controversy has been created by the discussion around the funding or reimbursement of the "swing" credits. The U.K. position is correct in pointing out that yearly reimbursements of the swing credits in hard currency would be equivalent to the introduction of an only lightly veiled gold standard system. The swings under the EPU should be nothing but the multilateral counterpart of the bilateral overdraft facilities or agreements to hold each other's currency up to a certain absolute amount, but without specific time limit.

4. It will be readily seen that the two devices discussed so far are essentially similar in their economic effects. It will probably be well to use either the one or the other but not the two in combination. It appears to the writer that the second device might be easier to negotiate.

5. A simple transfer of sterling balances to the EPU, unaccompanied by any of the above provisions, could in itself lead to either larger gold losses or larger gold gains than would have to be sustained otherwise by the Union. Thus, if Belgium rather than the U.K. develops an export surplus toward Italy after transfer of the latter's sterling holdings, the Union would soon have to pay gold to Belgium in settlement of its resulting credit while not receiving any gold from Italy. If, on the other hand, Belgium should run an *import* surplus with the U.K., Belgium would soon have to make gold payments to the EPU while the U.K. would finance its export surplus with Belgium by having its EPU debit balance drawn down and would not be entitled to gold receipts. Thus the arrangement would entail the possibility of both gold gains and gold losses for the EPU. Only if one of the above provisions in favor of the U.K. were adopted, would the probabilities definitely be weighted in the direction of gold losses by the EPU.

6. *Op. cit.* [OEEC Council, *European Payments Union*.]

# 17

## MULTILATERALISM AND EUROPEAN INTEGRATION

### MULTILATERALISM DEFINED

There is no need for me to restate here the advantages of multi-lateralism and the drawbacks of bilateralism. It really is obvious that the greatest advantages from world trade are realized when every country can buy in the cheapest market. To state this simple truth means to affirm the principle of multilateralism. For, when every importer in every country is free to buy wherever he chooses there is only a small probability that the purchases of country A in country B will be just equal to the purchases of B in A. It *could* happen and if it did nobody would object to the bilateral balance between A and B. More likely, however, each country, even when in overall balance, will have deficits in some directions and surpluses in others. The resulting pattern of trade is called a *multilateral* one and we generally designate by multi-lateralism the conditions in international trade and finance that make such a pattern possible.

---

Restricted. Lecture delivered by Mr. Hirschman on March 30, 1950, at the Foreign Service Institute of the Department of State.
*Review of Foreign Developments*, April 25, 1950.

Multilateralism, thus, is not identical with free trade although you will often hear that one of the goals of our foreign economic policy is the reestablishment of a "free, multilateral trading system." Free trade requires the absence of all barriers to trade whether they be tariffs, quotas, or exchange controls. A multilateral trading system, on the other hand, exists when the proceeds of exports (and, let us add, of foreign gifts or loans) do not have to be spent in the country which took the exports or which granted the loan, but may be used for procuring imports from anywhere in the world. Under this, possibly somewhat narrow definition of our concept, multilateralism would seem to be compatible not only with tariffs, but with certain types of exchange controls and quantitative restrictions. Thus a multilateral trading system does not necessarily conflict with administrative measures to keep *total* spending of foreign exchange within the limits of *total* foreign exchange receipts or with the imposition of global quotas, i.e. quantitative ceilings on commodity imports that do not specify the countries of origin where the commodities have to be bought.

In the usual broad sense, multilateralism is defined as a system under which traders can buy wherever they want *and* whatever they want to buy. In the more narrow sense, which I have elaborated here, multilateralism might be defined as a system in which traders can use wherever they wish those amounts of foreign exchange and of import licenses that are being made available to them. This narrower definition is useful because it permits one to perceive clearly the main conditions of multilateral trade, i.e. the convertibility of currencies and the absence of bilateral quotas. Actually, however, multilateralism has never taken this restricted and theoretically pure form. We have either had bilateralism or multilateralism in its broad sense. The simple reason for this is that foreign exchange difficulties invariably take the form of scarcities of *particular* foreign currencies, and this has resulted in restrictions being applied to those particular foreign currencies and, therefore, inconvertibility and bilateralism.

## THE LAST TIME WE SAW MULTILATERALISM

Before we look into the conditions and the methods for reestablishing a multilateral trading system I wish to go back a little bit in history and tell you how matters stood "the last time we saw multilateralism." For having immensely sharpened our vision in this respect we are heavily indebted to the economic research work of the League of Nations and in particular to Folke Hilgerdt, now with the United Nations.[1] By grouping the myriad data on world trade into a few significant groups, Mr. Hilgerdt has shown how a delicate mechanism of world-wide settlement of trade balances had grown up from 1860 to the nineteen twenties. I wish to retain in particular two lessons suggested by the fascinating material prepared by him.

It is often said that before the war the United States import surplus with the tropical areas permitted Western Europe to capture dollars through an export surplus with these areas and that Western Europe was in this way enabled to settle its deficit with us. One glance at the tables prepared by Mr. Hilgerdt shows that this is so simplified as a model of what was actually going on as to be seriously misleading. For instance, although the U.K. did have a small export surplus with the tropical countries in 1928 this is not true for the other European countries. The important export surpluses which enabled these countries to settle their overseas deficits were, for Germany, an export surplus with the Western European Continental countries and, for the latter, an export surplus with the United Kingdom. Finally, a most important link in the whole system of multilateral settlements was the interest and dividends receipts accruing to the U.K. as a result of its past foreign investments, which permitted the U.K. to have an import surplus with all its trading partner except the tropics. The U.K.'s import surpluses with the Continental countries of Western Europe permitted these countries to settle an important part of their import surpluses with the overseas countries and with Germany. Germany in turn was enabled to settle its overseas deficits by its export surpluses with Western Europe and the U.K. This sketch of some of the essential elements in the multilateral settlement mechanism of the interwar period is sufficient to show that the mechanism is virtually beyond repair. This is the first lesson. Britain's overseas investment and shipping income probably will never again enable it to sustain an import surplus of the prewar magnitude; consequently the Western European countries and, in turn, Germany will have to look in other directions for a balance in their international accounts.

This should not, however, lead us to conclude that there is no future in the multilateral trading system. To reach this conclusion would be equivalent to the popular fallacy of confusing the principle of the international division of labor with one particular manifestation of this principle, i.e. the division of labor between industrial countries on the one hand and agricultural and raw material producing countries on the other.[2] The very studies of Hilgerdt—and this is the second lesson I wish to draw from his work—show us that the multilateral pattern never stood still. The U.S. surplus with South East Asia, of which so much is being made in current literature, became important only in the twenties. Similarly, the U.K. completely changed its pattern of trade from the eighteen sixties to the years just before the first World War: in the course of this 50-year period, a deficit with Europe and with the United States replaced a deficit with Asia, Africa, and Latin America.

This variability in the pattern of multilateral settlement should give us confidence that the impossibility of recreating the particular pattern of multi-lateral settlement, which prevailed in the inter-war period, does not carry with it the end of multilateralism as such. I should also like to conclude from this that it is more important to concentrate our attention on the basic prerequisites of *any* multilateral trading system than to construct, and to aim at, any specific, "ideal" system of multilateral settlement with every country fitted into a neatly balanced "trade matrix."

## THE EMERGENCE OF BILATERALISM

There is perhaps no real need to pass in review the reason for the decay of the multilateral trading system in the thirties. It has often been told how, in the course of the Great Depression, France established import quotas and Central Europe exchange clearings and how these devices multiplied and spread to many countries during the thirties.[3] Nevertheless, the essential conditions for a regeneration of a multilateral system remained in existence until the outbreak of World War II: the pound sterling and the currencies of France, the Low and Scandinavian countries remained convertible. This state of affairs was terminated by the outbreak of the war when comprehensive exchange licensing was instituted everywhere in Europe.

At the end of the war, the trade of the European countries among themselves and with the outside world was resumed under a more pervasively bilateral system than ever before. Here again the reasons are well known: the devastations of war and the

general depletion of economic wealth required strict husband-
ing of foreign exchange resources; hard currencies were particularly sought after since they permitted the purchase of essential
food and raw materials and all countries were very reluctant to
part with these hard currencies in settlement of soft-currency
deficits; foreign exchange reserves were inadequate; exchange
rates were overvalued while internal purchasing power in most
countries was inflated; and tariffs were inoperative because price
inflations had reduced the incidence of the specific tariff rates
that were the rule in many countries. During the immediate
postwar period, therefore, only bilateral currency arrangements
combined with quantitative regulation of imports and exports
permitted the rebuilding of foreign trade.

Bilateralism, however, drew strength not only from the critical conditions of the world economy at the end of the war; it was
not universally regarded as a necessary evil. In spite of the experience of the thirties, during which time Germany had used bilateral trading as a means of dividing, exploiting, and dominating
its prospective victims, bilateralism had come to be advocated in
some quarters as a necessary complement to full employment
policies. I hasten to add that it was this type of theorizing—
which as all theorizing did have its effects on the daily decisions
of governments—that Lord Keynes branded in his last article as
"modernist stuff gone wrong and turned sour and silly."[4]

The reasoning on which this "stuff" is based can very suc-
cinctly be expressed as follows: at full employment, a country
will require a certain volume of imports to sustain production
at the required level; to obtain these imports a country needs
to market exports in the same amounts and in the appropriate
currencies; and to make quite sure that it will be able to do so,
the country cannot afford to throw itself on the vagaries of the
international market, but must strike a number of bilateral deals.

It does not take much time to point out that a policy based on this reasoning runs the great danger of sacrificing both real income and economic growth to full employment and that, moreover, it requires complete governmental control over foreign trade. No government has attempted to carry this policy out in its pure form. But the jarring experience of the Great Depression still lends considerable attractiveness to any policy that holds out the promise of insulation from the shocks of international depressions. In this sense, the reluctance to abandon bilateral trading today stems not only from the continuation of some of the immediate postwar conditions that compelled the recourse to bilateralism, but also from the fear that unconditional reintegration in a system of multilateral trade would result in frequent exposure to unemployment, particularly as a result of the "unstable character of the U.S. economy."

Before—at long last—getting into the real subject of our lecture let me shortly inquire into the character of the present trading system.

The principal European currencies remain inconvertible today. As a rule, they cannot be freely exchanged for each other, and even less for the dollar, either by nationals of the European countries or by the foreigners or foreign monetary authorities holding them. This absence of convertibility does not mean, however, that strictly bilateral balancing is enforced.

In the first place, the pound sterling is in fact freely transferable over a wide area through the mechanism of the sterling and transferable account systems; *within* these systems there is no payments obstacle to multilateral trade but there are important obstacles to true multilateral trade in the form of state trading and bilateral quotas.

Secondly, between most European countries there is no requirement of equality between exports and imports. These countries have usually granted each other so-called "swing credits" and additional funds for the financing of bilateral deficits have been provided by the "drawing rights" established for the past two years under the Intra-European Payments Schemes. The essence of bilateralism, however, is not the requirement of bilateral import-export balance, but the inability to spend available foreign exchange resources whether deriving from exports, from credits or from grants, anywhere but in their country of origin and by this criterion intra-European trade relations are purely bilateral except at the margin.

After the exhaustion of swing credits and drawing rights, a country must usually pay gold for further payments deficits, and from this point on, net exports to that country bring in gold or currency that is convertible. However, at that point, hurried conferences are usually called to "correct the situation" and further import restrictions are considered. With respect to the sterling area, there exists in general not even this marginal convertibility. For the countries belonging to the sterling area and to the transferable account system have taken upon themselves the commitment to hold sterling without limit; drawing on the sterling area dollar pool are [sic] the result of administrative decisions rather than the automatic outcome of the course of payments.

## HOW CAN WE THEN PROCEED FROM THE PRESENT SYSTEM OF BILATERAL QUOTAS AND INCONVERTIBLE CURRENCIES TO MULTILATERAL TRADING?

There probably is general agreement on the point that the so-called dollar shortage is the principal reason for inconvertibility and bilateralism in the world today. Our subject, therefore, could be covered fully only by indicating how to deal with the dollar shortage. It would thus seem to encompass all the crucial issues of international economics. I shall, however, attempt to limit myself to consider the various *gradual* approaches to multilateralism.

## THE ONE-BY-ONE VS. THE COLLECTIVE APPROACH

Two principal schools of thought may be distinguished in this respect: according to one school every country should work toward convertibility independently of other countries, while the other school advocates a collective approach, at least on the part of the Western European nations which participate in the European Recovery Program.

According to the first approach, each country can and should take a certain number of steps—primarily the elimination of inflationary pressures, and the adoption of a realistic exchange rate—which would enable it to ease trade and payments restrictions with the outside world. Essentially this assertion is based on the belief that each country can tackle and solve its own dollar shortage in isolation: by renouncing extravagant spending, by thus creating flexibility and appropriate incentives to the reshuffling of resources, every country will be enabled both to live within its means and to do so without stifling internal and external controls.

These are healthy precepts and for many countries they are much in need of being repeated. Nevertheless, there are many who doubt whether our goal can be reached by so direct a route. They think that the cost in internal rearrangement of resources, in redistribution of income, and in dependence from economic fluctuations originating abroad may be deemed too high a price to pay by many countries. Moreover they are convinced that the current restrictions do not have their origin solely in the demagogic extravagance of governments, but must be traced in part to the divergent trends—not to the different levels—of productivity that have prevailed over a long period in the United States on the one hand and the industrial economies of Western Europe on the other. It is this thinking which has led to the second approach to world-wide multilateralism: it consists primarily in creating first a "center of strength" in Europe through the lifting of intra-European obstacles to trade and payments; the resulting strengthening of the European economy would then make it possible to lift barriers against the outside world at a smaller cost in adjustments and real income and with more confidence in the permanence of such an arrangement than would be possible if every country were to "go it alone."

Here we have then a dispute which is essentially caused by two different diagnoses as to the severity of the economic disease afflicting the dollar-short countries. Those who think that the disease is deep-seated claim that only their medicine will work, and, in addition they would claim that even if their diagnosis should be overpessimistic, their proposed treatment would permit a less costly recovery than could be obtained by the traditional therapy.

In my opinion, far from being contradictory, the two treatments complement each other. It is highly desirable that each European country independently make as much progress as possible toward freedom from trade and payments restrictions with the outside world including the United States. Such a development is not inconsistent with even faster progress toward the abolition of intra-European restrictions. Only as the distant goal of complete European unification is being reached would there arise a conflict: since an economically united Europe would have a common set of tariffs, quantitative restrictions (if any), and exchange controls (if any) vis-a-vis the outside world, it is possible that some countries would have to reintroduce some restrictions which they might previously have lifted in their independent quest for multilateralism. If, as I hope to show, there is some virtue in European unification, such a partial reversal of earlier progress would be more than compensated by making possible more rapid progress in the right direction for the area as a whole.

But there is another reason for which it is not only not inconsistent, but highly desirable that the two roads toward worldwide multilateralism be travelled at the same time. If and when complete European economic unification will be within our immediate reach, it will be all to the good if individual European countries will have made on their own the maximum possible progress toward multilateralism. The common wall against the outside world, which will then be erected, will be some kind of average of the individual country walls in existence at the time of unification. The lower the walls of individual countries, the lower will be the resulting common wall, and the greater the assurance that the European economy will not look inward but outward. I thus believe that it is not necessary to choose between the one-by-one and the collective approach. But I have yet to make the full case for the latter.

## IS EUROPEAN INTEGRATION A STEP TOWARD MULTILATERALISM?

Is it possible to reach our goal of multilateral trade by slowly extending the *area* of multilateral settlement? A considerable controversy is now being waged on this point and because of its importance I shall devote the remainder of this lecture to its discussion. I submit that no general answer to the question can be given, and that the answer depends entirely on the specific region under consideration. A priori there is no reason whatever why the creation of a limited multilateral trading area should be a contribution to a world-wide system of multilateral trade. On the contrary, once the gravest inefficiencies of the bilateral system have been eliminated by the creation of a reasonably large area within which multilateralism prevails, the heat may well be off, so to speak, and we may get the building up of a largely self-sufficient regional bloc that does not look for further integration with the world economy. This has been the fear of many who have taken a negative view of the plans for "European integration."

There is, however, another possibility which would lead one to take a much more sympathetic view of current efforts: that is, the creation of an area in which the barriers to multilateral trade have been removed may help to remove many of the conditions which so far have held back progress toward general convertibility. This is precisely the theory underlying our efforts toward European integration. If it can be shown that the creation of a free multilateral trading area in Europe would make a contribution to the solution of the dollar shortage, then integration in Europe would definitely be a most valuable step toward general multilateralism and convertibility. We shall now examine whether this is likely to be the case.

By urging the countries participating in the European Recovery Program to abolish quantitative restrictions among themselves and to adopt plans looking toward the mutual convertibility of their currencies, we are proposing preferential or, if you like, discriminatory arrangements for the Western European area. This is, of course, a novel policy for us to advocate since we have long been staunch defenders of non-discrimination. Even our traditional stand, however, was not without important qualifications: thus it is well known that we are favorably disposed toward the most extreme form of discrimination, namely to customs unions, and that in the ITO Charter we have sanctioned even preferential arrangements provided they are meant as steps toward customs unions.

Past discussions of these matters look slightly out of focus today because, in the past, we did not subject everything to today's supreme test: the effect of a given policy on the dollar shortage.

Thus, one of the standard arguments against customs unions in the past was that the common tariff of the countries adopting the customs union might be higher on the average than the tariffs applying in the separate countries prior to the union. In this case the improvements in the division of labor within the customs union area may be more than compensated by a loss in international specialization between the area and the rest of the world. This argument is perfectly valid in itself, but it has a somewhat eerie quality in today's world when so large a part of "international specialization" consists of the United States providing goods and of the European countries receiving them.

We must thus examine the merits of European integration from the point of view of its possible contribution to the cure of the dollar shortage. The reasoning that has led the ECA to conclude that much was to be gained from European integration is well-known and quite simple in its outline: the establishment of a single large European market would, in general improve the allocation of European resources; it would create greater adaptability and mobility; it would make possible the economies of large-scale productions; and, most important, it would increase competition and would be a spur to entrepreneurial efficiency and initiative. As a result, productivity would be substantially increased and Europe's competitive position in world markets would be immeasurably strengthened.

What, if anything, is there wrong with this reasoning? It has been said the whole undertaking betrays the incorrigible naivete of the Americans ever bent on drawing false analogies from their environment and their history. In the first place, it is argued, the Western European economies cannot derive much benefit from integration since their economies are competitive rather than complementary. They cannot solve their problems by just trading more with each other for they must procure food and raw materials from abroad. In one effective formula: "a sum of 18 deficits is still a deficit."

It is not necessary to waste much time on this argument since those who propound it have taken so little time in examining the thesis which they attack. We have already seen that European integration is advocated not in order to make Europe self-sufficient but to enable it to compete more efficiently in world markets. It is also strange to cite the competitiveness of European economies as a proof that integration is purposeless. Presumably, the *more* competitive two economies separated by tariffs and other barriers, the greater will be the increase in real income to be expected from the removal of these barriers and from the subsequent reallocation of resources.

At this point in the discussion, the argument of the anti-integrationists shifts somewhat. The trouble with Europe apparently is not only that its component economies are not complementary enough, but in addition, they are *too* competitive. Its industries have grown up over decades behind tariff walls. Upon scrapping these walls, tremendous dislocation and unemployment would ensue so that the cure would definitely be worse than the disease.

After hearing these arguments one would never suspect that a flourishing inter-trade in manufactured goods has played an important part in the total European trade picture. The existence of this trade suggests that the Western European economies, while highly industrialized, have traditionally been "integrated" to a considerable extent and might be susceptible of further integration without too much trouble.

To pursue this thought a little further: it seems to me entirely possible and even probable that considerable benefits of increased specialization could be obtained in Europe as a result of relatively small reshuffling of resources.

In the first place, every national industry in Europe has grown up over a long period of time and the various firms and productive units composing it are often of very unequal productivity. An abolition of intra-European protection would therefore in many cases not lead to a whole national industry being completely outproduced by a more efficient one in another country, but to the disappearance of the most inefficient units in *both* countries.

In the second place, industrial economies as developed and well-rounded as, for example, the British, German, and French ones, can usually add one line of output without an undue loss in terms of comparative costs even if the article in question is more efficiently produced elsewhere. They can simply use and adapt existing machine tools and other equipment, and need but little protection for this purpose. In the aggregate, however, all these small departures from an optimum division of labor will represent a considerable loss in real income to the European economy as a whole. The situation can be compared to the inflationary process in which every investment considered by itself does not look particularly objectionable. If this diagnosis is correct then an abolition of restrictions among the European industrial economies would mean that this process would not only be stopped, but could even be reversed without undue cost. Considerable increases in real income and productivity could thus be expected to result from the rational location of new investment *and* from relatively minor and painless switches and reconversions within the existing industrial structure—without any wholesale destruction of fixed capital.[5]

The critics of European integration are not content with contesting the presumed benefits of a removal of intra-European trade and payments restrictions; in a counterattack many have expressed a concern that such a removal might actually intensify the dollar shortage and thereby render more remote the attainment of convertibility and multilateralism.[6]

The principal argument here runs as follows: the removal in isolation of intra-European trade and payments restrictions will lead to an expansion of intra-European trade. This expansion, according to our critics, may derive either from a substitution of the European countries for the United States as a source of supply or from a shift of European exports away from the United States to other European countries. But, it is argued, the first effect is likely to be negligible since all countries have already fully exploited the possibilities of procuring essential commodities outside of the United States. Therefore the net effect of the expected increase in European trade is likely to be a diversion of European exports away from dollar markets with a consequent intensification of the dollar shortage.

This reasoning may sound impressive, but I, for one, am not convinced by it. In the first place, if exports to the United States should really become less attractive as a result of the removal of barriers to intra-European trade, this could be remedied by an additional collective devaluation of European currencies. Secondly, the above analysis completely overlooks the *dynamic* elements in the situation. It treats the volume and kind of

European exports and imports as given and only admits of variability in their geographic distribution. This is of course highly
unrealistic. The main effect of the removal of intra-European
restrictions will no doubt be the emergence of new types of
commodity flows tied to the curtailment of certain types of output and the expansion of other types within the various European countries. Most of the new commodity flows will therefore
fit neither of the two types of shifts in trade detailed by our critics. They will bring about (and reflect) that more efficient specialization and distribution of productive functions which is the
prerequisite for the strengthening of Europe's competitive position in world markets.

In this connection, a parallel to the controversy about the
virtues of devaluation comes to mind: the anti-devaluationists
have often pointed out how low demand elasticities would make
devaluation ineffective in improving a country's balance of payments position. In logic they have had to recognize, however,
that if the elasticities were so low as to make devaluation a failure the opposite monetary move, i.e. appreciation, would result
in success.

Similarly, the critics of integration who maintain that the
removal of barriers would worsen the dollar shortage should in
logic advocate an increase of barriers among European countries. In fact why rest there and not come out in favor of a further
fragmentation of Europe? It is doubtless true that if the province
of Champagne were separated by high tariffs from the rest of
France some champagne that is now consumed in Paris, would
be shipped to New York. But it will probably be conceded that
the destruction of the previous integration between the province
of Champagne and the rest of France would weaken the viability of the whole area by far more than by the worth of such an
increase in champagne sales in this country.

This *reductio ad absurdum* leads us to a further important argument for integration. The choice before us is not integration or maintenance of the status quo, but rather whether we wish to stop and then reverse the slow process of *disintegration*, which has been taking place in Europe almost uninterruptedly at least since the First World War. As we have seen, disintegration is a dangerously easy path to go down on for the highly industrialized countries; if one of them produces cars, why should it not also turn out trucks? If trucks, why not also tractors? There are no big decisions to be taken as for instance when a country sets up its first steel mill; each step in the process looks like a relatively harmless interference with international specialization.

In the absence of positive steps, further disintegration is the likely course of affairs also for other reasons. At every shock, cyclical or otherwise, the national economies are likely to look to further insulation as a way out. Full employment is today an important national economic goal in most European countries. Few countries will hesitate to impose new restrictions on trade if they think that in this way they will safeguard employment. National sovereignty, combined with the rigid full employment postulate, is thus bound to lead to international economic disintegration. Our policy of integration is an effort to avert this development.

In the last analysis, our policy of integration is an effort to unleash and strengthen the dynamic forces of the Western European economy. Personally, I am inclined to place less trust in the economies of large-scale production that would be possible within a single free European market—for many industries the present markets of the U.K., Germany, and France are of a sufficiently large size—than in the general strengthening of the competitive spirit and of entrepreneurial initiative and in the productivity effects of an improved morale that would come with a free and united Europe. Of course, if there is no initiative to be strengthened and no morale to be improved, our efforts will be unavailing. The success of European integration thus hinges on the continued vitality of the Western European society. But belief in this vitality is at the same time the basis of our whole foreign policy and ought therefore to be taken for granted by our economic policy makers.

In advocating European integration as an important approach to the restoration of a multilateral trading system, we are, therefore, at least as right as we are in relying heavily on the recreation of a healthy Western European society in our struggle for peace.

## NOTES

1. See in particular, League of Nations, *The Network of World Trade* [(Geneva: League of Nations, 1942)]; and Folke Hilgerdt, "The Case for Multilateral Trade," *American Economic Review* [33, no. 1] (Supplement, March 1943) p. 393–407.

2. See A. O. Hirschman, "The Commodity Structure of World Trade," *Quarterly Journal of Economics*, [57, no. 4] August 1943, pp. 565–595.

3. League of Nations, *Commercial Policy in the Inter-War Period* [*Commercial Policy in the Inter-War Period: International Proposals and National Policies* (Geneva: League of Nations, 1942)]. Howard S. Ellis, *Exchange Control in Central Europe* [(Cambridge, MA: Harvard University Press, 1941)].

4. Lord [John Maynard] Keynes, "The Balance of Payments of the United States," *The Economic Journal* [56, no. 222] (March [the correct month is June] 1946) p. 186.

5. This point is overlooked in the interesting article of Henry C. Wallich and Frederick V. Loud, "Intra-European Trade and European Integration," *Columbia Journal of International Affairs* Vol. IV [no. 1] (Winter 1950), p. 43. Much of the unsatisfactory state of the discussion around "integration" can be traced to the oversimplified classification of pairs

of countries as either "competitive" or "complementary." The European economies are neither or both.

6. In a different context, I have myself argued that a policy of systematic discrimination against the United States might intensify the dollar shortage (cf. [Albert O. Hirschman,] "Disinflation, Discrimination, and the Dollar Shortage," *American Economic Review* [38, no. 5] December 1948, pp. 886–892). My reasoning was as follows: The reshuffling of resources necessary to export more to, and import less from, the United States might be prevented if the countries affected by the dollar shortage continue to import from each other items whose import from the United States they prohibit. For, as a result, the whole burden of readjustment would be thrown on the bilateral relationships between the dollar-short countries and the United States, whereas, if they were to cut back their purchases from each other along with their purchases from the United States, resources would be set free that might be applied to the production of goods for export to the United States or of substitutes for U.S. imports.

I still believe that there is truth in this argument. But it clearly has validity primarily to countries as broadly complementary as for instance the United Kingdom and the other sterling area countries. In particular, the argument applies to such commodities as the non-dollar countries already import and want to continue to import from each other even though they are not able, because of the dollar shortage, to import them from the United States.

The continuation of that trade (e.g. African tobacco against British manufactures) would not result in any shift in resources among these countries. On the contrary it would prevent certain shifts that may be desirable especially if we assume that these countries have not fully exploited the possibilities of exporting to the dollar area. The lowering of barriers between the highly industrialized European economies, on the other hand, would have quite different results; it would mean an expansion of types of trade between those countries which they so far have attempted to block and whose emergence would be tied to shifts in their productive resources toward a more efficient pattern. The resulting greater efficiency of their economies in general is, *in this case*, likely to outweigh decisively the possible unfavorable effects of discrimination on the cure of the dollar shortage.

# 18

# THE EUROPEAN
# PAYMENTS UNION

O n July 7, 1950, one week after the expiration of the second Intra-European Payments Scheme, the Council of the Organization for European Economic Cooperation reached full agreement on the establishment of a European Payments Union. This Union represents a radical innovation in the mechanism of intra-European payments and may have important repercussions on the whole system of international financial relations. The following paper does not give a systematic exposition of the EPU agreement.[1] It attempts to trace the rather tormented history of that agreement and to discuss in this connection some of the more important issues that had—and in part remain—to be faced.

Restricted. *Review of Foreign Developments*, August 15, 1950, later published as
Albert O. Hirschman, "The European Payments Union: Negotiations and the Issues,"
*Review of Economics and Statistics* 33, no. 1 (February 1951), pp. 49–55.

## BACKGROUND

Projects for multilateral clearing in Europe have been discussed ever since the European Recovery Program was
launched.[2] During the first two years of the European Recovery Program, however, the entrenched position of bilateralism
in the postwar trade and payments situation in Europe and
the United Kingdom's unwillingness to permit any transfers
of sterling that might result in gold obligations, prevented the
successful negotiation of any multilateral clearing arrangement. The intra-European payments schemes which have
been operating during the past two years were essentially ad
hoc arrangements providing some essential finance for intra-
European trade but, among many other shortcomings, they
failed to make any substantial advance toward multilateralization of payments.

In the course of 1949, it became clear that the main European problem had shifted from the area of production to that
of trade and payments. The currency adjustments of September
1949 not only improved the competitive position of the devalu-
ing countries with respect to the dollar, but also served to bring
about a greater degree of balance in intra-European payments.
At the same time, a number of efforts got under way to relax
the most irksome restrictions on trade and payments in Europe.
Mr. Hoffman's speech before the OEEC Council in Paris of
October 31, 1949, in which he advocated the economic "integration" of Europe through the creation of a single market freed
from restrictions, crystallized action in the two related fields of
trade and payments. With respect to trade, the OEEC countries
agreed (with some exceptions) to lift quantitative restrictions
on 50 per cent of their imports from each other. In the field of
payments, ECA drew up a blueprint for a European Currency

Union (later renamed European Payments Union) which was presented to the OEEC in December 1949.

## PRINCIPAL CHARACTERISTICS OF ANY SCHEME FOR MULTILATERAL CLEARING IN EUROPE

As was true of all similar previous plans for multilateral clearing, the EPU project consisted of two distinct parts: (1) an offsetting mechanism and (2) a settlement mechanism.

1.  *The offsetting mechanism* is designed to break through the bilateral channels within which intra-European trade has been constricted since the beginning of the war. It aims at permitting one country to offset a deficit in one direction by a surplus in another. This is not expected to be achieved by making European currencies directly convertible into each other and into the dollar, a step considered as premature by many European countries. Rather, each country, while maintaining its present system for controlling foreign exchange transactions, will have an account with a central Payments Union, and the debits and credits accumulated by each country's central bank in its bilateral relations with the central banks of other countries will be transferred at monthly intervals to its EPU account, which will thereby be debited or credited by the combined net result of its intra-European transactions. The great advantage of this method as contrasted with bilateralism lies in the fact that a country does not have to be concerned by deficits with some countries provided that these deficits are offset by surpluses in other directions. It thus eliminates bilateral bargaining and permits an expansion of useful trade. It also

means that a country that experiences a serious deficit with another country but remains in over-all balance will feel no need to resort to quantitative restrictions in order to correct this deficit.

2. *The settlement mechanism.* The settlement of the net balances emerging from multilateral clearing raises a number of important issues. One hundred per cent settlement in gold or dollars would amount to the establishment of one type of full convertibility of European currencies.[3] It has been generally agreed that such a step would not only be premature, but would also interfere with current efforts to liberalize intra-European trade. In a situation in which countries are faced with the obligation to pay gold for any additional import, they probably would be quite unwilling to undertake new risks by lifting existing trade barriers, even though this were done on a reciprocal basis.

On the other hand, there also was agreement that the terms of settlement of the net balances emerging from the clearing should not be too "soft." If countries knew that, as a result of large-scale credit facilities, they could run up a considerable net deficit with the other countries in the group without having to make gold payments, they might be tempted to pursue policies of monetary ease that would lead them straight back into the conditions of inflation from which they were just emerging.

These conflicting considerations led to the conclusion that the deficit countries should be granted some credit by the Union, but should make gold payments on an increasing scale as their deficit rose. Creditor countries also would finance their surplus partly by credits and would receive gold for the balance. The Payments Union would be endowed with an initial fund in dollars which would serve to make up any differences between gold payments by debtors and gold receipts by creditors.

## LAUNCHING OF THE EPU PROJECT
## AND FIRST DIFFICULTIES

In December 1949, the OEEC Council entrusted its Payments Committee to draft the outlines of a European Payments Union that would start operation on July 1, 1950. A general outline was produced and inserted into the *Second Interim Report of the OEEC*, which was published in January. In the meantime, however, the project encountered many difficulties. First, there was some concern within the U.S. government that the projected Payments Union would in some respects duplicate the functions of the International Monetary Fund; and, more important, it was feared that the arrangement, particularly in view of the inclusion of the whole sterling area, might lead to the establishment of a "high-cost soft-currency area" characterized by inflationary pressures and discriminatory restrictions against the dollar.

To counteract any tendency in this direction it was agreed that the EPU arrangement should not be of such a nature as to force countries that had already made considerable progress in the direction of convertibility to go back in the direction of soft-currency arrangements characteristic of (e.g.) the sterling area. Similarly, there was a consensus of opinion that any dollars contributed by ECA should not be provided to underwrite whatever net deficits would emerge but should only supplement the hard currency resources and mutual credits of the participants.

## BRITISH OPPOSITION

The most serious trouble arose for the EPU project as the result of British opposition. While British representatives had fully collaborated in outlining the project on a technical level within the OEEC, Sir Stafford Cripps declared during the session of the OEEC Council in January that the United Kingdom would be unable to accept substitution of the proposed clearing mechanism for the bilateral agreements involving sterling. He refused to accept an EPU that would supersede the existing bilateral agreements; rather, he favored one that would be superimposed upon these agreements as a "lender of last resort." It is easily seen that this concept of the EPU was directly opposed to the concept developed within the U.S. government. At the same time, Sir Stafford declared that the United Kingdom could not agree to restrict its freedom of action with respect to quantitative restrictions on trade.

It should be mentioned here that ECA was trying to obtain commitments from the OEEC countries to make further progress in abolishing quantitative restrictions in intra-European trade. Moreover, once these restrictions had been removed, it was deemed important that countries should not easily and unilaterally be able to restore them. It was in this respect that the United Kingdom served notice that it would have to retain its full freedom of action.

## THE EPU IN CONGRESS AND THE DOLLAR CONTRIBUTION

In spite of these difficulties, ECA went ahead with its project and made it figure prominently in the Congressional presentation of its request for funds for 1950/51. In order to make it possible to provide the Union with appropriated funds, ECA sponsored an amendment of the Economic Cooperation Act so as to permit a transfer of $600 million in free dollars from its appropriated funds to

> any central institution or other organization formed to further
> the purposes of this Act by two or more participating countries,
> or to any participating country or countries in connection with
> the operations of such institution or organization, to be used
> on terms and conditions specified by the Administrator and
> designed to promote multilateral intra-European trade, to facili-
> tate the transferability of European currencies, and progressively
> to eliminate the existing systems of bilateral trade, and to liberal-
> ize trade among participating countries and between them and
> other countries.

The Congress accepted this amendment and even provided that unless the $600 million were used for the purposes
mentioned in the amendment, they were to be returned to
the Treasury (ECA had only asked for *permission* to transfer
funds). Through this mandatory provision, the Congress no
doubt intended to exert some pressure on the United Kingdom, whose hesitations to join had in the meantime become
public.

ECA's dollar contribution will serve a triple purpose: (1) to
make up any difference between debtors' gold payments to EPU
and creditors gold receipts from EPU that might arise in the
course of EPU operations; (2) to provide funds for the redemption in certain conditions (see below, page 261) of existing
European-held sterling balances; and (3) to constitute a separate
fund which will permit ECA to intervene when a country experiences extraordinary and unforeseen difficulties in its intra-
European payments relations.

## AGREEMENT ON THE SPECIAL
## POSITION OF STERLING

With favorable action by the Congress, the principal immediate task was to break the deadlock with the British. It was recognized by United States and Continental officials that sterling was indeed in a special position with respect to the EPU project. In the first place, sterling, unlike any other European currency, is widely used as a means of settlement among third countries. Secondly, many countries have traditionally held sterling as part of their monetary reserve. Thirdly, several European countries had, during or after the war, accumulated considerable holdings of sterling. These holdings posed a special dilemma for the EPU: neither Britain nor the countries holding these sterling balances would consent to any blocking of such balances; but, in the absence of such blocking, the holders of these balances could continue to settle bilaterally with the United Kingdom and would thereby infringe on the principle that all countries had to settle multilaterally through the EPU.

On their side, the British realized that they could not maintain the negative attitude exhibited by Sir Stafford Cripps in January. In March, they came forward with a proposal of their own which advocated a limited participation of sterling in the scheme. Without going into its details, one may affirm that the proposal constituted considerable progress since, for the first time, the British showed themselves ready to accept transfers of sterling even when such transfers could involve them in losses of gold. The proposal, however, was rejected by both the American and the Continental negotiators since it did not go far enough in the direction of doing away with bilateral payments agreements.

After intensive further negotiations, in the course of which ECA, the Belgians, and the OEEC secretariat each produced tentative proposals, agreement was finally reached in May on the insertion of sterling into the EPU. The agreement provided that Britain would be a full member of the EPU: i.e., that it would establish a net balance with it for all the transactions of the sterling area with the other OEEC countries and would settle this balance through the EPU in accordance with the general procedure for settlements (part in gold and part in credits). The United Kingdom also agreed that it would reintroduce previously lifted quantitative restrictions only in the case of a serious drain on its reserves and then only on a multilateral as opposed to a discriminatory basis.

On the other hand, the "special" position of sterling was taken into account as follows:

(1) With respect to the use of sterling as a monetary reserve: it was agreed that, instead of holding EPU credits, creditors could make arrangements to hold in the form of sterling that part of their surplus which would correspond to their surplus in sterling;

(2) With respect to the existing sterling balances of the Continental members of the EPU: it was decided that these balances could be used only if the holders were in a net deficit position with respect to the EPU, but could then be used irrespective of whether the holders were in a deficit position vis-a-vis the sterling area. ECA agreed to indemnify the United Kingdom for any actual losses of gold that might result from such multilateral use of sterling balances.[4]

This solution of the vexing problem of the special position of sterling was generally found quite satisfactory. It was felt that the United Kingdom had indeed come a long way since Cripps' statement in January and that the price paid by ECA for the British concessions was a reasonable one.

## ADMINISTRATION OF THE EPU AND THE INTERNATIONAL MONETARY FUND

In the meantime, it had become clear that the issue of EPU's relationship to the International Monetary Fund, which had caused much concern at an earlier stage, would be disposed of without too much trouble. By general agreement, the EPU would be governed largely by automatic rules and would function under the supervision of the OEEC, a body that can make decisions only by unanimous vote. This arrangement did not seem likely to result in a powerful supranational monetary board whose authority would supersede that of the Fund.

Nevertheless, an attempt has been made to avoid the paralysis that has often been exhibited by international bodies tied to the rule of unanimity. On a number of important issues that must be deferred for decision to the OEEC Council, the final EPU agreement provides for the procedure of the "Special Restricted Committee." These Committees are to consist of "five persons chosen by lot from a list of persons nominated by each of the members for reasons of competence and standings." When the issue to be decided is a dispute involving one or several specific countries, none of the Committee members may be a national of one of the parties to the dispute. The Committee is to make a report to the OEEC Council on the issue at stake and the Council will then make a recommendation or take a decision "in the light of this report." The intention of this procedure is to invest the Committees with a moral authority which will make for unanimous acceptance of their reports within the OEEC Council.

## THE TERMS OF SETTLEMENT
## OF EPU BALANCES

One important question remained to be settled: that of the actual terms of settlement of EPU credits and debits. There was agreement that the gold payments by the debtor should increase as his deficit rose and that the creditor should extend some credit. But exactly what the ratio of gold settlement to credit settlement was to be, had been left undecided pending the solution of the sterling problem. The discussion started around a British proposal that was "soft" in the extreme: it called for a gold-free credit margin for debtors of 10 per cent of each country's total trade turnover (imports plus exports plus invisible current account items) with the other EPU members and, in addition, for another 5 per cent of credits which would go hand-in-hand with increasing gold payments. During subsequent discussions, these figures were whittled down to gold-free credit margins of 3 per cent of total turnover, with gold-assorted credits for an additional 6 per cent.

With respect to the gold-assorted credits the ratio of gold to credit settlement is to increase for debtors in equal installments from 1:4 over 2:3 and 3:2 to 4:1, whereas for net creditors the ratio is to remain fixed at 1:1 after exhaustion of the gold-free credit margin. The *quota* of each member country is defined as that range of its deficit within which it can command any credit from the EPU or, alternatively, as that range of its surplus within which it is committed to credit extension to EPU. This range is thus equal to 15 per cent (3 per cent gold-free credit margin plus 6 per cent credit tied to 6 per cent gold) of its total trade turnover.

After exhaustion of the quota, the debtor has to settle fully in gold unless the OEEC specifically decides otherwise. On the other hand, a net creditor who exhausts his quota has no assurance that he will automatically be paid 100 per cent in gold. It is merely provided that, at this point, the OEEC shall consider what arrangements can be made to enable the creditor to remain an effective member of the EPU.

The above asymmetries in the settling of debtors' and creditors' balances are only feeble reminders of the original blueprint idea that the EPU settlement mechanism should be such as to discourage equally the accumulation of excessive debit as well as of excessive credit positions. To this purpose, it was proposed that the debtors should settle increasing portions of their debit balances in gold while creditors should extend more and more and more credit. Naturally it proved impossible to obtain the unlimited commitments to extend credit that were implicit in this idea. Nevertheless, the mode of settlement as finally agreed goes farther than any previous international monetary mechanism in placing responsibility to maintain international balance on the creditor as well as on the debtor.

## THE QUESTION OF "SOFTNESS" OF THE TERMS OF SETTLEMENT

Even though the quotas and credits are established for a two-year period, it was felt in many quarters that the scheme still resulted in too large an injection of credit into the intra-European payments system. In view of the wide swings that have been characteristic of intra-European payments over the past few years, it is extremely hard to formulate a precise judgment as to the "generosity" of the credit margins provided under EPU. It seems safe to say, however, that the EPU system is, by itself, not "hard" enough to deter countries from following unduly expansionary policies. On the other hand, inflation is far too serious an affair to be started merely because of the existence of sizeable credit facilities for the settlement of intra-European deficits. This has been amply shown during the past years when countries have repeatedly failed to utilize drawing rights established for them under the Intra-European Payments Schemes.

With respect to debtor countries, the credit provisions of the EPU mean, that *one* of the many punishments for inflation will be mild, at least in the beginning. While this absence of punishment does not appear likely to induce countries to "commit" inflation, it does place more of a burden on their self-restraint than would have been the case with a harder system of settlement. The need for self-restraint will be even greater with the inflationary pressures that are likely to be generated by the additional military expenditures presently being planned.

## SPECIAL ARRANGEMENTS FOR BELGIUM

With respect to the probable creditors, the possible inflationary consequences of wide credit margins are more direct than in the case of the debtors. Whereas it was feared for the latter that the existence of over-generous intra-European credit facilities might fail to check, or might even elicit, inflationary developments, the commitment of the creditors to grant large credits could result directly in an unduly large volume of "unrequited" exports and thereby start inflation in the creditor country. The country that was most concerned with this danger was Belgium. Since Belgium's foreign trade with OEEC countries is particularly high in relation to its national income, the Belgians felt that credit extension by their country according to the general formula would represent a disproportionate contribution which might result in inflation and would thereby compromise the considerable progress Belgium had made toward non-discriminatory trade arrangements and currency convertibility. These feelings led to a last minute crisis in the EPU negotiations. The Belgian cabinet decided at first to reject the agreement but the deadlock was broken by a series of concessions to Belgium which considerably reduced its credit commitments. One of the concessions, later generalized for all countries, provided for repayment of Belgium's outstanding credits within two years unless special agreements providing for longer terms were concluded bilaterally between Belgium and its debtors. Provided that the two-year terms are not widely superseded by such bilateral agreements, this will result in making for somewhat less "softness" in general since part of the EPU credits will then be used for the repayment of old debts rather than for the financing of current deficits.

## FLEXIBILITY AND PROSPECTIVE FUNCTIONS OF THE EPU

The debate over the desirable degree of "softness" or "hardness" in the terms of settlement of EPU balances caused very specific provisions for review to be inserted into the final EPU agreement. In addition to regular periodic reports, a special comprehensive report is to be made as of June 30, 1951. All these reports will be devoted particularly to the question whether the credit facilities presently provided for will have proven to be excessive or inadequate.

These provisions for review underline the flexible nature of the EPU as a new international financial instrument. With multilateral clearing as its basic operating function, the ECA can indeed be adapted to play a useful role in a great variety of developments. With further progress toward freedom of trade within Europe and toward dollar solvability, the provisions for settlement could be progressively tightened. Such a process is likely to be hastened by the tapering off of ECA aid and would in the end convert EPU into a mere clearing house where income equals outgo. Even in such a situation EPU would still fulfill a useful function, since it would then represent a reliable mechanism for assuring the convertibility of European currencies.[5]

On the other hand, the EPU provides us in the present situation with an excellent instrument for giving precise financial meaning to such phrases as "European solidarity" and "equality of sacrifice." Because of the differences in the industrial and manpower resources of the various OEEC or Atlantic Pact countries, there are bound to be great differences in their individual contributions to a stronger common defense. The EPU, however, can serve as a ready instrument for equalizing these burdens by the channeling of EPU credits toward those countries shouldering the largest direct burdens and vice versa. In this way, the total volume of credit in the system need not be increased; but the available credit volume would be used and, if necessary, rearranged so as to provide the countries that devote most resources to defense with some resources of the other countries which would thus participate indirectly in the common effort.

Thus the EPU, whose original and central purpose is to make a contribution to the creation of a single European market, is well suited to play a useful role under conditions of worldwide convertibility as well as in the setting of a large defense effort. Naturally, there is no guarantee that the EPU will actually perform these useful functions. It could well develop into a brake on the progress toward convertibility if it were to refuse to introduce harder terms of settlement as such terms became possible. It could also interfere with a rational common defense effort if it permitted those countries that contribute least to the direct building up of armed strength to suck in additional resources from those countries already burdened by heavy defense expenditures.

To point out these possibilities, however, is merely to say that, like every human institution, the European Payments Union has potentialities for both good and evil. But, endowed with well-defined functions in response to pressing current problems and operating in an area ever more intimately bound together, the EPU at least promises to be that most difficult achievement: a genuinely alive international institution.

## NOTES

1. For a good description, see the article "Mechanics of EPU" in the *Economist* of July 15, 1950, pp. 130–132. The agreement is embodied in a 26 page-long OEEC Document, C (50) 190 (Final) Paris, July 7, 1950. The actual convention to be approved by the OEEC Council and to be signed by the member countries is still being drafted.

2. See, e.g., the paper by J. Burke Knapp on "Intra-European Financial Arrangements" in this *Review* of July 15, 1947 [J. Burke Knapp, "Intra-European Financial Arrangements," *Review of Foreign Developments*, July 15, 1947]; also Raymond F. Mikesell, "Regional Multilateral Payments Arrangements," *Quarterly Journal of Economics* Vol. LXII [no. 4] (August 1949 [the correct year is 1948]), pp. 500–18; and Robert W. Bean, "European Multilateral Clearing," *Journal of Political Economy*, Vol. LVI (Oct. 1948), pp. 403–15.

3. For a discussion of this and other varieties of convertibility, see "Types of Convertibility," *Review of Foreign Developments*, below in this issue [Albert O. Hirschman, "Types of Convertibility," *Review of Foreign Developments*, August 15, 1950, not published in this collection].

4. For suggestions for a solution along these general lines see "The European Payments Union—A Possible Basis for Agreement," this *Review*, February 28, 1950 [republished in this volume as chapter 16].

5. See article on "Types of Convertibility," in this issue, p. 4 [Albert O. Hirschman, "Types of Convertibility," *Review of Foreign Developments*, August 15, 1950, not published in this collection].

# 19

## SIZE AND DISTRIBUTION OF THE PUBLIC DEBT IN SELECTED COUNTRIES

E ver since the end of the First World War the existence of large public debts in the financial structure of the highly industrialized Western countries has created important new problems for the effective pursuit of policies aiming at monetary and economic stability.[1]

After the First World War, monetary instability was often caused or facilitated by sudden monetization of short-term debt held by banks and individuals. In the course of the twenties many governments concentrated their efforts on the consolidation of the large floating debt in order to curb these dangers. By reducing the real value of the debt, the post-war inflations themselves offered one type of solution—although an exceedingly costly one in economic, social, and political terms.

In the course of the thirties the practice of deficit financing increased public debts in almost all countries, but the problem at that time was one of translating monetary expansion into economic recovery, rather than one of preventing the existence of a growing public debt from interfering with anti-inflationary

Restricted. *Review of Foreign Developments*, February 13, 1951.

monetary policies. The increasing importance of the public debt in the financial structure of most countries was reflected by the declining role of the discount rate and the increasingly widespread use of open-market operations as an instrument of monetary policy during this period.

The huge growth of public debts during the Second World War created problems of far greater magnitude than those that characterized the post-1918 situation. In some countries the inflationary pressures generated by past and current deficit financing were so strong and the fiscal and other economic controls so weak that prices rose once more to a multiple of their prewar level. In these countries the relative importance of the public debt was again sharply reduced through inflation. Other countries escaped the dangers of open inflation through timely currency reforms, comparatively efficient control systems, and the disinflationary effects of budget and import surpluses.

Monetary policy generally played an important role in the breaking of open inflations, but—apart from the surgical intervention of currency reforms—was in general not heavily relied on in checking inflationary pressures in the countries whose price levels had not risen too sharply. This non-reliance on monetary policy took various forms. Negatively, it meant failure to resort to such instruments of monetary policy as, e.g., changes in the discount rate; but it also meant positive action on the part of several central banks which insured "pegged" market prices for government securities and thereby stabilized or depressed short-term and/or long-term rates of interest. Among the principal arguments adduced for these policies has been the importance and wide distribution of the public debt in the financial structure of the countries involved.

If only for this reason a comparative statistical study of public debts in various countries is of interest. Moreover, whether or not the existence of a large public debt justifies any particular type of monetary policy, it is clear that it brings about important changes in the conditions under which monetary policy must be pursued. To give but one example: several of the countries that have pursued active monetary policies in spite of large debts found it necessary to take special measures, such as the freezing of a portion of bank-held securities, to make monetary policy effective.

## THE STATISTICAL APPROACH

Public debt statistics are generally not comparable in scope and breakdown and most countries do not possess some of the statistics (e.g., distribution of the debt by types of holders) that would be most useful for the present inquiry. Nevertheless, an attempt is presented in the table [table 19.1] to circumscribe the concept [of the] "importance of the public debt" by a number of ratios relating the public debt or significant portions of it to various economic magnitudes. The two appendix tables contain the data on the basis of which these ratios have been calculated.

The first ratio is that showing the percentage relationship of the total public debt to national income; this ratio has little precise meaning except that it provides the most general yardstick for what we have called the importance of the public debt. In order to obtain a more meaningful and roughly comparable concept of public debt for the various countries in this study, external, non-interest bearing and intra-governmental debt has been deducted from the gross debt.

The second ratio, that of the public debt to the total money supply, is another general measure of the importance of the

## TABLE 19.1 INDICATORS OF SIZE AND DISTRIBUTION OF PUBLIC DEBT IN SELECTED COUNTRIES (PERCENTAGE RATIO AT THE END OF 1949)[a]

| Country | Public[b] debt to national income | Public[c] debt to money supply | Interest on debt to budgetary revenue | Commercial-bank-held debt to total com[m]. bank assets | Bank-held debt to total debt[b] |
|---|---|---|---|---|---|
| United Kingdom | 208 | 408 | 14 | 48 | 27 |
| Netherlands | 123 | 205 | 15 | 55 | 34 |
| Australia | 116 | 211 | 11 | 15 | 41 |
| Canada | 108 | 275 | 17 | 36 | 36 |
| United States | 100 | 179 | 14 | 43 | 45 |
| Belgium | 53 | 79 | 14 | 47 | 42 |
| Sweden | 46 | 120 | 6 | 12 | 45 |
| Italy | 30 | 65 | 8 | 15 | 37 |
| France | 30 | 62 | 4 | 20 | 47 |
| Denmark | 18 | 48 | 5 | 8 | 50 |

[a] For basic data as well as for explanatory and qualifying notes see appendix tables.
[b] Exclusive of non-interest-bearing and intra-governmental debt.
[c] Exclusive, in addition, of central-bank-held debt.

public debt but at the same time it can be interpreted in more concrete terms: it shows the extent to which the money supply would be expanded in the event of monetization of the public debt. To permit this interpretation, that part of the public debt which has already been monetized, i.e. which is held by the central bank, has been excluded from the calculations.

The third ratio is a simple one: it shows the portion of total budgetary revenue that is absorbed by the cost of carrying the public debt. This figure naturally gives one indication of the reluctance of national treasuries to see interest rates rise. Another important indication would be the portion of the total debt that is due to be refunded in the relatively short-term future; unfortunately the national statistics giving breakdowns of debt into long- and short-term are too heterogeneous to permit a comparison.

A further indication as to the importance of the debt in the financial structure is given by the ratio of commercial bank-held debt to total commercial bank assets. This ratio is useful in evaluating the extent to which banks are able to expand their reserves, particularly in conditions under which the central bank assumes the role of a residual buyer of government securities at fixed prices.

Finally, one of the most interesting questions concerning public debt structure is the distribution of the debt by types of holders. If the public debt is held by a great many institutions and individuals, the reactions to changes in interest rates and the chances of successful conversion are necessarily quite different from a situation in which an overwhelming portion of the debt is held by a few financial institutions. Unfortunately adequate data on the distribution of the debt by holders are available only in a very few countries. In general, all that it has been possible to do was to collect data on the amount of government securities held by the banking system (central bank and commercial banks). This information yields a residual figure which includes holdings of insurance companies, business corporations, and individuals.[2]

A further important distinction is that between marketable and non-marketable debt. The non-marketable security redeemable on demand at a fixed price has assumed considerable importance only in the public debt structure of the United States. The existence of large amounts of such securities creates special problems for monetary and debt management policies. These problems, however, are not too dissimilar to those created by savings in the form of deposits with state savings banks which in turn invest largely in government securities—the situation prevailing in many European countries.

## RESULTS

The statistics which have been brought together in the table above [table 19.1] for 10 selected countries, suggest a number of comments:

(1)  As could be expected, the importance of the public debt is much greater for the countries that were active belligerents and avoided a multiple rise in prices than for those countries that experienced ruinous inflation or that did not participate actively in World War II.

(2)  Among countries in the former category, the United Kingdom appears to be the country where the public debt is largest in relation to both national income and money supply. Partly because of the low interest rates paid and partly because of the comparatively large size of the U.K. budget, the interest burden in relation to budget revenue is not higher for the U.K. than for the other countries in the group.

(3)  Coming some distance behind the United Kingdom, the United States belongs to the group of countries comprising also Canada, Australia, and the Netherlands whose public debt is roughly of the same order of magnitude as the national income. In these countries the public debt held outside the central bank is two to three times as large as the money supply. The similarity among this group of countries extends to the ratios of debt service to budget revenue (about 15 per cent) and of bank-held to total commercial bank assets (about 50 per cent). As to the latter ratio, the only exception is Australia with the

remarkably low figure of 15 percent which results from the tying up of large banking funds through the "special accounts" technique.

(4) Finally, there is a remarkable similarity of practically all countries examined with respect to the distribution of the debt between bank and non-bank holders. It appears that from one-third and one-half of the total debt is held in all these countries within the banking system, the remainder being subdivided among insurance companies, business corporations, and individuals.

## CONCLUSIONS

It has sometimes been said that, in view of the extraordinarily large size and distribution of the public debt in the United States, foreign experiences with debt management and monetary policies cannot furnish any useful lessons for this country. A first conclusion of the statistics given above is that this argument has no basis of fact. While, in absolute terms, the U.S. public debt far outdistances that of any other foreign country, our comparison shows that in relative terms the problems raised by the size of the public debt can be no greater in the United States than in a number of advanced industrial countries. With respect to the one aspect of *distribution* of the public debt for which we are able to provide comparative statistics, the position of the United States is similar to the position of an even larger number of foreign countries than is the case with respect to the size of the debt.

A second conclusion, closely related to the first, is that there appears to be no clear-cut correlation between size and distribution of the public debt of individual countries and their monetary policies.

It is true that the countries having relied most actively on monetary policy—France, Italy, Belgium—are also those whose debt is comparatively small. But, at the same time, Sweden, with a similarly light debt, has pursued until quite recently a policy of pegging the whole interest-rate structure.

If we now consider the countries with relatively large debts, we find that, while only the United States has consistently pegged the long-term rate of interest, the Netherlands and Canada have pursued, at least until the very recent past, a rather passive monetary and credit policy. Australia, on the other hand, has resorted to an extremely rigorous method of restraining bank credit.

Finally, at the far end of the scale, the United Kingdom with a debt relatively much larger than the United States, has not attempted to stabilize the long-term (as opposed to the short-term) rate since the failure of Dalton's "cheap money" drive. In fact, it has been argued with considerable force that the United Kingdom could not afford to peg the long-term rate precisely *because* of the huge volume of outstanding securities and the consequent danger of inflation in case of large central bank purchases.[3] In the United States, on the contrary, it has often been said that the large size and wide distribution of the debt made firm support operations necessary to maintain orderly conditions in the security market.

Not only, therefore, have countries with similar debt burdens pursued widely divergent monetary policies (and vice versa); but we also find that the same facts with respect to public debts have been cited in different countries in support of opposite policies.

**APPENDIX TABLE I PUBLIC DEBTS OF SELECTED COUNTRIES—BASIC DATA (IN BILLIONS OF NATIONAL CURRENCY, END OF 1949)**

| Country | Total domestic debt | Non-interest bearing debt[a] | Intra-governmental debt[b] | Interest-bearing debt held by central bank |
|---|---|---|---|---|
| | (1) | (2) | (3) | (4) |
| United Kingdom[c] | 23.7 | — | 2.5[d] | 1.6[e] |
| Netherlands | 19.4 | 1.5 | 0.5[f] | 1.8 |
| Australia[g] | 2.4 | — | 0.2 | 0.3[h] |
| Canada | 14.9 | — | 0.8 | 2.0 |
| United States | 257 | — | 39 | 19 |
| Belgium | 207 | 68 | 0.6[i] | 6 |
| Sweden | 12.1 | 0.1 | 1.8 | 2.5 |
| Italy | 2,275 | 479 | n.a. | 235 |
| France | 2,724 | 634 | 128[j] | 279[k] |
| Denmark[l] | 8.0 | 4.7 | 0.2 | n.a. |

[a] Mostly large blocks of direct central bank advances to national treasuries in connection with war or occupation expenditures.
[b] Debt held by government agencies and trust funds other than state savings banks.
[c] Data relate to March 31, 1949.
[d] Estimate of *The Economist* (April 8, 1950, pp. 784–786) adjusted to exclude holdings of savings banks which are included in holdings of banking system ["Who Holds Gilt-edged?," *The Economist*, Apr. 8, 1950, Vol 158, Issue 5563, pp. 784–786].
[e] Issue and Banking Departments.
[f] The only intra-governmental debt which it has been possible to identify consists of 502 million guilders of securities held by the State Insurance Bank.
[g] Data include both Commonwealth debt and state debts, for the reason that loan programs of the state and Commonwealth Governments are coordinated under the single authority of the Australian Loan Council; moreover, all securities are floated in the name of, and are guaranteed by, the Commonwealth Government.
[h] Holdings of Central Banking Division, Commonwealth Bank only.
[i] Estimated holdings of Caisse Générale d'Epargne et de Retraite for accounts other than savings institutions.
[j] Holdings of Caisse des Depots et Consignations other than holdings for account of savings institutions which amount to 365 billion francs.
[k] Includes 51 billion francs advances from various Central Banks of French Union.
[l] Data as of March 31, 1950.

APPENDIX TABLE II PUBLIC DEBT AND RELATED ECONOMIC DATA FOR SELECTED COUNTRIES—BASIC FIGURES FOR RATIOS SHOWN IN TEXT TABLE [TABLE 19.1] (IN BILLIONS OF NATIONAL CURRENCIES, END OF 1949)

| | Public debt I[a] | National income | Public debt II[b] | Money Supply | Interest on debt | Budget revenue | Debt held by commercial banks | Total commercial bank assets | Debt held by banking system[c] |
|---|---|---|---|---|---|---|---|---|---|
| United Kingdom[d] | 21.2 | 10.2 | 19.6 | 4.8 | 0.5 | 3.7 | 3.2[e] | 6.6[e] | 5.8 |
| Netherlands | 17.4 | 14.1 | 15.6 | 7.6 | 0.5 | 3.3 | 4.2 | 7.6 | 5.9 |
| Australia | 2.2 | 1.9 | 1.9 | 0.9 | 0.07 | 0.63 | 0.18[f] | 1.2[f] | 0.9 |
| Canada | 14.1 | 13.0 | 12.1 | 4.4 | 0.4 | 2.3 | 3.1 | 8.7 | 5.1 |
| United States | 218 | 217 | 199 | 111 | 5.3 | 38.2 | 67 | 156 | 97 |
| Belgium | 133 | 252 | 127 | 160 | 8.4 | 60.4 | 34 | 72 | 56 |
| Sweden | 10.1 | 22.0 | 7.7 | 6.4 | 0.3 | 4.8 | 1.3 | 10.9 | 4.5 |
| Italy | 1,796 | 5,927 | 1,561 | 2,375 | 91 | 1,108 | 298 | 1,961 | 663 |
| France | 1,962 | 6,573 | 1,683 | 2,713 | 58 | 1,434 | 275 | 1,357 | 919 |
| Denmark[g] | 3.1 | 16.8 | 3.1 | 6.4 | 0.17 | 3.1 | 0.6 | 7.3 | 1.5 |

[a] Total domestic debt minus non-interest-bearing and intra-governmental debt (see appendix table I for basic data).
[b] Total domestic debt minus non-interest-bearing, intra-governmental, and central-bank-held debt (see appendix table I for basic data).
[c] Includes holdings of commercial banks, savings banks, and central bank. Ratio (5) in text table [table 19.1, column "Bank-held debt to total debt"] is obtained by dividing figures in this column by public debt I.
[d] Data as of March 31, 1949.
[e] Estimates for London clearing banks.
[f] Includes holdings and assets, respectively, of General Banking Division, Commonwealth Bank.
[g] Data as of March 31, 1950.

## NOTES

1. The statistical material on which this study is based was prepared by various members of the Division of International Finance and of the research staff of the Federal Reserve Bank of New York.

2. As mentioned previously the total debt figures exclude debt held by government agencies and trust funds.

3. R. S. Sayers, "Central Banking in the Light of Recent British and American Experience," *Quarterly Journal of Economics* [63, no. 2], May 1950 [the correct year is 1949], p. 204.

# IV

## THE ECONOMIC CONSEQUENCES OF U.S. HEGEMONY

# 20

# THE LONG-RUN EFFECT
# OF DEVELOPMENT AND
# INDUSTRIALIZATION ABROAD
# ON THE UNITED STATES

## I. HISTORICAL ATTITUDES OF
## INDUSTRIAL COUNTRIES TOWARD
## INDUSTRIALIZATION ABROAD

"Is Export of Machinery Economic Suicide?" This succinct question was the title of a little tract published at the beginning of the century by one of the lone free trade economists of Imperial Germany.[1] The tract ably answered the question in the negative, but its publication was symptomatic of the widespread alarm that was felt at the time in Germany about the industrialization of new areas of the world and about the "suicidal," though, in the meantime, highly profitable help in this process extended by the older industrial countries.

In truth, the technically more advanced countries have been remarkably inconsistent in their attitude toward the less advanced countries ever since the rise of manufacturing: they have alternatively and often simultaneously helped, feared, and attempted to block, the efforts of these countries to acquire industrial techniques and equipment. The most consistent attempt at blocking was made during the mercantilist period when all manufacturing nations issued prohibitions against the exports of machinery and the emigration of skilled artisans; these regulations could not be enforced with the coming of the industrial age and evasions became so widespread that they either fell into disuse or were formally repealed as happened in England a century ago.[2] But while England did nothing to prevent the spreading of industrial methods to other nations that marked the second half of the nineteenth century, this development did not fail to arouse many misgivings. No less an economist than Stanley Jevons warned in 1865 that the emigration toward the United States would "develop, or rather complete, abroad systems of iron and coal industry in direct competition with ours."[3]

The rapid rise of German and American industry benefited the British economy in many respects, but at the same time alarmed British opinion; an extensive literature grew up toward the end of the century describing in particular the disastrous dangers of the German trade rivalry.[4]

But the fears of the industrialization of undeveloped countries found their most outspoken expression in Germany itself; with remarkably bad taste, that country had hardly joined the small band of industrialized countries when it was already intent on slamming the door behind it in the face of any additional newcomers. German foreign economic policy before both World Wars I and II actually contains several instances of direct attempts at preventing industrialization of other countries.[5]

With the possible exception of their own colonies it proved, however, generally impossible for the older industrial countries to prevent the spread of industrialization to other countries and, once this was clear, every industrial country wished for its own manufacturers to capture the profitable market in capital goods that was the consequence of world-wide industrialization. Nevertheless, opinion in the industrial countries always remained apprehensive about the ultimate outcome of the process. The effect in the interwar period of the Japanese trade expansion on specific old established industries such as the British cotton mills seemed to justify the pessimistic forecasts about the eventual doom of the older industrial countries who had allowed their secrets to be copied.

## II. THE UNITED STATES ATTITUDE

Among the many expressions of these gloomy views, one voice is almost consistently absent: that of the United States.[6] Indeed, once this country turned its attention to the problem, it was in order to foster the development of undeveloped countries through the promotion of the International Bank for Reconstruction and Development, through the development loans of the Export-Import Bank, and finally through the elaboration of the Point Four Program. It is of considerable interest to analyze the probable reasons for the apparent absence of concern in the United States over any untoward effect of foreign development and industrialization on the U.S. economy. For, in the course of this analysis, we will not only discover why we have been traditionally exempt of a fear that has afflicted most other industrial countries, but we will also find out whether we have any reasons to change our traditional outlook on this problem.

Possibly the most important reasons for our lack of concern about industrialization abroad is the composition of our exports. In contrast with a country such as the United Kingdom, our exports of manufactures consist typically of articles that are geared either to increases in production (machine tools and other capital goods), or to high and expanding levels of income (automobiles and other consumers' durables). For this reason, our exports are not only not endangered by industrialization and development abroad, but on the contrary stand to gain considerably from expanding production and rising incomes in other parts of the world. This is in marked contrast with those industrial countries whose exports were mainly based on such goods as textiles, hardware, glassware, etc., the production of which is usually among the first undertaken by newly industrializing countries. Moreover, the United States also exports substantial quantities of industrial raw materials, such as cotton, petroleum, sulphur, etc. and these exports therefore are likely to gain directly from an expansion of manufacturing abroad.

The industrial countries of Europe, in particular England and Germany, viewed with concern and alarm the building of foreign industries not only because of the prospective competition for their own export industries; there was the additional fear that, once the foreign markets were lost, they would not have any countervalue to offer for the foodstuffs and raw materials on whose massive imports they had come to rely for the sustenance and employment of their people. Actually, the "fear of becoming a predominantly industrial state," often voiced in Germany during the period of rapid industrialization toward the end of the 19th century, had in part its roots in this vision of a country that finds itself suddenly deprived of the essential supplies because it can no longer market its manufactures abroad. Such apprehensions gave considerable impetus to the German policies of agricultural protection and of colonialism.

In the United States, such fears could never become very oppressive: for the dependence of our economy on foreign supplies has always been quantitatively and qualitatively of a much smaller order than that of the Western European industrial countries. There would be no starvation in the United States even if we were to be cut off overnight from our foreign sources of supply as a result of industrialization abroad.

There are other less tangible factors that are equally important in explaining the United States attitude toward foreign development.

After all, the differences in foreign trade structure between Germany and the United States, important as they are, are not so great as to explain why Germany should have been generally alarmed and the United States largely unconcerned by industrialization abroad. For if the United States had good reasons for its attitude, the German fears were largely unfounded. Even some contemporaries pointed out, statistics in hand, that industrial countries usually are each other's best customers. The truth is that German writers took a certain delight in showing that the industrial countries were digging their own grave through the export of machinery and industrial techniques. This propensity for discovering apocalyptic historical vistas has been a general trait of German historical and sociological writing since the 19th century. It can, e.g. also be found in the familiar Marxist analysis which showed how capitalism was preparing its own destruction through the creation of a proletariat and how competition was destined for extinction because of the way in which the competitive struggle led to monopoly. These numerous prophecies of doom do not teach us so much about the real nature of industrialism, capitalism, and competition as about the state of mind of their intellectual authors, ill at ease in the industrial age, and therefore inordinately fertile in finding proofs for its inevitable dissolution.

The fundamental reason why these theories have never gained much credence or influence in the United States is to be found in the absence of the many conflicts and strains—deeply embedded in history—that in Germany and many other European countries resulted in a widespread intellectual hostility toward industrial capitalism. In this country, any difficulties accompanying our economic development were generally interpreted as difficulties of growth, remedies for which could readily be found from case to case, rather than as deep-seated cracks fated to bring about the collapse of our whole economic structure.

Instead of casting an uneasy eye toward the industrial advances of other countries we have always believed in the possibilities of further economic and technological progress and in our ability to maintain industrial leadership. Moreover, our economic history testifies abundantly to the benefits of vigorous industrial expansion; and a theory maintaining that any further extension of industrialism, be it within or without our borders, is disastrous or even dangerous, is *prima facie* suspect to us.

These historical and psychological reasons are at least as important as the purely economic ones in explaining why we not only have *practiced* foreign economic and industrial development, but why, unlike other industrial nations, we have generally not been alarmed by this practice and have lately taken the lead in advocating it as a matter of public policy.

## III. THE ARGUMENTS AND THE FACTS

In the preceding paragraphs we have already had occasion to mention some of the arguments that have been used in demonstrating either the dangers or the benefits of foreign industrialization and development for the older industrial countries. We shall now review the controversy in a more systematic fashion.

*The market-destroying effects.* It is easy enough to understand how industrialization of new areas can be harmful for the established industrial countries. Certainly the local refining of ores and canning of food will take work away from the refineries and canneries of the countries that previously imported materials and foodstuffs in their raw state. No doubt, the setting up of cotton mills in the developing countries reduces the market of the old established cotton industries. It is also possible that the country with the newly established industries may eventually compete successfully with the older industrial countries in third markets and we cannot even exclude the possibility that it may do so in the market of the very country that originally supplied it with finished goods as well as with the capital necessary for industrialization. Is it not natural enough then to cast the industrializing country in the role of the snake reared and nursed at the bosom of the older industrial countries?

The strength of this argument lies in its simplicity and directness. In this, it has a striking affinity to the early arguments against the introduction of labor saving machinery. The counterarguments are very similar in both cases: it is shown first that the harmful direct effects described above are more than compensated by a number of beneficial indirect effects. Secondly it is argued that the incriminated process is already underway, that it cannot be halted, and that therefore it is far better to lead it into beneficial or at least innocuous channels rather than futilely to oppose and bemoan it.

*The market-creating effects.* The first market-creating rather than market-destroying effect of industrialization (here again the analogy with the argument for the introduction of labor-saving machinery is obvious) relates to the demand for capital goods in the newly industrializing country. This demand clearly has been for some time of the greatest importance for the continued vitality of the exports of older industrial countries. Nevertheless, in itself the new demand for, say, textile machinery cannot lastingly compensate for the loss of old markets for finished textiles.[7]

The second and more powerful market-creating effect of industrialization rests on its income-generating aspects. It is easily shown how for many countries a soundly conceived process of industrialization is a necessary component of any development that would lift these countries to higher levels of real income. These increases in income will result in higher demands for all kinds of goods, including imports. In this fashion new markets will be created all around and in the end the older industrial countries will find that they can export new varieties of manufactures in far greater quantities than previously.

These arguments are valid enough and they are made even more convincing by the statistical evidence that has been accumulated in their support.

*The statistical evidence.* The statistical material has brought out the following facts:

(1) Not only do imports of all kinds show a universal tendency to rise with per capital [sic] income,[8] but imports of manufactured goods have generally increased in countries progressing along the road of industrialization. The increase in imports of manufactures generally lagged behind the increase in local manufacturing, but it is worthy of note that imports of manufactures generally showed a tendency to rise most in countries where a rapid process of industrialization took place. This relationship is illustrated by the following table [table 20.1] taken from the League of Nations report on industrialization and foreign trade.[9]

(2) World trade is not by any means confined to the exchange of manufactures against foodstuffs and raw materials. This

### TABLE 20.1 MOVEMENT OF MANUFACTURING AND TRADE IN MANUFACTURED ARTICLES, UP TO 1926-29 (1926/29 AS PERCENTAGE OF 1891/95)*

|  | Manufacturing | Imports of manufactures |
|---|---|---|
| Japan | 1,932 | 628 |
| Finland | 583 | 473 |
| United States | 436 | 230 |
| Sweden | 405 | 480 |
| Italy | 394 | 189 |
| Germany | 279 | 185 |
| France | 260 | 127 |
| United Kingdom and Ireland | 143 | 195 |

\* Hirschman's report did not include the title of the table from the original source, which we have reinstated; see League of Nations, *Industrialisation and Foreign Trade* (Geneva: League of Nations, 1945), p. 93.

"traditional type of interchange," in fact, amounts to only about one-third of total world trade; the remaining two-thirds consist of the exchange of some foodstuffs and raw materials against other foodstuffs and raw materials on the one hand, and, on the other, of the exchange of some manufactures against other manufactures. It has been shown that approximately one-half of the manufactures entering world trade are exchanged against other manufactures, and only the other half against foodstuffs and raw materials.[10] In a more detailed way, it has been shown that many countries "export and import what are apparently the same commodities" whereas in fact they are only broadly similar but differ in quality, price, design, and in other respects.[11]

These statistical findings show only that *on balance* industrial countries have nothing to fear, and much to gain, from the industrialization of other countries. Naturally they do not and cannot show that there will be no harm to any industry or firm. It is clear that industrialization will mean smaller markets and more competition for *some* industries of the old industrial countries.

In order to maximize the net gain to be derived by the industrial countries from the industrialization of underdeveloped countries, the old industrial countries must strive to fulfill three conditions:

(1)  The exports of these countries should specialize as much as possible in such lines as are likely to be benefited, rather than hurt, by industrialization abroad. These lines are capital goods and such consumers' goods whose production is rather complex and whose consumption is sensitive to rises in income.

(2)  These countries must actively develop new and improved processes and products so as to maintain their trade position with as little disturbance as possible.

(3)  Finally, these countries must maintain a sufficient degree of mobility and adaptability in their economy so as to be able to shift resources away from those branches which are threatened by foreign industrialization.[12]

It is quite evident that among all industrial countries it is the United States which comes nearest to fulfilling all three of these conditions.

## IV. THE "MAGIC" OF INDUSTRIALIZATION

So far we have only given the reasons for which the industrialized countries should not fear development and industrialization abroad. There are, in addition, powerful reasons why they should promote it so as to be able to influence it in the right direction.

The leaders of the under-developed countries throughout the world have been caught by the magic of the words "development" and "industrialization." Whether or not they have studied the relevant correlations and scatter diagrams[13] they are fully aware that there exists an almost straight line relationship between per capita income and percentage of the population *not* absorbed in agriculture.

They are, if anything, overaware of this relationship: industrialization, the creation of any industry whatsoever, is often held [as] the only key to the escape from age-old poverty. Given this mentality two dangers have to be guarded against:

(1)  Too much emphasis should not be placed on industrialization in development programs, and over rapid and uneconomic industrialization must be avoided. This double danger has been clearly recognized by the United States. In the Point Four Program, for instance, the accent is as much or more on teaching the undeveloped countries to do more efficiently the things they are already doing (in agriculture and small-scale industry) than on the setting up of entirely new industries.

(2)  The second danger is that, in their haste to industrialize, the undeveloped countries will be tempted to adopt the totalitarian methods which, without doubt, have been highly successful in Russia. It is in this connection that the timely provision of technical and financial assistance from the older industrial countries, can be decisive in convincing the undeveloped countries that they do not need to buy economic progress at the exorbitant political and human cost which has been paid by the Russian people.

## V. INTERNATIONAL TRADE IN
## AN INDUSTRIALIZED WORLD

In view of the predisposition of the United States in favor of development and industrialization, there is little need further to elaborate on our argument. On the contrary, a useful purpose may be served by concentrating attention on some of the problems raised by the process. The need for the industrial nations to preserve mobility and to encourage further technological progress as well as the dangers of unsound industrial development for non-industrial countries have already been pointed out. At the end of our short survey, we may perhaps speculate about the institutional changes required in a world where the prime determinants of international trade would no longer be differences in climate and natural resources and where there would no longer be just one or even a small group of nations that can claim being "the workshop of the world." Let us say from the outset that such is far from being the present condition of the world. An inspection of any table showing a few basic indexes of industrialization (horsepower per capita, etc.) reveal[s] the huge disparity in industrial development among nations. It is even far from certain that this disparity has substantially decreased during the past generation or two. Nevertheless, if we advocate world-wide industrialization, we should look forward to a world economy where many of the presently underdeveloped countries will have become proficient in a number of industrial processes.

Such a development does not hold sinister implications for the future of international trade since there will certainly remain room for a profitable division of labor among nations. But it may be asked whether a division of labor based essentially on differences in skill and on the past history of industrial development is not likely to be more unstable than the simple

and "natural" division of labor between industrial and agricultural nations. Countries with an established system of industry,
with a good transportation system, with a pool of engineers and
technically skilled workers can usually graft additional lines of
output onto their existing industrial structure without too much
difficulty. In every single instance the loss from the pre-existing
international specialization is likely to be small although in the
aggregate these losses may be quite considerable. For this reason,
disintegration of the finely wrought international division of
labor which we have in mind here, is dangerously likely as long
as nations remain entirely free to pursue autonomous domestic
economic policies, as long as sectional interests can push for special advantages under the cover of national interest, and as long
as the special risks affecting international as opposed to internal
trade have not been eliminated.[14]

One example may perhaps make clear this proposition. Slot
machines are produced in the United States today exclusively in
Chicago while Hollywood has a virtual monopoly on the production of movies. This division of labor is based more on historical accident than on any basic difference in the distribution of
natural or human resources. Nevertheless, it is presumably beneficial to both movie-goers and slot machine addicts and there is
little prospect that Los Angeles will add the production of slot
machines and Chicago that of movies thereby destroying these
benefits. But would this still be the case if a national boundary
line were drawn tomorrow along the water shed of the Rocky
Mountains? Is it not likely that at one time or the other the West
Coast state would then experience balance of payments difficulties with the Middle West state and would restrict the importation of such "non-essentials" as slot-machines? Would not then
a profitable internal market be created in the West Coast state
for the "domestic" production of such machines just as, in the

absence of European imports during World War II, California was quick to build up a ceramics industry? And once such an industry had come into being would it not be likely to be protected by the West Coast state, to "safeguard employment" and for similar well-known reasons even after the balance of payments difficulties have long been overcome? Are we not then confirming, through a slightly more sophisticated route, the very thesis which we thought we had refuted, namely, that worldwide industrialization makes the future of international trade dark and hazardous indeed?

In answering this question we must first repeat that this danger is remote insofar as the undeveloped countries are concerned. It has taken on actuality only for the small, but important group of countries formed by the United States and Western Europe. Within this group we have indeed already experienced a substantial regression from the delicate integration that existed within it before the First World War or again in the twenties. But within this group also we are now witnessing the beginning of a major effort to reverse this process by changing the institutional framework within which the intertrade of the group operates. By creating closer forms of economic association, it is hoped that serious divergences of national economic policies can be avoided, that sectional interests can be held in check, and that the special risks affecting foreign trade can in general be reduced.

It remains to be seen to what extent this aim can be achieved through cooperation in the economic field alone. Closer forms of political association may be required to convert what is today international trade into the interregional trade of tomorrow. But, in any event, current efforts are encouraging evidence that we are not passive in the face of the dangers threatening fruitful specialization among advanced industrial countries.

Rather than dejectedly contemplating the operation of another dismal historical law, we are busily and, let us hope, successfully engaged in proving that the only historical laws are those which we ourselves accept and create.

## NOTES

1. Heinrich Dietzel, *Ist Maschinenausfuhr volkswirtschaftlicher Selbstmord?* (Berlin [Verlag von Leonhard Simion Nf.], 1907).

2. "The export of machines was prohibited because it was feared that this would help a competing industry in another country. One of the first examples of this was the export prohibition . . . against stocking frames in England (1695/96), followed by a similar measure in France in 1724. About this time there was also a considerable fine in France on the export of textile implements in general. In various other ways, too, every possible obstacle was placed in the way of this export. At the beginning of the 1720's, Jonas Alstromer, the most enthusiastic protagonist of manufactures in Sweden in the 18th century, experienced the greatest of difficulties in smuggling from France and Holland the equipment which he needed for the formation of the Alingsas textile works. In England it was not until a somewhat later date (1750 and 1774) that the export of various textile machines and instruments was forbidden and there soon followed similar prohibitions against the export of iron-producing machinery (1781). Once this policy had been set going it was elaborated on all sides and pursued for a considerable time. In England, the country where an independent machine industry originated, the prohibition against its export was not abandoned in effect before 1825, while officially it persisted until 1843." Eli F. Heckscher, *Mercantilism* (London, 1934), Vol. II p. 147 [Eli F. Heckscher, *Mercantilism*, vol. 2, trans. Mendel Shapiro (London: George Allen & Unwin, 1934), p. 147].

3. Stanley Jevons, *The Coal Question*, Third Edition Revised, (London [Macmillan], 1906), p. 424. See also the interesting quotation from Torrens provided by J. [Jacob] Viner in "The Prospects for Foreign Trade in the Post-War World," *Transactions of the Manchester Statistical Society* (1946), reprinted in *Readings in the Theory of International*

*Trade* (Philadelphia, 1949) [Howard S. Ellis, Lloyd A. Metzler, American Economic Association, eds., *Readings in the Theory of International Trade* (Homewood, IL: Richard D. Irwin, 1949)], p. 520. It is possible that some classical economists adopted the pessimistic view as a result of their habit of reasoning in terms of the two-country, two-commodity model of foreign trade. Another reason for their preoccupation was the way in which the law of diminishing returns was expected to operate in reducing the profitability of agriculture in the food-exporting countries. But this source of alleged danger for the international division of labor between industrial and agricultural countries has in general played a far less important role in the discussion than the industrialization argument. The latter argument would be strengthened by the existence of diminishing returns in agriculture, but does not depend on it.

4. See Ross J. S. Hoffmann [correct spelling: Hoffman], *Great Britain and the German Trade Rivalry, 1875–1914* (Philadelphia [University of Pennsylvania Press], 1933).

5. For German policy prior to World War I see J. Viner, *Dumping: A Problem of International Trade* (Chicago, 1924) [Jacob Viner, *Dumping: A Problem in International Trade* (Chicago: University of Chicago Press, 1923)], p. 52. Literature on Germany's foreign economic policies before World War II in this respect is too voluminous to be quoted here.

6. There has been one recent exception: during the congressional debate on the bill vesting in the Export-Import Bank the power to guarantee private capital invested abroad against certain risks peculiar to foreign investment, the opposition used the argument that foreign investment would create competition for domestic industry through the use of cheap foreign labor. (See the speech by Rep. Wolcott, *Congressional Record*, July 11, 1950, p. 10031 f.) Other examples of such arguments can probably be found, but there has never existed in this country anything approaching the national anxiety, fostered by leaders of public opinion, that has been characteristic of some European countries.

7. A. J. Brown, *Industrialization and Trade* (London [Royal Institute of International Affairs], 1943), pp. 36–39.

8. With respect to the United States, for instance, it has recently been calculated that, from 1936 to 1940, "the people of the well-developed areas bought from the United States, on the average, $5.80 worth of goods per person per annum. The people of the intermediate areas bought, on the

average, only $1.25 worth and those of the underdeveloped areas only 70 cents worth." Department of State, *Point Four* (Washington [DC: Department of State], 1950), p. 10.

9. Princeton 1945, p. 93 [League of Nations, *Industrialisation and Foreign Trade* (Geneva: League of Nations, 1945), p. 93].

10. A. [Albert] O. Hirschman, *National Power and the Structure of Foreign Trade* (Berkeley [University of California Press], 1945), pp. 117–157.

11. H. [Herbert] Frankel, "The Industrialization of Agricultural Countries," *Economic Journal* [53], June–Sept. 1943, pp. 188–201.

12. See in particular, Eugene Staley, *World Economic Development* (Montreal [International Labour Office], 1944) pp. 159 ff.

13. For these, see Louis H. Bean, "International Industrialization and per Capita Income," Nat. Bur. of Econ. Research, *Studies in Income and Wealth*, Vol. VIII, 1946, pp. 121–144 [National Bureau of Economic Research, *Studies in Income and Wealth* 8 (1946), pp. 121–144].

14. D. H. Robertson diagnosed this danger in his article "The Future of International Trade," *Economic Journal* (1938) [D. H. Robertson, "The Future of International Trade," *Economic Journal* 48, no. 189 (1938), pp. 1–14], reprinted in *Readings in the Theory of International Trade*, Philadelphia 1943 [Ellis, Metzler, American Economic Association, *Readings in the Theory of International Trade*], pp. 505–506.

# 21

# THE INFLUENCE OF
# U.S. ECONOMIC CONDITIONS
# ON FOREIGN COUNTRIES

## I. THE UNITED STATES IN THE WORLD
## ECONOMY—A FEW FACTS AND FIGURES

With six per cent of the world's population, the United States produces roughly one-half of the world's income.[1] The overwhelming importance of the United States in the world economy is illustrated in Table I [table 21.1] which shows, for a number of important industrial commodities, the share of this country in world production and/or consumption. For a long list of finished industrial products, headed by television[s] and passenger cars, the United States produces and consumes an even larger share of the world's total output.

Table I [table 21.1] also indicates that the relative weight of the United States in world production and consumption has increased significantly since 1937.

While these data point up the dominance of the United States as the foremost producing and consuming nation of the

Restricted. *Review of Foreign Developments*, September 12, 1950.
Prepared in June 1950 by Albert O. Hirschman and Robert Solomon
at the request of the staff of the Gordon Gray Project.

### TABLE 21.1 U.S. SHARE IN WORLD PRODUCTION AND CONSUMPTION (EXCL. USSR)

| Commodity | Production 1937 % | Production 1948 % | Consumption 1947 % | Consumption 1948 % |
|---|---|---|---|---|
| Electricity | 36 | 46 | 36 | 46 |
| Coal and lignite | 36 | 44 | — | — |
| Crude petroleum | 69 | 63 | — | — |
| Natural rubber[a] | — | — | 50 | 44 |
| Cotton | 45 | 57 | 29 | 45 |
| Copper | 37 | 38 | — | — |
| Zinc | 31 | 42 | — | — |
| Tin | 0.1 | 21[b] | 38[c] | 46[c] |
| Lead | 28 | 33 | — | — |
| Cement | 28 | 39 | — | — |
| Steel | 44 | 59 | 41 | 55 |
| Automobiles & trucks | 78 | 82 | — | — |

[a] Includes USSR.
[b] 1949
[c] Primary tin consumption.

Sources: *Major Economic Changes in 1948*. U. N. Dept. of Econ. Affairs (Jan. 1949) [UN Department of Economic Affairs, *Major Economic Changes in 1948* (Lake Success, NY: UN Department of Economic Affairs, January 1949)]; *European Steel Trends*, ECE, Geneva (1949) [UN Economic Commission for Europe, Department of Economic Affairs, *European Steel Trends in the Setting of the World Market* (Geneva: UN Department of Economic Affairs, 1949)]; *Commodity Yearbook, 1949*, Commod. Res. Bur. N. Y. (1949) [Commodity Research Bureau, *Commodity Yearbook 1949* (New York: Commodity Research Bureau, 1949)].

world, it does not bring out the fact that the rest of the world is highly dependent on the United States both as a market and as a source of supply. Thus in 1949 over 20 per cent of the imports of the rest of the world came from the United States. On the other hand, about 14 per cent of the exports of the rest of the world were purchased by the United States.

As is shown in Table II [table 21.2], with the increased weight of the United States in the world, the dependence of other countries on the United States has also increased since before the war, when the United States accounted for about 14 per cent and 12 per cent of the imports and exports respectively of the rest of the world.

Behind these aggregate figures there is great variety in the degree of dependence of other countries on the United States.

TABLE 21.2 U.S. SHARE IN TOTAL EXPORTS AND IMPORTS
OF OTHER COUNTRIES

|  | Exports | | Imports | |
|---|---|---|---|---|
|  | 1938 | 1949 | 1938 | 1949 |
|  | % | % | % | % |
| *Rest of world* | 11.7 | 14.7 | 13.9 | 21.9 |
| *Africa* | 5.4 | 8.7 | 7.5 | 11.7 |
| *Latin America: Total* | 24.0 | 38.4 | 29.3 | 45.1 |
| Brazil | 33.1 | 50.6 | 20.9 | 34.1 |
| Chile | 20.1 | 59.4 | 24.3 | 49.3 |
| Cuba | 74.6 | 81.0 | 71.7 | 75.1 |
| Mexico | 44.5 | 52.9 | 56.4 | 90.6 |
| *Asia: Total* | 16.5 | 17.3 | 15.0 | 24.1 |
| Indonesia | 18.2 | 22.9 | 10.4 | 24.9 |
| Japan | 15.5 | 15.0 | 30.1 | 53.9 |
| Malaya | 35.6 | 27.4 | 3.2 | 4.6 |
| Philippines | 81.7 | 86.7 | 65.6 | 67.0 |
| *Europe: Total* | 5.4 | 4.3 | 9.3 | 14.6 |
| OEEC countries | 5.3 | 4.5 | 9.6 | 16.4 |
| *Oceania: Total* | 2.1 | 5.7 | 12.2 | 9.4 |

Thus the United States is a market for over one-half the exports of Canada, the Philippines and a number of the Latin American countries. On the other hand Greece, Portugal and Switzerland appear to be the only European countries which send even 10 per cent of their exports to this country. However, for most countries of the world, with the notable exception of Europe, the share of total exports going to the United States has increased since 1938.

On the side of imports, the rest of the world has of course increased its dependence on the United States to a greater extent than for its exports. In fact, with the exception of the United Kingdom, Sweden, the countries in the Russian sphere, Australia and New Zealand, virtually all other countries got a larger share of their imports from the United States in 1949 than in 1938. Again there is diversity in the degree of dependence, with Canada and some of the Latin American countries taking over one-half of their imports from the United States.

While the information shown in Table II [table 21.2] indicates the degree of *direct* dependence of the various regions and countries of the world on trade with the United States, it does not of course indicate the full extent to which changes in the level of activity in this country would affect the other countries of the world. Because of the close interdependence of all countries participating in world trade, changes in the U.S. economy which affect the regions most highly dependent on this country will have important repercussions elsewhere. For example, a decline in U.S. imports will *directly* affect the level of economic activity in Chile more than in Europe, but Chile's imports from Europe are likely to decline as its economic activity slows down.

A further crucial, though statistically almost inaccessible aspect of the dominant position of the United States in the world is its share in world savings. It was mentioned earlier that a very rough calculation indicates that the share of the United

States in the income of the world is about one-half. Within a nation the concentration of savings has tended to be far higher than the concentration of income itself.[2] A similar relationship is quite likely to prevail among nations and it may therefore be assumed that the share of this country in world savings is far higher than one-half—maybe as high as two-thirds or three-fourths. The predominance of the United States in the savings of the world has found its expression in the unique contribution of the United States to international aid in the postwar period. This contribution can be estimated at 80 per cent.[3] Moreover, much of the remaining 20 per cent was given by countries receiving aid from the United States and might therefore not have been forthcoming in the absence of U.S. aid.

## II. U.S. FOREIGN TRANSACTIONS—THEIR IMPORTANCE FOR OTHER COUNTRIES

No further figures are needed to demonstrate the weight of the United States in the world economy. A general lesson which is not always clearly perceived, may be drawn: economic intercourse between the United States and foreign countries is, as a rule, far more important for the prosperity of the foreign countries than for ourselves. In an elementary way, this fact finds its expression in the very large shares of total trade occupied by trade with the United States in the case of many foreign countries as compared to the much lower percentages occupied by the same trade in our total exports and imports. It must also be remembered that for most of our trading partners foreign trade is larger in relation to national income than in this country.

But our foreign trade is more important for foreign countries than for ourselves also in a less statistical and more specific and concrete sense. As the most advanced industrial country we are able to export goods and techniques which enable other countries to increase their standard of living much more rapidly than would otherwise be possible for them; whereas for us it would in general be easier to find alternative sources of supply, develop substitutes for, or to do without, many of our imports from any one foreign country. This relationship was described several decades ago in the following general terms by the British economist Alfred Marshall:

> The rich country can with little effort supply a poor country with implements for agriculture or the chase which doubled the effectiveness of her labor, and which she could not make for herself; while the rich country could without great trouble make for herself most of the things which she purchased from the poor nation or at all events could get fairly good substitutes for them. A stoppage of the trade would therefore generally cause much more real loss to the poor than to the rich nation.[4]

The importance to foreign countries of our economic intercourse with them is even greater if we turn from foreign trade to foreign investment. Economic progress in many foreign countries is held back by the fact that their economies are unable to lift themselves to higher levels of living by their own forces: they could do so only by producing an adequate volume of savings but their very poverty prevents the formation of savings on any substantial scale, at least in the absence of the most radical political regimes; by being able to provide such savings the United States creates the very possibility of progress for many countries.

This disproportion between the importance for *us* of our foreign economic relations and their importance for our trading partners abroad is strikingly illustrated by the economic history of the last few years. There is no instance in the postwar period of any decisive influence of our foreign transactions on our domestic economy. In 1946 and 1947 our export surplus exerted no doubt an inflationary influence, but there is general agreement that this influence was quite small compared to the purely domestic expansionary forces of the economy; in 1948, the reduction of our export surplus by $5 billion from its 1947 peak did not interfere with a further expansion of total activity whereas the increase in the export surplus in the first half of 1949 coincided with a decline in economic activity; at present, as in 1948, a considerable decline in exports and export surplus from previous levels does not prevent a vigorous business upswing.

Abroad, in the contrary, economic developments are closely related to our foreign transactions. In 1947, the near-exhaustion of our immediate postwar measures of assistance leads to an economic crisis and to serious social and political dangers in Western Europe. In 1948, reconstruction proceeds vigorously thanks, to a considerable extent, to the renewed flow of American aid; in 1949, the American inventory adjustment throws the sterling area's external economic relations into a turmoil and precipitates the widespread devaluation of currencies in September.

## III. FOREIGN EFFECTS OF PROSPERITY AND DEPRESSION IN THE UNITED STATES

It should be clear by now that foreign countries have good reasons for watching economic development in the United States with the utmost attention. Since our foreign transactions mean so much to them, any sudden substantial change in the flow and direction of these transactions raises the most delicate problems. A decline in sales to the United States is not easily compensated by a more active sales effort at home or in other foreign markets; and the resulting loss of the dollar proceeds of exports, may mean that the affected country will not be able to buy certain imports essential to the smooth functioning and the progress of its economy. Similarly serious are the problems with which foreign countries could be faced in the event of a sudden drying up of U.S. capital inflow on which they count for the development of their resources.

In general, a high and expanding level of economic activity in the United States means a high and expanding level of foreign transactions: high levels of production and income in this country will, in the first place, result in strong U.S. demand for foreign goods and services. This in turn will make dollars available to foreign countries for their purchases here. It will also lead to less discrimination in the treatment of U.S. exports and to a more liberal policy with respect to the transfer of earnings of U.S. capital invested abroad. These developments will no doubt stimulate the outflow of private capital from the United States. This outflow is also likely to be stimulated by the search for, and development of, new sources of raw materials abroad and, even more, by the spirit of enterprise and willingness to assume risks that are characteristic of prosperous business conditions. Under prosperous conditions, moreover, the special risk factors affecting foreign trade and, in particular, foreign investment are considerably reduced since economic well-being generally decreases political and social tensions of all kinds. These stimulating effects of a high level of U.S. economic activity on our foreign trade and investment are far more important in a dynamic environment than the limitation on exports and investment that might be caused by an active domestic demand for exportable goods and investment funds. A high level of business activity in the United States could arouse the concern of other countries only as a result of fears that everyday brings them nearer to the "inevitable" U.S. depression that would disrupt and cripple their economies.

The sensitivity of other countries to the possibility of a U.S. recession or depression is thus based in the first place on the benefits enjoyed by them in the course of their economic relations with us during prosperous times. The widespread fear of a U.S. depression—an emotion so thoroughly exploited by Soviet propaganda—is, in a way, an eloquent testimony to the magnitude of the gains derived by foreign countries from their intercourse with us when business conditions are favorable. Therefore, the United States could actually take some pride in the foreign fears of a U.S. depression, but at the same time we must recognize that sovereign nations dislike even more than individuals the feeling that the foundation of their well-being is precarious and may suddenly collapse as a result of events which are entirely beyond their control.

We shall show below that a certain amount of fiction has grown up around the general theme of the devastating foreign effects of a U.S. depression. But first of all it must be said quite clearly—at the risk of repeating the obvious—that a serious depression would indeed have calamitous repercussions abroad.

The reduced volume and prices of foreign countries' exports to us would result in unemployment and distress in the foreign exporting industries; effects of these developments would of course be felt throughout the foreign economies. Except where U.S. aid is on a substantial scale (see below), reduced dollar proceeds from exports will not permit the foreign countries thus affected to purchase the same volume of dollar imports as prior to the depression level. This situation will lead in the first place to drafts on generally scanty foreign exchange reserves and possibly to some drawings on the Fund. An attempt will and should thus be made to "ride out" the recession but it is by no means certain that this will be feasible. If not, the countries hit by the depression will inevitably impose additional discriminatory restrictions on imports from the United States. Not only would this further affect economic activity and living standards abroad, but our hopes of establishing a workable economic world order on the basis of multilateral trade and currency convertibility would suffer a setback that would be more than temporary. For foreign countries may decide that stability in trade relations is preferable to the occasional benefits of a high level of trade with the U.S. As a result they may tend to reduce permanently the intensity of their intercourse with us and will be only too ready to join with others in a "high-cost soft-currency area."

A serious depression would also lead to a drying up of the outflow of private capital. Although this would not mean too substantial a loss of dollars to foreign countries at the present time (see below) such a development would inevitably dash our hopes of reviving private foreign lending on a substantial scale as a means of bridging permanently part of the dollar gap.

Thus several important goals of our foreign economic policy would be rendered unattainable by the consequences of a serious depression; a final blow would be dealt to that policy by the probable revival of economic protectionism and isolationism that would almost certainly take place in this country in the wake of mass unemployment and distress.

The political consequences of a serious U.S. depression are even more obviously disastrous than its disruptive economic effects: no development could play more into the hands of the Soviet Union. For all the world to see, Democratic Capitalism would have lost in its "competition of performance" with Totalitarian Planning.

No matter how high the standard of living in the United States in prosperous times, our system would hold little attraction for other countries if it were shown to be subject to violent shocks which periodically expose large masses of the people to unemployment and insecurity, if not misery.

At the same time, since a serious depression in the United States would cause important economic setbacks to foreign countries it would be likely to endanger their social and political stability. Such a development would clearly undo all our current efforts to build up "centers of strength" in the free world.

## IV. THE OBSESSION WITH A U.S. DEPRESSION: EXAGGERATIONS AND MISCONCEPTIONS

Frankly to recognize the deleterious economic and political consequences of a serious U.S. depression is quite a different matter from partaking in the strange obsession with this subject which has developed in some quarters. This obsession not only magnifies the dangers and the probable foreign effects of a U.S. depression, but often leads to the adoption of precautionary measures which are in effect equivalent to the undesirable policies that foreign countries would be forced to adopt in the event of a real depression. To act in this way is very much like the policy of Gribouille, who, according to a French tale, threw himself into the water in order not to get wet from the rain.

It is therefore important to see our subject in its proper perspective, free from exaggerations and misconceptions. The following sections are devoted to this task.

1. *Balance of payments effects of a U.S. depression.* It is true that a depression in the United States would normally result in a

reduction of our demand for imports and would therefore cause a loss in employment and incomes in the foreign industries that are geared to our demand. It is not true that such a development would of necessity in all cases cause balance of payments difficulties since in a depression foreign countries would also be able to buy from us at reduced prices and could thereby save dollars. When foreign countries import much more from the United States than they export to it, the dollar savings resulting from declines in import prices could be larger than the loss of dollars resulting from the falling off of exports. In 1949 the balance of payments position of the Continental countries of Western Europe actually profited from our short recession in this way whereas the sterling area which covers a much more substantial portion of its dollar imports by exports (rather than by U.S. aid) suffered a net loss in dollars.

Another more general factor that is likely to ease balance of payments difficulties of foreign countries arising from a U.S. depression is connected with the type of goods predominantly exported by the United States. A large and increasing fraction of our exports is indeed formed not by basic foodstuffs and materials, but by goods geared to expanding production (such as machinery) or tied to high and rising living standards (such as consumers' durables). Given the highly elastic demand for these products with respect to income changes, the purchases of both types of goods are likely to be *spontaneously* and drastically decreased by our foreign customers as soon as our depression spreads to their countries. While such a development would no doubt create additional problems in this country, it would tend to reduce such dollar deficits as may have been caused to foreign countries by the fall in their exports to the United States.

2. *The "special sensitivity" of U.S. foreign transactions to fluctuations in national income.* It is true that our imports exhibit a

tendency to exaggerate the swings in our total economic activity as measured, for instance, by national income statistics. A succinct statement of this fact was recently provided in the following terms by the report on *National and International Measures for Full Employment* prepared by a group of experts under the auspices of the United Nations:

> Between 1929 and 1932, while the United States national income fell by 52 per cent, the dollars supplied by the United States to foreign countries through purchase of goods and services and new investments abroad fell by 68 per cent. This implied a reduction in the dollars available to foreign countries after meeting fixed debt service obligations of no less than 77 per cent. Between 1937 and 1938 the United States national income declined by some 10 per cent, while the dollar value of commodity imports fell by 35 per cent. Between the fourth quarter of 1948 and the second quarter of 1949, the United States national income fell by 5 per cent, the value of imports by 15 per cent.[5]

While this particular relationship thus seems to be well proven by recent experience, the explanations offered for it have often been faulty. The reason given by the U.N. experts themselves is that our imports "consist largely of commodities in which the bulk of requirements is satisfied out of domestic production."[6] This is clearly not the case. As ought to be expected in a country with a long history of protection behind it, by far the larger portion (approximately 75 per cent) of our imports consists of commodities the domestic production of which is either nil or entirely inadequate to meet even depressed consumption levels. But even if the statement of the experts were correct it would not necessarily follow that the brunt of any decline in domestic demand would fall on the imported rather than on the domestically produced articles. This would depend entirely on the comparative prices of the imported as compared to the domestically produced product. Another explanation that is often given for the relatively wide swings in the value of our imports is the mistaken idea that our imports are prevalently composed of such items as lace, perfumes, and similar luxuries the demand for which is very sensitive to rises and falls in personal incomes. While some of our imports from Europe and much of our travel abroad fall into this particular category, the bulk of our imports certainly cannot be characterized as luxuries.

The real reason for the variability of our imports in the course of the business cycle is to be found in the fact that in the course of the cycle, inventory fluctuations are far more pronounced than fluctuations in economic activity in general. In fact, both the 1937/38 and 1949 recessions have often been characterized as inventory cycles or adjustments. Now, imports go in the first instance to swell the inventories of importers, industrial producers, and distributors. Imports *are* inventories and thus naturally partake in the swings characteristic of inventories. Moreover, inventory and price fluctuations are most pronounced in the case of industrial materials and it so happens that this category occupies over one half of our total import trade. It is not necessary to look any farther for an explanation of the sensitivity of our imports to economic fluctuations. But the explanation suggests also that this sensitivity is not particularly characteristic of the U.S. economy, but applies to a greater or smaller degree to all countries and in particular to industrial countries importing large quantities of raw materials.

It might also be noted that even though decreases in our domestic economic activity are likely to lead to more than proportional decreases in our foreign purchases, the decrease in the national income of the supplying countries is in turn likely to be smaller than the decrease in their exports to us. Where a country's economic life is entirely based on exports of, say, coffee to the United States it is fair to surmise that the rise and fall in its national income will roughly parallel the movements in coffee shipments to the United States. Even in such a country the relative stability of government services and of some private industrial and commercial transactions are likely to amortize to some extent any shocks administered from abroad. In other countries, where exports to the United States provide an important, but not the principal support of economic activity, total income is likely to be much less variable than the income derived from trade with the United States. Moreover, aside from the natural or "built-in" stabilizers, governments are likely to engage in compensatory policies intended to counteract the spread of depression. The fluctuations of our foreign transactions—in particular of our import trade—may therefore be compared to a fast moving transmission belt connecting, through the appropriate gears, with two mechanisms which, themselves, revolve at considerably lower speeds.

3. *The "perverse behavior" of capital flows.* It is frequently pointed out that a downturn in the U.S. economy would lead almost instantly to a drying up of U.S. private investments and that, for this reason, foreign countries would be deprived of an inflow of foreign capital at precisely the moment when they need it most, i.e. when their transactions on current account will show a tendency toward imbalance as a result of declining exports to the United States. It will certainly be granted that private U.S. investment abroad is indeed not likely to flourish when our domestic economy is depressed. We have listed above the reasons for which a high level of domestic business activity is likely to lead to an expansion of U.S. investment. All the arguments made there can be easily inverted.

Nevertheless, the fears concerning the "perverse behavior" of U.S. capital seem to be considered exaggerated in the current setting. In the first place U.S. private investments abroad do not currently provide a really substantial volume of dollars to foreign countries. (In 1949, they amounted to $500 million). Secondly, lending by such institutions as the International Bank and the Export-Import Bank is not likely to be affected much by the cycle; while these lending agencies have shown no disposition to engage on any large-scale lending specifically for anti-cyclical purposes, their operations are tied to the development programs of the borrowing countries and can be expected to proceed reasonably undistributed by fluctuations in the level of activity in the United States. The operations of these agencies will thus exert at least a steadying influence during a cycle. The same may be said of the various programs of direct U.S. aid to foreign countries.

The International Monetary Fund, on the other hand, can be expected to play a more active role. While its resources are hardly sufficient to take care of all international monetary contingencies that might arise in the course of a major depression, the Fund is designed to provide liquidity for temporary balance of payments disequilibria and can be expected to do so when these disequilibria are clearly of a cyclical nature. In fact the caution hither to displayed by the fund is precisely meant to enable it to play an active role in meeting requests for foreign exchange that originate in temporary (including cyclical) rather than fundamental balance of payments difficulties.

In conclusion it appears therefore, that the fears of the unstabilizing influence of U.S. capital outflow in the course of a depression have been somewhat exaggerated.

4. *Foreign effects of minor U.S. recession.* Finally, the experience of last year shows that we need not be too concerned about a *minor* recession in the United States. Last year's inventory

adjustment in the United States did have some serious foreign repercussions. As noted above, our imports, particularly of raw materials, decreased sharply as a result of a fall in both volume and price. In part, however, this decrease was also due to the speculative anticipation of devaluation on the part of U.S. importers. In particular, our recession had only a relatively minor share of responsibility in the loss of monetary reserves experienced by the United Kingdom in the second and third quarters of the year. The speculative reaction to devaluation rumors and a temporary increase in imports *from* the United States during the same period were more important causative factors.

Nonetheless, it is probably correct to say that our recession helped to precipitate the foreign currency devaluations of September 1949. And far from deploring this repercussion, we can now clearly see that it was a healthy development which helped in readjusting world price levels and permitted not only a substantial narrowing of the world dollar gap, but gave new strength to many foreign economies in their efforts to lift themselves to higher levels of output and productivity. This episode, therefore, is heartening. It shows that relatively minor fluctuations in American economic activity not only need not be disastrous for foreign countries, but may actually serve a useful purpose in placing both the American and foreign economies on foundations more solid than those provided by conditions of inflation and physical shortages in this country.

## V. TOWARD FREEDOM FROM FEAR OF A U.S. DEPRESSION

What can the United States do to relieve other countries of the fear of suddenly being deprived of part of their well being and livelihood as a result of a U.S. depression? Naturally, the most important and only secure way of avoiding the foreign repercussions of a U.S. depression is to prevent a U.S. depression in the first place. It is indeed important for us fully to realize that the prevention of a major depression has become of crucial importance not only in the management of our domestic affairs, but also as a matter of our international responsibilities: it is a commanding task for us in our leadership of the free world. Apart from this obvious duty what can be done to mitigate the unfavorable foreign effects of a U.S. depression if it should come despite all our efforts? By drawing on our previous analysis we may supply a few tentative answers:

1. We can do only little to mitigate the first direct impact of our recession i.e. the falling off of our foreign purchases. In as much as we carry out stockpiling programs it may be possible to use such programs to some extent for countercyclical purposes (i.e. to buy less when private demand is high and vice versa). The primary aim of these programs is, however, unconnected with the business cycle. As long as stockpiling programs are in existence, we may expect them to give some underlying stability to the volume of our foreign purchases, but should not hope for much more from them.

The preceding analysis (cf. p. 307 above) provides us with another possible line of attack. We have traced the variability of our imports to their inventory character and, in particular, to the predominance in our imports of industrial raw materials the prices and quantities of which traditionally exhibit particularly wide fluctuations. It follows that the average stability of our foreign purchases would probably be strengthened if we were to increase the share of manufactured articles in our imports. This result could be secured through further lowering of our import duties which are almost exclusively directed against foreign manufactures. It is possibly not always realized that reductions in our protective duties would not only provide the world with more dollars (so that the need for aid would be reduced) but would also help in making the outflow of dollars more even than it has been.[7]

2. More can be done to safeguard other countries against the possible *repercussions* of the fall of U.S. imports. These repercussions include losses in monetary reserves and any resulting deflationary action or import cuts adopted as counter-measures by foreign governments.

It is now recognized that in a situation where a country experiences reserve losses as a result of a cyclical fall in foreign demand, it would be wrong for it to "play the rules of the gold standard" and to deflate merely to counteract the reserve outflow. Such actions would not be corrective, but would only spread and deepen the depression. The proper policy for the country is, on the contrary, not to resist the loss in reserves so as to "ride out" the foreign depression. This, however, is feasible only if the country has ample reserves at its disposal or has ready access to the "second line" reserves held by the International Monetary Fund. For this as for many other reasons it will therefore be important for the United States to encourage the accumulation of an adequate volume of monetary reserves which foreign countries could freely spend to finance balance of payments deficits arising from a depression in the United States. Similarly, the resources of the Fund should be preserved for such a contingency, but should then be made available on a substantial scale.

Naturally over the past years, all countries have become conscious of the dollar problem and of the desirability to husband their dollar reserves. They may therefore be expected to restrict American imports rather than to run the risk of exhausting their dollar reserves. Restrictions against imports from the United States would have adverse effects not only on the United States, but also on the economic activity of the restricting country. This is particularly likely if even before the onset of the depression dollar imports are subject to severe restrictions so that any further import cut will eliminate highly "essential" items. If on the contrary dollar imports are relatively free, then restrictions can be temporarily adopted without unduly harming economic activity. It would seem therefore that a country which has established conditions of relatively free trade with the dollar area is likely to be able to defend itself better against the consequences of a U.S. recession than a country that has already, so to speak used up all its ammunition before the outbreak of the recession. Therefore, the more successful a country has been in making its currency convertible into the dollar both internally and externally, the better armed will it be against the dangers of a depression originating in the United States.

In summary it appears therefore that a number of policies presently pursued, programmed, or advocated by the United States have the incidental effect of affording foreign countries some protection against the effects of a domestic depression. Thus our stockpiling programs can provide some stability where it is most needed, i.e. in our foreign purchases of industrial raw materials. Our policy of encouraging imports should eventually result in a higher share of manufactures in our total imports and will thereby reduce the overall variability in our foreign purchases. As noted earlier, the lending policies of the International Bank for Reconstruction and Development and of the Export-Import Bank are likely to help in stabilizing the outflow of capital from the United States. The existence of the International Monetary Fund as well as our policy of encouraging the rebuilding of adequate foreign reserves should go some way in enabling countries which develop balance of payments deficits during a worldwide depression to avoid deflationary action. Finally, our policy aiming at restoring multilateral trade and convertibility will, if successful, result in greater adaptability of foreign balances of payments to world economic conditions.

In short, we do not have in the foreign field a unified policy of avoiding the repercussions of a domestic depression just as in the domestic field we hardly can claim having a "master plan" for preventing a depression; but, again as in the domestic field, we have a series of policies which, if energetically and successfully pursued, should in combination greatly reduce foreign fears of the world effects of a U.S. depression.

## NOTES

1. Rough estimate for 1948 on the basis of data assembled at Federal Reserve.

2. In the United States, for instance, it was found for 1948 that the top fifth of income receivers which took nearly one half (47 per cent) of all incomes, accounted for 60 per cent of all positive savings and for as much as 99 per cent of all net savings—the latter figure being explained by the large amount of dissaving that occurs among the lower income groups especially on the part of those who are only temporarily members of these groups. See *Federal Reserve Bulletin*, January 1950, p. 23 [Board of Governors of the Federal Reserve System, "1949 Survey of Consumer Finances—Part VIII. Distribution of Consumer Saving in 1948," *Federal Reserve Bulletin* 36, no. 1 (January 1950), p. 23].

3. Estimate based on *Major Economic Changes in 1948* (U.N. Jan. 1949) [UN Department of Economic Affairs, *Major Economic Changes in 1948* (Lake Success, NY: UN Department of Economic Affairs, January 1949)] and brought up to date by the authors.

4. Alfred Marshall, *Money, Credit and Commerce* (London [Macmillan], 1923) pp. 109–110.

5. *National and International Measures for Full Employment*, United Nations, New York, December 1949, p. 30 [United Nations, *National and International Measures for Full Employment* (New York: United Nations, December 1949), p. 30].

6. Ibid. [United Nations, *National and International Measures*], p. 29.

7. Some of the manufactures imported by the United States are of a luxury character and their volume would therefore be likely to fluctuate rather sharply in the course of the cycle. To the extent, therefore, that any additional imports are in this category, little would be achieved in steadying the total volume of our imports. Fortunately, however, there exists a wide range of non-luxury manufactures—of a handicraft or other type—which could find an expanding and more stable market in the United States.

# INDEX

50 per cent system (Italy), 8, 53–63, 64n4, 66–67, 69, 94

fostering, 24; Hirschman's
reports a window into debate
on, 33; inflationary effect of
reconstruction aid, 132–33;
infrastructure repair/rebuilding,
6, 72, 77; lack of resources
(dollar shortage), 11–15;
modernization needed, 158, 162
(*see also* investment); phases of,
5–6; slowing of, in 1949, 162.
*See also* industrial production;
Marshall Plan; production;
*specific institutions*
European recovery. *See* European
economic recovery
European Recovery Program
(ERP), 141–43, 172, 213, 239–40,
249. *See also* bilateralism; *Interim
Report on the European Recovery
Program*; Marshall Plan
European trade. *See* trade, European
European Union, 22
exchange control, in Italy, 53–70; 50
per cent system, 8, 53–63, 64n4,
66–67, 69, 94; accumulation
of reserves resulting from, 172;
devaluation and, 93–94; franco
valuta system, 65–70, 70n3,
70nn3–4
exchange controls (elsewhere):
EMA and, 204, 207; European
integration and, 238; France,
64n3; multilateralism and, 229;
Spain, 64n3
exchange rates and policies: in
1945, 232; currency adjustments
(1949), 249; dollar shortage and,

11–13; EMA and, 21, 206–7;
France, 7, 48–49, 110; Italy, 7–8,
53–63, 56t; single vs. multiple
exchange rates, 60–62; and
trade imbalances, 13, 131, 166
(*see also* balance-of-payments
problems). *See also* devaluation
of currencies
Export-Import Bank, 89–90, 279,
292n6, 309, 313
exports: aggressive sales policy
needed, 153–54; bilateralism,
production, and, 233; countries'
long-term goals/programs,
149–54; and devaluation, 174;
direction of OEEC countries'
exports, 150t; European
integration and exports to the
U.S., 243–44; expansion of,
165–66; higher to well-
developed areas, 292–93n8;
increased as supply problems
solved, 212; and the Intra-
European Payments Scheme,
192 (*see also* Intra-European
Payments Scheme); of
machinery, 277–78, 291n2; prewar
export surpluses, 230; share of
world exports purchased by
U.S., 295–97, 296t; U.S. exports,
recession, and OEEC countries'
dollar position, 177–83, 179t,
181t, 305. *See also* balance of
payments; balance-of-payments
problems; Export-Import Bank;
trade, European; trade, world;
*specific countries and commodities*

rail transportation: electrification of, 148; France, *74t*, 75, 85, 96, 100–101, 103, 162; Italy, *74t*, 75, 85, 162; repair and rebuilding, 72, 162; war damage, 6

Ramadier, Paul, 101

rationing, 11, 78, 105, 115

recession, 161–76; in Belgium, 162; and devaluation, 174–76, 310; dollar shortage and, 165–66; evidence of, 161–62; in foreign countries, effects of, 171–74; and investment, 162–63; in Italy, 112, 116–18, 162; mitigating repercussions of a future U.S. recession, 311–14; policies to address, 164; stability of foreign economies, 161–66; U.S. recession, international effects of, 166–71, 176n2, 177–83, *179t*, *181t*, 300, 305, 309–10 (*see also* depression). *See also* deflation; depression; depression, U.S.

reconstruction. *See* European reconstruction; *specific countries*

recovery, economic. *See* European economic recovery

reserves: ECA funds and, 210–13; EMA and national reserve requirements, 199; of Italian banks, 112–13, 114–15, 117, 119n1; limited, in early postwar period, 11–14, 38n27; pooling of, 21–22, 204–6; in sterling, 255, 256. *See also specific countries*

resources, postwar lack of, 11–16

*Review of Foreign Developments*, vii

rice, 146, 148

Rosenstein-Rodan, Paul, 13

Russia. *See* Soviet Union

Salant, Walter, 2

savings: and economic progress, 299; in France, 108–9; inflation and, 163–64; and investment, 108, 157, 162–65; private (individual; personal), 14, 108–9, 132, 157, 163–64; state savings banks, 268–69; U.S. share in, 297–98, 314n2

Schuman, Robert, 48, 97, 101–3

securities: central banks and (generally), 200; France, 101, 108; Italy, 84, 112, *113t*, 114–15; prices "pegged," 265, 271; and public debt, 84, 266, 268–69, 271. *See also* bonds

sequences, in Hirschman's thought, 9–11, 15

shipping, 90, 148, 151, 162

Snoy-Marjolin report, 177

Solomon, Robert, 31–32

South America, *150t*, 151–52. *See also* Latin America; *specific countries*

South Rhodesia, 153–54

sovereignty: economic sovereignty, 19–20, 23, 196–97, 201–2, 209; and employment and economic disintegration, 245

Soviet Union, 31, 287, 297, 303

Spain, 64n3

specialization, international, 242–43, 245, 288–90

Spinelli, Altiero, 24, 41n65

Sri Lanka (Ceylon), 153–54

U.S. aid (*continued*)
    inability to absorb/utilize, 172–73;
    as share of foreign aid in postwar
    period, 298; and the U.S. export
    surplus, 168; U.S. recession
    and, 168–71. *See also* Economic
    Cooperation Administration;
    European Recovery Program;
    Marshall Plan

vegetable oils, 146, *146t*, 151

wages, 76, 85, 100, 103, 116
weighted volume indexes, 93
Western Germany: Bizone, 155,
    189; imports from Eastern
    Europe, 150; unemployment, 148,
    160; U.S. recession and dollar

position of, 180, *181t*. *See also*
    Germany
wheat, 76–77, 84, 99. *See also*
    agriculture; grains
wool, 55, 90, 145, 151. *See also* textile
    industry
workforce. *See* labor
World Bank, 13–14, 32, 102
world economy, U.S. importance to,
    30, 92, 294–300, *295t*, *296t*
*Worldly Philosopher: The Odyssey of
    Albert O. Hirschman* (Adelman),
    37n16
world trade. *See* trade, world
World War II, 3–4, 6, 78, 232–33,
    265, 269

Zellerbach, James D., 176n3

Printed and bound by CPI Group (UK) Ltd, Croydon, CR0 4YY

23/04/2025

14660942-0001